THE CONFESSIONS
OF ST. AUGUSTINE

The Confessions *of* Saint Augustine

ST. AUGUSTINE OF HIPPO

Edited by Hal M. Helms, Foreword by Fr. Mark Henninger

CONTEMPORARY ENGLISH EDITION

PARACLETE PRESS
BREWSTER, MASSACHUSETTS

The Confessions of St. Augustine

2010 First Printing

ISBN 978-1-55725-695-9

Library of Congress Cataloging-in-Publication Data
Augustine, Saint, Bishop of Hippo.
  [Confessiones. English]
  The confessions of Saint Augustine / St. Augustine of Hippo ; edited by Hal
M. Helms ; foreword by Mark Henninger. -- Contemporary English ed.
    p. cm. -- (Paraclete essentials)
  Includes bibliographical references (p.   ).
  ISBN 978-1-55725-695-9
1. Augustine, Saint, Bishop of Hippo. 2. Christian saints--Algeria--Hippo
(Extinct city)--Biography. I. Helms, Hal McElwaine. II. Title. BR65.A6E5
2010
  270.2092--dc22
  [B]   2010003247

10 9 8 7 6 5 4 3 2 1

Published by Paraclete Press
Brewster, Massachusetts
www.paracletepress.com

Printed in the United States of America

CONTENTS

FOREWORD

I was introduced to St. Augustine's *Confessions* in college, and to this day I'm surprised at the impact this book had on me. Sometimes, as the saying goes, "heart speaks to heart." And although there were many voices calling to me in those years—voices of the popular culture, voices from other writers and teachers, voices of friends—that of Augustine spoke to more levels of my personality and more powerfully than any that I recall. I am not alone.

It is still a mystery how St. Augustine has managed to do this, generation after generation, for over fifteen hundred years. It is similar to going to a movie and hearing spoken and acted out feelings and desires, thoughts and intimations that you were only dimly aware of and could never articulate, but knew were having a profound impact on your life. How could the screen-writer possibly know me so well? we might wonder to ourselves. The answer lies, of course, in the fact that we are not islands; we are not alone; rather, we are, all of us, human.

But what is it to be human? St. Augustine understood it in terms of what is called Christian neo-Platonism, a synthesis of Christianity and the philosophy of neo-Platonism originating in the pagan mystic and thinker Plotinus. Neo-Platonism can be summarized in these terms:

- a theory of the universe
- a theory of human nature
- a diagnosis of what is wrong with us; and
- a prescription of what is to be done about it.

For Augustine, the answers to these four issues were roughly as follows:
- The whole cosmos is made up of a material, changing world and a spiritual, unchanging world.

- We are basically souls, belonging to the spiritual world.
- But we have "fallen" into this changing, material world.
- And it is only with God's help in Jesus Christ that we can "turn back" to the true homeland, the place where we really belong—our spiritual home.

Hence, to be human, for St. Augustine, is to be caught up in the drama of a soul, fallen yet called to beatitude, true and abiding happiness. All the longings, missed opportunities, and looking for love in all the wrong places that characterize our existence, he sees within this framework.

It is perhaps for this reason that so many people have been moved and changed by reading the *Confessions*. For those caught up in the whirlwind of their own unhappiness, the *Confessions* afford not an artificial safe harbor, but a real and profound understanding of their predicament.

St. Augustine knows from his own experience how bitter it can be to be "lost in a dark wood," as Dante wrote about nine hundred years later. But he also knows of God's saving grace that never left him, and does not leave us today. This grace finds us in such a miserable state, and yet it reaches down, calling us to "turn away" from our over-the-top desires for the beautiful things of this world; with his mighty hand God breaks the chains, the obsessions, that bind us.

The *Confessions* are, in essence, a hymn to this grace of God, and a confession—not primarily of Augustine's sins—but of a God who is great in his compassion. Like the Good Samaritan in St. Luke's Gospel who stops on his way to help the traveler lying at the side of the road, God pours out the oil of his grace to heal our self-inflicted wounds.

St. Augustine wrote his *Confessions* when he was bishop in the small northern African town of Hippo, as he was looking back on his life, astounded at what had happened to him. It was the record of an encounter with God. Not only one encounter, but many! He saw his life in a new light, discovering to his delight and astonishment that God had been calling him constantly: through his mother Monica, through the death of a friend, through his disillusionment with Faustus (the leader of the sect of the Manicheans with which Augustine spent many years), through hearing the stories of St. Anthony in the desert, through listening to the homilies of St. Ambrose in Milan, and through his mind-and-heart-wrenching battles with his own sexuality.

Only as bishop, after his conversion, halfway through his life, did St. Augustine realize that each of these experiences, and countless more, were so many ways God had been calling to him. "And behold, you were within, but I was outside, searching for you there. . . . You were with me, but I was not with you." How deaf he had been to God's inner call! "Too late have I loved you, O Beauty, ancient yet ever new. Too late have I loved you!"

We need not adopt the whole of the neo-Platonic outlook, with its devaluation of the body and material reality, to be moved by St. Augustine's account of his life. For he wrote the *Confessions* to awaken others to this inner voice of God, insistently calling us to true inner peace and our inheritance as children of God. We who are made for communion with a loving God are called to a life much better than we ever imagined. The life of a Christian is to be a disciple of Jesus Christ, the "inner teacher." Listen to this voice, for as Augustine famously says, "You have made us for Yourself, and our hearts are restless until they rest in You."

—*Rev. Mark G. Henninger, SJ*
Martin Chair of Medieval Philosophy
Department of Philosophy
Georgetown University

INTRODUCTION

A ugustine stands as one of the greatest and most influential of Christian theologians. "It may be safely predicted, that while the mind of man yearns for knowledge, and his heart seeks rest, the *Confessions* will retain that foremost place in the world's literature which it has secured by its sublime outpourings of devotion and profound philosophical spirit."[1]

It should be borne in mind that the *Confessions* was not intended to be an intellectual exercise, removed from the everyday realities of life. In it, Augustine seeks to lay bare his heart, his soul—before God and before his fellow men. It is an honest book and a book that speaks to the heart first of all.

We moderns may find some difficulty in his allegorizations, especially those found in the last three books. But one translator aptly remarked, "Where the strict use of history is not disregarded, (to use Augustine's expression), allegorizing, by way of spiritual meditation, may be profitable." Certainly his insights are not to be despised!

Born in 352, in the small city of Tagaste, Africa (in what is now Algeria), Augustine lived in the time of the growing ascendancy of the Christian Church and the growing decline of the Roman empire. It was scarcely a quarter of a century earlier that the great Council of Nicaea had been held, and there were heresies and schisms throughout the Christian world that still held sway over hearts and minds. Donatists continued to hold that many Catholic orders were invalid because they came through *traditori* (those who had denied the faith during the severe persecution and had later repented and been restored to the Church). In his later years Augustine would spend much effort in fighting for the unity of the Church against their schismatic beliefs. Arianism (denying the full divinity of Christ) succeeded in winning the allegiance of the Emperor and his mother, and echoes of that threat to the peace and unity of the Church continued to resound throughout Augustine's lifetime. But for Augustine personally, his sojourn among the Manicheans gave the background for much of the material we find in the *Confessions*. After his schooling under a harsh tutor in Tagaste, he was sent to Madaura for a time. Family finances forced his return home and resulted in an idle year, 369–70. He was then sent to Carthage, to what would be equivalent to a university, where he distinguished himself in the rhetorical school. His father died in 371, but his mother continued to support his schooling with the aid of a wealthy patron, Romanianus. It is evident that she continued to cherish high ambitions for his worldly success. While at Carthage, Augustine came under the influence of the Manicheans and took a mistress, to whom he was faithful for fifteen years. To them was born one son, Adeotus.

After some years of teaching at Carthage, Augustine decided to go to Rome. His mother opposed the idea, but could not dissuade him. After a brief stay in Rome, he was appointed in 385 as Public Teacher of Rhetoric at Milan, where he first came under the influence of St. Ambrose. In 385–86, the Empress Justina demanded the surrender of two churches to the Arians. Ambrose led his people in a refusal to surrender the churches, even when confronted by military force. Augustine was aware of this crisis, but he was not personally involved.

Ten years spent with the Manicheans had brought Augustine many intellectual difficulties with their system. Although they had encouraged his own skeptical approach to the Holy Scriptures, they had not satisfied his thirst for sure knowledge nor his growing uneasiness with his disorderly life. With his mother's help, Augustine's mistress was dismissed and arrangements were made for his marriage, which had to be postponed because his intended was underage. But his struggles with the flesh resulted in his taking a new mistress, because he felt morally incapable of making a better choice. He chronicles the inner struggles which led, with timely help from Ambrose, to his departure from the Manicheans and his conversion to the Catholic faith. He was baptized at Easter, 387, along with his son, Adeotus. Having resigned his position as professor of rhetoric, he and his company were waiting for a ship to make their way back to Africa when his mother suddenly became ill and died at Ostia, the port of Rome.

The next year, having returned to Tagaste and sold his property there, Augustine set up a monastic kind of community with a few friends, continuing his writing. In 391, with much misgiving on his part, he consented to be ordained presbyter at Hippo, a nearby city of about 30,000. The Church was not strong there, its population being a mixture of pagans, Jews, several schismatic sects, and a large group of Donatists. In 395 (in violation of the eighth canon of Nicaea) he was made assistant bishop to the aged Valerius, and succeeded him as bishop the following year.

It was not long after his election as bishop that he began the *Confessions*, completing them probably in 398. Thus they represent his thought and the account of his life in its midstream. He wrote this book "at the request of friends who begged him to commit to writing those recollections of his former life to which he often referred in private conversation. He consented for the characteristic reason that he desired his friends to mourn and rejoice along with him as they followed his retrospect of past years, and on his behalf to give thanks to God."[2]

Augustine's years as bishop involved struggles with errors he believed to be a threat to salvation and to the welfare of the Church on several fronts: Manicheans, Donatists, Arians and Pelagians. In addition to these very real battles, the Roman empire itself was under mortal assault. It is one of the great ironies of history that as Augustine finished his immortal *City of God* in the quiet of his monastic residence, the Vandals were pillaging the countryside of North Africa. "While the Vandals besieged Hippo, St. Augustine died (August 28, 410) in the sanctity and poverty in which he had lived for many years. Shortly afterward, the Vandals destroyed the city, but left his cathedral and library untouched."[3]

Sending the *Confessions* to a friend, Augustine wrote, "In these behold me, that you may not praise me beyond what I am. Believe what is said of me, not by others, but by myself."[4]

ACKNOWLEDGMENTS

The older translations of the *Confessions* are, unfortunately, obscure in many places, making it increasingly difficult for the modern reader to see Augustine as the living, vital person he must have been. I have made free use of all the English versions available (and am indebted to them all), comparing them with the Latin version by Gibb and Montgomery. As in other modern versions, I have taken the liberty of removing some of the unnecessary conjunctions and shortening some of the most lengthy and difficult sentences. Throughout, the pronoun *you* is used rather than *Thee* in addressing God, consistent with a growing practice among Christians.

The manuscript has been read by several friends and colleagues (several times!). They are the Revs. H. Arthur Lane, Ronald Minor, Shelton Johnson, and Dr. William Showalter, and Sister Constance Ayers—all of whom made helpful suggestions. Miss Gertrude Andersen has graciously and efficiently proofread my typewritten texts at several levels of their evolution. To all of them I give "humble and hearty thanks." I am grateful, too, to the people of Paraclete Press who suggested that we add this volume to the Living Library series. It goes forth with the prayer that those who read it will not only come to know Augustine better, but be encouraged to know better the same Lord he knew and loved.

—Hal M. Helms

The Confessions *of* Saint Augustine

BOOK I

Infancy to Age Fifteen

ONE

You are great, O Lord, and greatly to be praised. Great is your power, and your wisdom is infinite.[1] And man would praise you; man, who is but a small particle of your creation; yes, man, though he carries with him his mortality, the evidence of his sin, the evidence that you resist the proud; yet man, but a particle of your creation, would praise you.[2]

You awake us to delight in your praise; for you made us for yourself, and our hearts are restless until they rest in you.

Grant me, Lord, to know and understand which of these is most important, to call on you or to praise you. And again, to know you or to call on you. For who can call on you without knowing you? For he who does not know you may call on you as other than you are. Or perhaps we call on you that we may know you? *But how shall they call on him in whom they have not believed? or how shall they believe without a preacher?* And *they who seek the Lord shall praise him.* For they that seek shall find him, and those who find shall praise him. Let me seek you, Lord, by calling on you, and call on you believing in you, for you have been preached to us. My faith calls on you, Lord, the faith you have given me, the faith you have breathed into me through the incarnation of your Son, through the ministry of the preacher.[3]

TWO

But how shall I call upon my God, my God and Lord? For when I call on him, I ask him to come into myself. And what room is there in me, where my God can come—God who made heaven and earth? Is there anything in me, O Lord my God, that can contain you? Indeed, do heaven and earth which you have made, and in which you made me, contain you? Or, since nothing could exist without you, does every existing thing contain you? Why, then, do I ask that you come into me, since I, too, exist—I who could not exist if you were not in me? Why do I say this? Because even if I were in hell, yet you would be there also. For *if I go down into hell, you are there.* I could not exist then, O my God, could not exist at all, unless you were in me. Or should I not rather say, I could not exist unless I were in you, *from whom are all things, by whom are all things, and in whom are all things.*

Even so, Lord, even so. Where do I call you to come, since I am in you? Or whence can you enter into me? For where beyond heaven and earth could I go that my God might come there into me, who has said, *I fill the heaven and the earth?*

THREE

Do the heaven and earth then contain you, since you fill them? Or do you fill them and yet overflow, since they cannot contain you? And where, when the heaven and earth are filled, do you pour forth that which remains of yourself? Or indeed, is there no need that you who contain all things should be contained by anything, since those things you fill, you fill by containing them? For the vessels that you fill do not sustain you, since even if they were broken, you would not be poured out. And when you are poured out on us, you are not cast down, but we are uplifted. You are not dissipated, but we are drawn together. But as you fill all things, do you fill them with your whole self, or, since all things cannot contain you wholly, do they contain part of you? Do they all contain the same part at once, or has each its own proper part—the greater more, the smaller less? If this is so, then is one part of you greater, another less? Or are you wholly everywhere, while nothing altogether contains you?

FOUR

What are you then, my God—what, but the Lord God? *For who is Lord but the Lord? Or who is God save our God?* Most high, most excellent, most powerful, most almighty, most merciful, and most just; most hidden, yet most present; most beautiful, and most strong; stable, yet mysterious; unchangeable, yet changing all things; never new, never old; making all things new and *bringing age upon the proud, though they know it not;* ever working, yet ever at rest; still gathering, yet lacking nothing; sustaining, filling and protecting; creating, nourishing, and maturing; seeking, yet possessing all things. You love without passion; you are jealous without anxiety; you repent, yet have no sorrow; you are angry, yet serene; change your ways, yet your plans are unchanged; recover what you find, having never lost it; never in need, yet rejoicing in gain; never covetous, yet requiring interest. You receive over and above, that you may owe—yet who has anything that is not yours? You pay debts, owing nothing; remit debts, losing nothing. And what have I now said, my God, my life, my holy joy—what is this I have said? Or what do any say when they speak of you? Yet woe to those who keep silence, since those who say most are as the dumb!

FIVE

Oh, how shall I find rest in you? Who will send you into my heart to flood it, that I may forget my woes and embrace you, my only good? What are you to me? In your pity, teach me to speak. What am I to you that you demand my love, and if I do not give it are angry with me and threaten me with great sorrows? Is it then, a slight sorrow not to love you? Oh, alas! for your mercies' sake, O Lord my God, tell me what you are to me. *Say to my soul, "I am your salvation."* When I hear this word, may I run and lay hold of you. Hide not your face from me. Let me see it, though I die, for I shall assuredly die if I do not see it. [4]

The house of my soul is narrow; enlarge it, that you may enter in. It is in ruins! Repair it! It has in it that which must offend your eyes. I confess and know it. But who shall cleanse it, or to whom shall I cry, but to you? *Lord, cleanse me from my secret faults and spare your servant from the power of the enemy. I believe, and therefore I speak.* Lord, you know. *Have I not confessed against myself my transgressions to you, and you, my God, have forgiven the iniquity of my heart? I do not contend in the judgment with you,* who are the Truth; I am afraid to deceive myself, lest my iniquity lie against itself. Therefore *I do not contend in judgment with you, for if you, Lord, should mark iniquities, O Lord, who shall stand?*

SIX

Yet allow me to speak before your mercy, me—*dust and ashes.* Allow me to speak for I speak to your mercy and not to man's scorn. You too, perhaps, despise me, but when you turn to me, you will have compassion on me. For what would I say, O Lord my God, but that I know not from whence I came into this—shall I call it "dying life," this "living death"? Yet as I was told by my earthly parents out of whose substance you fashioned me (for I do not remember it), the comforts of your compassion sustained me. Then I received the comfort of human milk, for neither my mother nor my nurses filled their own breasts, but you bestowed the nourishment of my infancy through them, according to your ordinance and that bounty of yours which underlies all things.

You also caused me to want no more than you provided; and those who nourished me gave me willingly what you gave them, for they, with a heaven-taught affection, willingly gave me what you had abundantly supplied. It was good for them that my good should come from them, though in truth it was really not from them but by them, for all good things are from you, O God, and *from God is all my health.* This is what I have learned since, as you have declared yourself to me through your blessings within me and from without, which you have bestowed on me. For at that time I knew only how to suck, to be satisfied when comfortable and to cry when in pain—nothing more.

Afterward I began to smile, first in sleep, then awake. This was told me of myself, and I believe it (though of myself I do not remember it), for we see the same thing in other infants. So, little by little, I realized where I was and wanted to express my desires to those who could satisfy them, but I could not! For my wants were inside me and they were outside and could not by any faculty of their own enter my soul. So I flung my limbs and voice about at random making the few signs I could, suggesting (though very inadequately) by signs or sounds what it was I wanted. And when I was not presently satisfied (because what I wanted either was not understood or was not good for me), I grew indignant that my elders were not subject to me, angry with those who owed me no service, for not serving me, and avenged myself on them by tears. Such have I learned infants to be by watching them, and that I was the same way myself;

they, though unknowing, have shown me better than my nurses who knew me.

But lo! my infancy died long since, and I live on. But you, Lord, live for ever, and in you nothing dies, since before the foundation of the world, and before all that can be called "before," you are, and you are God and Lord of all which you have created. With you, fixed forever, abide the first causes of all passing things, the unchanging sources of all changeable things; the eternal reasons of all things unreasoning and temporal.

Tell me, Lord, your suppliant; O all merciful One, tell your miserable one—tell me, did my infancy succeed another age of mine that died before it? Was it that which I spent within my mother's womb? For of that I have heard something and have myself seen pregnant women. And what before that life, O God, my joy? Was I indeed anywhere or anybody? For no one can tell me this, neither father nor mother, nor experience of others, nor my own memory. Perhaps you laugh at me for asking such things and bid me praise you and acknowledge you for what I do know.

I give you thanks, Lord of heaven and earth, and praise you for my first being and my infancy, of which I remember nothing. You have appointed that mankind should learn much about themselves from others and believe many things on the authority of frail women. Even then I had life and being, and at the close of my infancy I was already looking for ways to make my feelings known to others. Where could such a creature come from, Lord, but from you, or shall any of us be skillful enough to fashion himself? Or can any stream be found anywhere else that brings being and life into us, except this, that you, O Lord, have made us, with whom being and life are one, because you yourself are supremely being and life? For *you are most high and do not change*, neither does today come to a close in you, and yet it does come to a close in you, because all such things are also in you. For they would have no way even to pass away unless you sustained them. And since *your years do not fail,* your years are as an ever-present today. How many of our years and our fathers' years have flowed away through your today, and received from it their measure and shape of being; and still others to come shall receive the shape of their degree of being and pass away. But *you are still the same,* and all tomorrows and what is beyond them, and all yesterdays and what is behind them, you make to be in your today. What does it matter to me, even if none of us can understand this? Let us still rejoice and say, "What *is* this?" Let us be content by not understanding to find you, rather than by understanding not to find you.

SEVEN

Hear me, O God! Alas for the sin of mankind! We speak this way and you have compassion on us, for you made us, but you did not make sin in us. Who reminds me of the sins of my infancy? *For in your sight, no one is free from sin, not even the infant whose life is but a day upon the earth.*

Who reminds me? Does not each little infant in whom I see what I do not remember about myself? What was my sin then? Is it that I cried for the breast? For if I should cry that way now for food suitable to my present age, I should be laughed at and rebuked. What I did then deserved rebuke, but since I could not understand reproof, custom and reason forbade my being rebuked. For as we grow, we root out and cast away such habits.

Now no man, though he prunes, wittingly throws away what is good. Or was it good then, even for a time, to cry for what, if given, would be hurtful—to bitterly resent that those free persons, elders—even my own parents who gave me birth—did not serve me? That many others besides, wiser than I, did not obey the beckoning of my good pleasure? That I did my best to strike and hurt because my commands were not obeyed, which would only have been to my hurt if carried out? Then in the weakness of infant limbs, not its will, lies its innocence.

I myself have seen and known an infant to be jealous, even though it could not speak. It turned pale and looked bitterly at its foster-brother. Who does not know this to be true? Mothers and nurses tell you that they appease these things by all kinds of remedies. Is that innocence when the fountain of milk is flowing in rich abundance, not to allow one to share it, though it needs the nourishment to sustain its life? We look leniently on all this, not because we fail to recognize the presence and degree of the evils, but because they will disappear as age increases. For although they are allowed in infancy, the very same tempers are utterly intolerable when they appear in an older person.

O Lord my God, who gave life to my infancy, furnishing the body you gave with senses, knitting its limbs together, shaping its proportions and implanting in me all the impulses necessary to the maintenance of the integrity and safety of a living being— you command me to praise you in these things, *to give thanks unto the Lord and to sing to your name, O Most High.* For you are God, almighty and good, even if you had done nothing but these things which no one but you could do. You alone made all things, O most Fair, and you make all things fair; and by your law you order all things.

This period of my life, then, Lord, of which I have no remembrance, which I take on others' word and which I guess from observing other infants—true though the guess may be—I do not care to reckon as a part of my life which I live in this world. For it is hidden from me in the shadows of forgetfulnes no less than that which I spent in my mother's womb. But if *I was shaped in iniquity, and in sin did my mother conceive me,* where, I pray, O my God, where, Lord, or when, was I, your servant, innocent? But I pass that period by. What do I now have to do with that, the memories of which I cannot recall?

EIGHT

Passing on from infancy, I came to boyhood, or rather it came to me, succeeding my infancy. The infancy did not depart (for where did it go?) and yet it was no more. For I was no longer a speechless infant, but a chattering boy. This I do remember and have since observed how I learned to speak.

My elders did not teach me words by any particular method (as a little later they taught me other things); but when I was unable to say all I wished and to whomever I desired by whimperings and broken sounds and various gestures which I used to enforce my wishes, I myself began to repeat the sounds in my memory according to the understanding which you, my God, gave me. When they called anything by name and turned toward it as they spoke, I saw and gathered that the object they were pointing out was called by that name. And I understood by their gestures that they meant this thing and nothing else, movements that are the natural language as it were of all nations, expressed by the countenance, glances of the eyes, movements of the limbs, and tones of the voice, indicating the feelings of the mind as it seeks, gets, rejects or avoids certain things. And so by frequently hearing words as they occurred in various sentences, I gradually gathered what they meant. Having formed my mouth to make these sounds, I could then give voice to my will. Thus I exchanged with those about me these current expressions of our wants, and so advanced deeper into the stormy fellowship of human life, still subject to parental authority and the bidding of my elders.

NINE

O God, my God! What miseries and mockeries I now experienced, when obedience to my teachers was set before me as proper to my boyhood that I might prosper in this world and excel in the science of speech which would gain the praise of men and deceitful riches. After that, I was put in school to get learning whose usefulness I could not imagine (useless as I was), and yet if I was idle in my studies, I was flogged![5] For our forefathers deemed this the right way, and many, passing the same way before us, had laid out the weary paths through which we were obliged to pass, multiplying labor and grief on the children of Adam.

But, Lord, we found that men prayed to you, and we learned from them to think of you according to our abilities, to be some Great One who, though hidden from our senses, could hear and help us. So I began, even as a boy, to pray to you, my help and refuge; and I let my tongue freely call on you, praying to you, even though I was small, with no small earnestness, that I might not be beaten at school. And when you did not hear me (not *giving me over to folly thereby*), my elders, yes, my own parents who certainly wished me no ill, laughed at my stripes, which were then my great and grievous ill.

Is there anyone, Lord, bound to you with such greatness of soul and with so strong an affection (there is a sort of stupidity that may do that much)—is there anyone who is endowed with so great a courage from clinging devoutly to you that he can think lightly of racks and hooks and other tortures? For throughout the whole world men pray fervently to be saved from such tortures and can they as bitterly mock those who fear them as our parents mocked the torments which we suffered from our teachers in boyhood? For we did not fear our torments any less, nor did we pray less to you to escape them. And yet we sinned in writing, reading, or studying less than was required of us. For we did not lack memory or ability, Lord, of which, by your will, we possessed enough for our age. But we delighted only in play, and for this we were punished by those who were doing the same things themselves. But older people's idleness is called business, while boys who do the same, are punished by those same elders; and yet no one expresses pity, either boys or men. For will any one of good sense approve of my being whipped because as a boy I played ball, and so made less progress in studies which I was to learn only so that, as a man, I might play at more shameful games? And what else was my tutor doing who beat me, who, if defeated in some trifling controversy with his fellow tutor, was more embittered and angry than I was when I was beaten in a game of ball by a playmate?

TEN

And yet I sinned in this, O Lord God, Creator and Disposer of all things in Nature (but of sin only the Disposer). O Lord my God, I sinned acting against the commands of my parents and of my teachers. For what they, with whatever motive, wanted me to learn, I might have put to good use later on. But I disobeyed, not because I had chosen a better way, but from love of play, loving the honor of victory in my contests, and to have my ears tickled with fables that they might itch for more. The same curiosity burned in my eyes more and more for the shows and sports of adults. Those who gave these shows were held in such repute that almost everyone wished the same for their children, and they were very willing that the children be beaten if these very games kept them from their studies by which they wanted them to reach the point of being teachers to others.

Look down with compassion on these things, Lord, and deliver us who call upon you now. Deliver those, too, who do not call on you, that they may call on you and that you may deliver them.

ELEVEN

As a boy, then, I had heard of eternal life promised us through the humility of the Lord our God stooping to our pride. Even from the womb of my mother, who greatly hoped in you, I was signed with the mark of his cross and seasoned with his salt.[6] You saw, Lord, how at one time while yet a boy I was suddenly seized with pains in the stomach and was near death. You saw, my God, for you were my Keeper, with what eagerness of mind and with what faith I besought the baptism of your Christ, my God and Lord, from the piety of my own mother and of your Church, the mother of us all. At this time, my mother was very anxious, since she labored more lovingly in travail for my salvation than in my natural birth. She would have provided for my cleansing initiation by your health-giving sacraments, confessing you, Lord Jesus, for the remission of sins, if I had not suddenly recovered. And so, as if I must needs be further polluted if I should live, my cleansing was deferred, because the defilements of sin would bring greater and more perilous guilt after that washing.[7] I already believed at that time, with my mother and the whole household except my father. Yet he did not overcome the power of my mother's piety in me so as to prevent my believing in Christ. The fact that he did not yet believe did not make me think that I should not. For it was her earnest concern that you, my God, should be my Father rather than he. In this you enabled her to overcome her husband to whom, though the better of the two, she yielded obedience because in this she obeyed your commandment as well.

I beseech you, my God, for I would like to know if it is your will, for what purpose was my baptism then deferred? Was it for my good that the reins were loosened on me, as it were, for me to sin? Or were they not slackened at all? If not, why does it still echo in my ears on all sides, "Let him alone, let him do as he will, for he is not yet baptized"? But as to bodily health, no one says, "Let him be wounded even more seriously, for he is not yet healed." How much better then would it have been for me to have been healed at once and then, by my friends' diligence and my own, my soul's recovered health had then been kept safe in your keeping who gave it! Better truly. But how many great waves of temptation seemed to hang over me after my childhood! My mother foresaw these and preferred to expose the unformed [unregenerate] clay to them rather than to the very image itself after it was made.

TWELVE

In my childhood, which was less dangerous for me than my adolescence, I had no love of learning and hated to be forced to it. Yet I was forced to it, and this was good for me, though I did not do well. For I would not have learned unless I was compelled. But no one does well against his will, even though what he does may be well. Yet they who forced me did not do well either, but the good that came to me was from you, my God. For they were totally uncaring of how I should use what they forced me to learn, except to satisfy the inordinate desire of a rich beggary and a shameful glory. But you, *by whom the very hairs of our head are numbered,* used for my good the error of all those who urged me to learn; and my own error in my unwillingness to learn, you used for my punishment—a fit penalty for one, so small a boy and so great a sinner. So by the instruments of those who did not do well, you did well for me; and by my own sin you justly punished me. For you have appointed and it is so, that every inordinate affection should be its own punishment.

THIRTEEN

But why did I hate the Greek language so much, which I studied as a boy? I do not yet fully know the answer. For I loved the Latin; not what my first masters taught me, but what the so-called grammarians teach. For those first lessons, reading, writing and arithmetic, I thought as great a burden and punishment as any Greek studies. And yet where did all this come from, too, but from the sin and vanity of this life, because *I was but flesh and a breath that passes away and does not come again.* For those primary lessons were better, certainly, because they were more certain. By them I obtained and still retain the ability to read what I find written, and the ability to write what I will. On the other hand, I was forced to learn the wanderings of one Aeneas, forgetful of my own, and to weep for Dido, dead because she killed herself for love; while at the same time with dry eyes, I brooked my wretched self dying among these things, far from you, O God of my life.

What is more wretched than a wretch who does not pity himself, weeping over the death of Dido for her love of Aeneas, but shedding no tears over his own death in not loving you, O God, Light of my heart, Bread of my inmost soul, Power that weds my mind with my inmost thought? I did not love you, and I committed fornication against you, and all those around me who were doing the same, echoed, "Well done! Well done!" for *the friendship of this world is fornication against you*, and "Well done! well done!" echoes on till one is ashamed not to be such a man. And for all this I did not weep, though I wept for Dido, slain as she sought death by the point of a sword, myself seeking the extremest and lowest level of your creatures, having forsaken you, earth sinking to earth. And if I were forbidden to read all this, I grieved that I was not allowed to read what grieved me. Madness like this is considered more honorable and more fruitful learning than that by which I learned to read and write.

But now, my God, shout aloud in my soul and let your truth tell me "It is not so! it is not so! Far better was that first study!" For I would rather forget the wanderings of Aeneas and all such things than how to read and write. Over the entrance of the Grammar School a veil is hung, it is true, but this is not so much a sign of honor of the mysteries taught in them as a covering for error. Let not those whom I no longer fear cry out against me while I confess whatever my soul desires to you, my God, and let them agree in the condemnation of my evil ways, that I may love your good ways. Let neither buyers nor sellers of grammar education cry out against me. For if I question them as to whether Aeneas came once to Carthage, as the poet tells, the less learned will reply that they do not know; the more learned, that he never did. But if I ask with what letters the name "Aeneas" is written, everyone who has learned this will answer me rightly, in accordance with the conventional understanding men have settled on as to these signs. If, again, I ask which might be forgotten with the least detriment to the concerns of life—reading and writing, or these poetic fictions, who does not foresee what all must answer who have not wholly forgotten themselves? I erred then, when as a boy I preferred those vain studies to the more profitable ones, or rather loved the one and hated the other. "One and one are two; two and two are four." This to me was a hateful sing-song; but such vanities as the wooden horse full of armed men and the burning of Troy and the "spectral image" Creusa were a most pleasant but vain spectacle.

FOURTEEN

Why then did I hate the Greek classics, which have the same kind of tales? For Homer also skillfully wove the same fictions, and is more sweetly vain, yet he was disagreeable to my boyish taste. And so I suppose would Virgil be to Grecian children, if forced to learn him as I was Homer. The difficulty, in truth, of learning a foreign tongue mingled, as it were, with all the sweetness of the Grecian fable. For I did not understand one word of it, and to make me understand I was urged vehemently with cruel threats and punishments. There was a time, of course, when as an infant I knew no Latin. But this I acquired without fear or torment, by mere observation, amid the caresses of my nurses and jests of those who smiled on me, and the sportiveness of those who encouraged me. I learned all this without any pressure of punishment, for my own heart urged me to bring forth its own conceptions, which I could only do by learning words—not of those who taught me, but of those who talked to me, into whose ears also I brought whatever thoughts I had. No doubt then, a free curiosity has more influence in our learning these things than a frightful enforcement. But this enforcement restrains the overflowing of unrestrained freedom. Your laws, O God, your laws—from the teacher's cane to the martyr's trials—are able to turn bitternes into a wholesome thing, and call us back to yourself from the pernicious pleasures that lure us from you.

FIFTEEN

Hear my prayer, O Lord; do not let my soul faint under your discipline. Do not let me faint in confessing before you all your mercies by which you have saved me from my most evil ways, that you might become sweet to me above all the seductions which I once followed; and that I may love you entirely and clasp your hand with whole heart; and that you may yet deliver me from every temptation, even to the end. For lo! O Lord, my King and my God, let whatever useful thing I learned as a child be for your service, and for your service whatever I speak, write, read or count. For you granted me your discipline while I was learning vain things. You have forgiven my sin in taking delight in those vanities. Indeed, I learned many a useful word in them, but these may better be learned in things that are not vain; and that is the safe path for youths to walk in.

SIXTEEN

But woe to you, stream of human custom! Who can stay your course? How long will it be before you are dried up? How long will you carry the sons of Eve into that huge and hideous ocean which even they who are embarked on the Tree can scarcely pass over? Did not I read in you of Jove the thunderer and adulterer? Both, doubtless, he could not be, except to have the real adultery supposedly countenanced and pandered by the feigned thunder. And now which of our gowned masters lends a sober ear to one who from their own school cries out, "These were Homer's fictions; he transferred things human to the gods; I wish that he had transferred divine things to us"? Yet it would be more truthful if he said, "These are indeed his fictions; but he ascribed divine attributes to wicked men, that crimes might not be accounted crimes, and that whoever commits them might appear to imitate the celestial gods, not forsaken mankind!"

And yet, O hellish stream of custom, into you are cast the sons of men with rich rewards for learning such things. And much is made of it when this is going on in the forum in the sight of laws which grant salaries in addition to the scholars' payments. And you lash upon your rocks and roar, "Here words are learned! Here eloquence is attained, essential to gain your ends or to persuade people to your way of thinking." So in truth we would never have known such words as "golden shower," "bosom," "intrigue," "temples of the heavens," or other words in that passage, if Terence had not brought a good-for-nothing youth on the stage to set up Jupiter as his example of lewdness.

Viewing a picture, where the tale was drawn,
Of Jove's descending in a golden shower
To Danae's bosom . . . with a woman's intrigue.

And then notice how he excites himself to lust as if by celestial authority, when he says,

Great Jove,
Who shakes the heaven's highest temples with his thunder
And I, poor mortal man, do not the same?
I did it, and with all my heart I did it.

Not one whit more easily are the words learned for all this vileness; but by their means the vileness is perpetuated with more confidence. Not that I blame the words. They are, as it were, choice and precious vessels. But the wine of error was poured out to us in them by intoxicated teachers; and if we, too, did not drink, we were beaten, and had no sober judge to whom we could appeal. Yet, O my God, in whose presence I now can remember this without hurt, all this, unhappily, I learned willingly with great delight, and for this was called a promising boy.

SEVENTEEN

Bear with me, my God, while I speak a little of those talents you have bestowed on me, and on what follies I wasted them. For I was given a task, troublesome enough to my soul (in hope of praise or fear of shame or stripes), to speak the words of Juno, as she raged and mourned that she could not

Bar off Italy
From all approaches of the Trojan prince.

I had learned that Juno never uttered these words, but we were forced to wander in the paths of these poetic fictions and say in prose much of what the poet expressed in verse. And the one whose speaking showed most the passions of rage and grief, and best reproduced the dignity of the character, was most applauded. What is it to me, O my true Life, my God, that my declamation was applauded above that of many of my own age and class? Is not all this smoke and wind? And was there nothing else on which I could exercise my wit and my tongue? Your praises, Lord, your praises might have supported the yet tender shoots of my heart by your Scriptures, so that it might not have been dragged away among these empty trifles, a shameful prey for the fowls of the air. For there are more ways than one of sacrificing to the fallen angels.

EIGHTEEN

What wonder is it that I was carried away to vanity and strayed from you, O my God, when men were set before me as models, who, if in relating some action of theirs, not evil in itself, they committed some barbarism or solecism, and being censured, became embarrassed? But when they made a full and ornate oration in well-ordered words, telling of their own disordered life, and were applauded for it, they boasted. These things you see, Lord, and hold your peace, *longsuffering and plenteous in mercy and truth*. Will you keep silent for ever? And even now you draw out of this vast deep the soul that seeks you, that thirsts for your pleasures, *whose heart says to you, I have sought your face; "Your face, Lord, will I seek."* I was far from your face, for darkened affections mean separation from you. For it is not by our feet or change of place that we either leave you or return to you. That younger [prodigal] son did not look out for horses or chariots or ships, fly with visible wings, or journey by the motion of his limbs, so that he might waste all he was given in riotous living in a far country at his departure. You were a loving Father when you gave, and more loving to him when he returned empty. So then in lustful—that is, in darkened passions—lies the true distance from your face.

Behold, O Lord, God; yes, look patiently as you are wont to do how carefully the sons of men observe the conventional rules of letters and syllables received from those who spoke prior to them, yet neglect the eternal rules of everlasting salvation received from you. So true is this that a teacher or student of the hereditary laws of pronunciation will offend others more by saying "'uman being" without the "h" in violation of the laws of grammar, than if he, a human being hated another human being in violation of your law. As if indeed, any enemy could be more destructive than the hatred with which he is incensed against him, or could wound more deeply the one he persecutes than he wounds his own heart by his enmity. Of a truth, there is no knowledge of letters so inborn as the writing of our conscience, "that he is doing to another what he would hate to receive from another." How mysterious are your ways, O God: you only are great, who sit silent on high and by an unwearied law dispense punishing blindness to illicit desires. In seeking the reputation of eloquence, a man standing before a human judge, surrounded by a human throng, inveighing against his enemy with the fiercest hatred, will take the greatest care not to let his tongue slip into grammatical error, lest he murder the word "human," but takes no heed lest, through the fury of his spirit, he murder the real human being.

NINETEEN

These were the customs in the midst of which I, an unhappy boy, was cast, and on this stage it was that I feared more to commit a barbarism than, having committed one, to envy those who had not. These things I declare and confess to you, my God; for these I was applauded by those whom I then thought it my whole duty to please. For I did not perceive the abyss of infamy into which I was cast away from your eyes. In your eyes who could be more infamous than I already was, displeasing even those who were like me, deceiving with innumerable lies my tutor, my masters and my parents from love of play, the desire to see stage shows, and a stage-struck restlessness to copy them? Pilferings also I committed from my parents' cellar and table, enslaved by gluttony, or that I might give something to boys who sold me their playthings, which all the while they liked as little as I. In these games, too, I often sought dishonest victories, conquered as I was by a vain desire for first place. And what could I endure less in others or, when I detected it, criticize so fiercely, than the very thing I was doing to others? And if I was detected and I too, was upbraided, I chose rather to quarrel than to yield. Is this the innocence of childhood? Not so, Lord, not so; I entreat your mercy, O my God. For these same sins, as we grow older, these very sins are transferred from tutors and masters, from nuts and balls and sparrows, to magistrates and kings, to gold, and lands, and slaves, just as severe punishments displace the cane. It was then the low stature of childhood which you, our King, commended as the emblem of humility, when you said, *Of such is the kingdom of heaven.*

TWENTY

Yet O Lord, Creator and Ruler of the universe, most excellent and good, thanks had been due to you even if you had destined me only for childhood. For even then I had being, I lived and felt; and even then was solicitous for the care of my own well-being—a trace of that mysterious unity from whence I was derived. I guarded by intuition the wholeness of my senses, and in these insignificant pursuits, and also in my thoughts on trivial things, I learned to take pleasure in truth. I hated to be deceived, had a vigorous memory, was gifted with the power of speech, soothed by friendship, avoided sorrow, meanness and ignorance. In so small a being, was this not wonderful—even praiseworthy? All are gifts of my God; I did not give them to myself; and they are good, and these together constitute myself. He who made me, then is good, and he is my Good; I will rejoice before him for every good gift I enjoyed as a boy. For in this lay my sin, that I sought pleasures, honors and truths in his creatures rather than in him—in myself and the rest—and so fell headlong into sorrows, troubles and errors. Thanks be to you, my joy, my glory and my confidence, my God; thanks be to you for all your gifts. But do preserve them for me. For in so doing, you will preserve me and those things which you have given me will be developed and perfected, and I shall be with you. For my very being is from you.

BOOK II

Object of These Confessions

ONE

I will now call to mind my past foulness and the carnal corruptions of my soul, not because I love them, but that I may love you, O my God. For love of your love I do it, reviewing my most wicked ways in the very bitterness of my memory, so that you may grow sweeter to me; O sweetness never failing, blissful and abiding Sweetness, gathering me again from my dissipation in which I was torn to shreds while I was alienated from you, the one Good. I wasted myself among a multiplicity of things. For I burned in my youth to take my fill of hell, and ran wild into a rank profusion of various and dark loves. My beauty consumed away, and I was rotten in your eyes, pleasing myself and wanting to please others.

TWO

And what was it that I delighted in, but to love and be loved? But I did not keep within the limits of love—of mind to mind —friendship's bright boundary. Out of the muddy concupiscence of the flesh and the bubblings of youth, mists fumed up which clouded and overcast my heart, so that I could not discern the clear brightness of love from the fog of lustfulness. But confusedly boiling inwardly, and hurrying my reckless youth over the precipice of unholy desire, I sank in a gulf of shameful and scandalous wickedness. Your wrath hung over me, but I did not know it. I had grown deaf to the clanking of the chain of my mortality, the punishment of the pride of my soul.[1] I strayed further from you, and you let me alone. I was tossed about, wasted, dissipated, and I boiled over in my fornications. But you held your peace, you who are too lately my joy! You held your peace and I wandered further and further from you into more and more fruitless seed-plots of sorrows with a proud depression of spirit and a restless weariness.

Oh, that someone had then regulated my disorder and turned to some good the passing beauties of these, the least exalted things of your creation! Would that someone had put bounds to their delightfulness to me, so that the urges of my youth might have cast themselves on the marriage shore if they could not be calmed, and kept them within the confines of a family, as your law prescribes, O Lord![2] For this is the way you form the offspring of this our death, and are able with a gentle hand to blunt the thorns by which we were excluded from your paradise. Your almighty power is not far from us, even when we are far from you. But I should have heeded more carefully the voice from the clouds which said, *Nevertheless such shall have trouble in the flesh, but I would spare you,* and *It is good for a man not to touch a woman,* and further, *He who is unmarried thinks of the things of the Lord, how he may please the Lord; but he who is married cares for the things of this world, how he may please his wife.* I should have listened more attentively to these words and, being separated for the sake of the kingdom of heaven, I would have waited more happily for your embraces.

But I, poor fool, seethed like a troubled sea, following the rushing of my own tide. Forsaking you, I went beyond all your limits. Yet I did not escape your scourges! What mortal can? But you were always with me, mercifully severe, and you sprinkled all my unlawful pleasures with a most bitter disgust, so that I should seek pleasures free from anxiety. But where to find such, I could not discover, except in you, O Lord. You teach by sorrow and wound us in order to heal, and slay us that we may not die from you. Where was I, and how far was I exiled from the delights of your house in that sixteenth year of my mortal life, when the madness of lust (to which human shamelessness gives license, although forbidden by your Law) held complete sway over me and I surrendered myself to it entirely? My friends meanwhile took no care to save me from ruin by marriage. Their only concern was that I should learn to speak excellently and become a persuasive orator.

THREE

That year my studies were stopped for a time, after my return from Madaura (a neighboring town where I had been sent to learn grammar and rhetoric).[3] My father then provided expenses for a journey to Carthage—out of his determination rather than his means, for he was but a poor freeman of Tagaste. To whom do I tell this? Not to you, my God, but before you to my fellow men, or at least to that small portion of them who may see these writings of mine. And for what purpose? So that whoever reads this may consider out of what depths we are to cry to you. For what comes nearer to your ears than a confessing heart and a life of faith? Who did not praise my father for the fact that he went beyond his ability and means to furnish his son with all the necessities for a long journey for the sake of his education? Many far abler citizens did no such thing for their children. But yet this same father had no concern as to how I grew toward you, or how chaste I was, as long as I was skillful in speech, however fruitless I might have been to your cultivation of my heart, which is your field, O God, the only true and good Lord.

But while in my sixteenth year, I lived with my parents, leaving all school for a while. A season of idleness was caused by my parents' financial circumstances. During that time the briers of unclean desire grew rank over my head, and there was no hand to root them out. When my father saw me at the baths, perceiving that I was becoming a man and was endued with a restless youthfulness, he, as if already anticipating his future grandchildren, gleefully told my mother about it, rejoicing in that intoxication of the senses in which the world forgets its Creator and falls in love with the creature instead of you—the intoxication of the invisible wine of a perverse and downward-tending will which stoops to the very basest things. But in my mother's breast you had already begun your temple, and the commencement of your holy dwelling place. My father, on the other hand, was as yet only a catechumen, and even that but recently. She was startled then with a holy fear and trembling, and though I was not yet baptized, she feared those crooked ways in which they walk who turn their backs to you rather than their faces.

Woe is me! Do I dare say that you held your peace, O my God, while I strayed farther from you? Did you then indeed hold your peace to me? And whose but yours were the words which you sang in my ears by my mother, your faithful handmaid? But none of them sank into my heart to make me perform them. For she despised these strayings, and I remember she warned me in private with great solicitude, *not to commit fornication*; but especially never to defile the wife of another. These seemed womanish words to me, which I should blush to obey. But they were yours, and I knew it not. I thought you were silent and that it was she who was speaking. Yet all the time you were speaking to me through her, words that were despised by me, *the son of your handmaid, your servant*. But I did not know it.

I ran headlong with such blindness that among my peers I was ashamed to be less shameless than they when I heard them boast of their disgraceful acts. The greater the degradation, the more was their boast. And I took pleasure both in the deed and in the praise.

What is worthy of blame but vice? But I made myself out to be even worse than I was so that I might not be dispraised. When I had not sinned in some way like the others who were more abandoned in their sin, I would say that I had done what I had not done so that I should not seem contemptible to them in my relative innocence, or esteemed less for being somewhat more chaste.

Behold with what companions I walked the streets of Babylon, and wallowed in its mire, as if in a bed of spices and precious ointments! And so that I might be knit more firmly to the very root of sin, my invisible enemy trod me down and seduced me, and I was then easy to seduce!

But although my mother had now fled out of the "center of Babylon," she still went more slowly in the skirts of it.[4] She advised me to be chaste, but paid no heed to what her husband had told her about me, so as to restrain within the bounds of married love what she felt to be presently destructive and dangerous for the future (if it could not be pared away to the quick). She did not heed this, for she feared that a wife might prove a clog and hindrance to my hopes—not the hopes of the world to come, which my mother had in you, but the hopes of education, which both my parents were too anxious for me to acquire—my father because he had little or no thought of you and only vain thoughts for me, and my mother because she thought that those usual courses of learning would not only be no drawback, but even of some help toward my attaining you. I am guessing about this, recalling as well as I may the respective dispositions of my parents.

The reins, meantime, were slackened toward me beyond all proper restraint, to spend my time in sport, yes, even to dissoluteness, to do whatever I wanted. And in all this was a darkness, coming between me and the brightness of your truth, O my God; *and my iniquity grew enormous as with fatness.*

FOUR

Theft is punished by your law, O Lord, and the law written on the hearts of men which iniquity itself cannot blot out. For what thief can stand another thief? Not even a rich thief will tolerate one who steals through need. Yet I had a desire to steal, and did so, compelled neither by hunger nor poverty, but through a boredom of well-doing and a lust for iniquity. For I pilfered something of which I had enough and much better. I did not care to enjoy what I stole, but rather to enjoy the act of stealing and the sin itself. There was a pear tree near our vineyard, heavily loaded with fruit that lacked both color and flavor to tempt us. To shake and rob this, some of us worthless young fellows went late one night, having prolonged our games in the streets till then, as our disgraceful habit was, and took huge loads of these pears, not to eat ourselves, but to throw to the hogs, having only tasted them, and to do this pleased us all the more because it was forbidden.

Behold my heart, O God, behold my heart, which you had pity on when it was in the bottomless pit. Let this heart of mine tell you what it sought there, that I should be evil for naught, and that my sin should have no cause but the sin itself.[5] It was foul and I loved it; that is, I loved my own perishing, I loved my own fault—not that for which I committed the fault, but the fault itself. Foul soul, leaving security with you and leaping down into destruction, seeking nothing through shame but the shame itself!

FIVE

There is an attractiveness in all beautiful bodies, in gold and silver and all things. Bodily contact has its own powerful influence, and each other sense has its proper purpose when used temperately. Worldly honor also has its glory, as have the power of command and strength to overcome. But from these also comes the desire for revenge. Yet, to acquire all these, we must not depart from you, Lord, nor violate your law.

The life we live here has its own attractiveness through a certain measure of beauty of its own and its correspondence with all beautiful things here below. Human friendship is endeared with a sweet tie in a unity formed of many souls. On account of this, sin is committed when through an immoderate appetite for these goods of the lowest order, we forsake the better and higher ones—yourself, our Lord God, your truth and your law. For these lower things have their delights, but not like my God, who made all things. *The righteous rejoice in the Lord and he is the joy of the upright in heart.*

So when we ask why a crime was done, we assume that it could have been done only through some desire of obtaining some of those things which we call lesser goods, or out of fear of losing them. For truly they are beautiful and comely, even though compared with those higher and beatific goods they are abject and low. A man has murdered another. Why? He coveted his wife or his estate. Or a man would rob for his own livelihood, or the fear of losing something of the kind through the action of the one he was robbing; or, having been wronged, he burned for revenge. Would anyone commit murder for no cause at all, simply delighting in murdering? Who would believe it?

As for that furious and savage man [Catiline], of whom it is said that he was evil and cruel without cause, a cause is nevertheless assigned. "I did it," he says, "to keep my hand and heart from becoming inactive." And to what end? That, when once he had taken the city through his practice of crimes, he might gain honor, empire, riches, and be freed from fear of the laws which he feared because he knew his own villainy; and that he and his family might be freed from the possibility of want. So, even Catiline himself did not love his own villainies, but something else, and to obtain these he became wicked.[6]

SIX

What then did I, wretched as I was in that sixteenth year of my life, so love in my theft, you deed of darkness? You were not beautiful; you were theft. But are you anything at all, that I should argue with you in this way? The pears that we stole were fair to look at, because they were your creation, O fairest of all, Creator of all, God of goodness, God, the highest Good and my true Good. Those pears were pleasant to the sight, but my soul did not want them. I had ample quantities better than they. I picked them only in order to steal. For, when I had stolen them, I threw them away. My only gratification was my own sin which I was pleased to enjoy. For if any of those pears entered my mouth, what sweetened their taste was sin.

Now I ask, O Lord my God, what was it in that theft that delighted me? It has no beauty in it[7]—I mean not such beauty as there is in justice and wisdom; nor such as is in the mind, the memory and the animate life of man; nor yet such as is in the stars, glorious and beautiful in their orbits; nor the earth or sea, full of fresh offspring ever taking the place of what is being used up. No, not even that false and dark beauty which belongs generally to deceptive vices.

Thus pride imitates exaltedness, but you alone are God, exalted above all. And what does ambition seek but honor and glory, whereas you alone are to be honored above all and are glorious forevermore? By cruelty the powerful want to be feared, but none is to be feared but God alone, out of whose power nothing can be wrested or snatched away—when, where, whither, or by whom? The enticements of the lascivious person want to be counted as love, but nothing is so enticing as your love, nor is anything loved more healthfully than your truth, bright and beautiful above all. Curiosity pretends to be a right desire for knowledge, but it is you who understand all things supremely. Yes, even ignorance and foolishness cloak themselves under the name of simplicity and harmlessness, but nothing is more singular than you, and what is more harmles than you, since it is their own works that bring harm to sinners? Yes, sloth seems to long for rest, but what rest is there, but in the Lord? Luxury parades as plenty and abundance, but you are the fullness and never-failing abundance of pleasures that are incorruptible. Wastefulness presents a semblance of liberality, but you are the most overflowing Giver of all good. Covetousness would possess many things, but you are the Possessor of all things. Envy wrangles for first place, but who can be before you? Anger seeks revenge; who can avenge justly but you? Fear jumps with alarm at the unexpected and sudden which threaten things beloved, and is wary of their security, but who can separate those you love from you? Grief pines away for the lost delight of its desires, and wishes not to be deprived of anything more than you can be.

In this way the soul commits fornication when we turn from you, seeking without you what we cannot find pure and untainted until we return to you. Thus all who separate themselves far from you and raise themselves up against you, imitate you. But even by imitating you in these ways, they acknowledge that you are the Creator of all nature, and that there is no place where they can flee from you altogether.

What, then, did I love in that theft, and how did I even corruptly and perversely imitate my Lord? Did I wish to break your law by a kind of trick because I could not do it by a strong hand? While I was no better than a bond slave, did I counterfeit a false liberty by doing without punishment what I could not do without sin, in a shadowy imitation of your omnipotence? Behold this slave of yours, running away from his Lord, and laying hold on a shadow! O rottenness! O monstrosity of life and depth of death! Could I like what was unlawful only because it was unlawful?

SEVEN

What shall I render unto the Lord, that while my memory recalls these things, my soul is not appalled at them? *I shall love you, O Lord, and thank you, and confess your name*, because you have forgiven me these wicked and heinous deeds of mine, and have melted away my sins as if they were ice. To your grace I ascribe whatever sins I have not committed; for what might I not have done, who even loved a sin for its own sake? Yes, I confess all to have been forgiven me; both the evils I committed by my own willfulness and those which, by your help, I did not commit. What man is he, who, reflecting on his own weakness, dares to ascribe his chastity and innocency to his own strength, so that he should love you the less, as if he needed your mercy less, the mercy by which you forgive the sins of those who turn to you? For whoever, being called by you, has followed your voice and avoided those things which he finds me remembering and confessing concerning myself, let him not despise me. Sick as I was, I was healed by that same Physician whose aid is the reason he was not sick at all, or rather was less sick; but let him love you as much as I do, yes, all the more, since he sees that I have been rescued from such deep destruction of sin by him who preserved him from a like destruction.

EIGHT

And what return did I get from those things which, when I remember them, cause me shame—above all that theft which I loved for the theft's sake. Since the theft itself was nothing, I who loved it was all the more wretched! I would not have done it alone. Such as I remember myself to have been then, I would never have done it alone. So I loved in it the companionship of my accomplices with whom I did it. Did I then love something else besides the theft? No, I loved nothing else; for that circumstance of the company was also nothing. Who can teach me the truth except him who enlightens my heart and uncovers its dark corners? What is it that has come to mind to inquire about, discuss and consider? For if I had loved the pears I stole and wished to enjoy them, I could have done it alone. The mere commission of the theft might have given enough pleasure to satisfy me. I would not have needed to inflame the itching of my desires by the stimulus of association in evil. But since my pleasure was not in those pears, but in the offense itself, it needed the concurrence of the company of fellow-sinners.

NINE

What was this pleasure, then? Surely it was shameful, and woe is me that I had it! But yet, what was it? *Who can understand his errors?* It was the sport which, as it were, tickled our hearts at the thought that we were deceiving those who knew nothing of what we were doing and would have vehemently disapproved of it. Yet again, why was my delight of such sort that I did not do it alone? Because no one ordinarily laughs alone? Ordinarily no one does, though laughter sometimes overcomes men when no one else is with them, if something very ludicrous presents itself to their senses or mind. But I would not have done this alone. Alone I could never, never have done it. Behold my God, before you, the vivid remembrance of my soul! Alone, I would never have committed that theft. For what I stole did not please me.

O friendship, you are too unfriendly! You mysterious seducer of the soul! Out of mirth and wanton recklessness grew the desire to do harm to others, without wanting our own gain or revenge. But when it is said, "Let's go, let's do it," we are ashamed not to be shameless.

TEN

Who can unravel that twisted and tangled knottiness of my soul? It is foul. I hate to think of it or look at it. But I long for you, O righteousness and innocence, fair and comely to all pure eyes, and a satisfaction that never cloys. With you is complete rest and untroubled life. He who enters into you, enters into the joy of the Lord, and shall have no fear, and shall do excellently in the most Excellent. I strayed far from you in those days of my youth, and wandered too far away from you, O my God, my Stay, and I became to myself a barren land.

BOOK III

From Age Sixteen to Eighteen

ONE

I came to Carthage, where a caldron of unholy loves bubbled up all around me. I did not yet love, but I loved to love, and out of a deep-seated want I hated myself that I did not want. I looked around for something to love, in love with the idea of loving, despising a safe way without snares. For my soul was starving for that inward food, yourself, O my God, though that famine caused me no hunger. I had no appetite for incorruptible food, not because I was filled with it, but the more empty I was, the more I loathed it. For this reason my soul was sick and, full of ulcers, it cast itself forth miserably, craving to be excited by the touch of feeling creatures. Yet, if they had not had souls, they would not have been objects of love.

To love and be loved was sweet to me, and all the more when I succeeded in enjoying the person I loved. So I polluted the waters of friendship with my unclean appetite, and I dimmed its brightness with the hell of lustfulness. Foul and dishonorable as I was, I wanted, through my great vanity, to be elegant and courtly. I fell headlong then into the love in which I longed to be trapped. My God, my mercy, with how much bitterness did you, out of your great goodness, sprinkle me for that sweetness! For I was loved by another and we secretly formed a bond of pleasure. Thus I was blissfully bound with sorrow-bringing ties, so that I might be scourged with the burning rods of jealousy, suspicions, fears, anger and quarrels.

TWO

Stage-plays also carried me away, full of representations of my miseries, fuel to my fire. Why is it that man likes to be made sad by beholding doleful and tragic scenes which he himself would by no means suffer? Yet he wishes as a spectator to feel sorrow at them, and this very sorrow is his pleasure. What is this but wretched madness? For they who are most affected with these actions are those who are most plagued with the actual emotions. When a man suffers personally, it is considered misery; when he sympathizes with another who is suffering, it is called mercy. But what sort of compassion is this for fictitious and pretended sufferings? The hearer is not called on to relieve such suffering, but only to grieve. And the more he grieves, the more he applauds the actor of these fictions. If the calamities of those characters (whether of ancient times, or mere fictitious ones) are acted in such a way that the spectator is not moved to tears, he goes away disappointed and critical. But if he is moved to grief, he sits it out attentively and weeps for joy.

Are sorrows, then, also loved? Surely all people desire joy. Surely no one likes to be miserable, but is pleased to be merciful. But is it because mercy cannot be without sorrow that sorrow is loved? This also springs from the vein of friendship. But where does that vein go? Whither does it flow? Why does it run into that torrent of pitch, bubbling forth those monstrous tides of loathsome lustfulness into which it is deliberately changed and transformed, precipitated and corrupted from its heavenly clearness by its own will? Shall we put away mercy then? By no means! Let us rather be content to love grief sometimes. But beware of uncleanness, O my soul, under the protection of my God, the God of our fathers, who is to be praised and exalted above all forever. Beware of uncleanness!

I do not take myself to be without pity; but then in the theaters I sympathized with lovers when they sinfully enjoyed one another, although this was done fictitiously in the play. And when they lost one another, as if pitying them, I grieved with them, yet had my delight in both. But nowadays I feel much more pity for the one who rejoices in his wickedness than for the one who is thought to endure hardship by missing some pernicious pleasure and the loss of some miserable happiness. This is surely the truer mercy, but in it grief does not delight us. For though he grieves for a person in misery, yet he who is genuinely compassionate would rather there were nothing for him to grieve for. Some sorrow may then be allowed, but none loved. Thus, O Lord God, you who love souls far more purely than we, are more incorruptibly compassionate on them, and yet you are wounded with no sorrow. But who is sufficient for these things?

But I, miserable one, then loved to grieve and sought things to grieve at; that acting pleased me best and attracted me most powerfully which drew tears from me. And what wonder was it, that an unhappy sheep, straying from your flock, restless under your care, should become infected with a foul disease? And hence my love of griefs—not such as should probe me too deeply, for I did not love to suffer what I was looking on. But I loved such grief as upon hearing their fictions should lightly scratch the surface, on which, like nails full of venom, there followed burning, swelling, putrefactions, and horrible corruption. Such was my life! But was it really life, O my God?

THREE

And your faithful mercy hovered over me afar. With what grievous iniquities I wasted myself, following an unholy curiosity, that, having forsaken you, it might bring me to the treacherous abyss and to the beguiling service of devils to whom I sacrificed my evil actions. In all these things you scourged me! I even dared, while your solemnities were celebrated within the walls of your Church, to seek and to conclude a business sufficient to procure me the fruits of death, for which you scourged me with grievous punishments, but nothing in comparison with my fault, O my exceeding mercy, my God, my refuge from those terrible hurts! Among them I wandered with stiff-necked presumption, straying farther from you, loving my own ways and not yours; loving an aimless liberty.

Those studies, too, which were considered commendable, were directed at excelling in the courts of law. The more crafty I was, the greater would be the praise. Such is the blindness of men, that they glory even in their own blindness. And now I was head in the School of Rhetoric, at which I rejoiced proudly and was inflated with arrogance, though (Lord, you know) far quieter and altogether removed from the undermining of those "underminers" with whom I lived, whose stupid and devilish name was held to be the very badge of gallantry. I felt ashamed that I was ashamed not to be just what they were. I lived with them and was sometimes delighted with their friendship, but I always abhorred their acts, that is, their "underminings"with which they insolently attacked the modesty of strangers, disturbing others by pointless jeering, gratifying their devilish mirth by it. Nothing can be more like the very actions of devils than these. What then could they be more truly called than "underminers," undermined and altogether perverted themselves in the first place by the deceiving spirits who derided and seduced them, and then delighting themselves in jeering at and deceiving others?

FOUR

Among such companions as these, at that unstable period of my life, I studied books of eloquence in which I wanted to be outstanding, from a damnable and vainglorious ambition, a delight in human vanity. In the ordinary course of study, I fell upon a certain book of Cicero, whose language almost everyone admires, though not his heart. This book of his contains an exhortation to philosophy, and is called *Hortensius*. But this book, in truth, changed my affections and turned my prayers to you, O Lord. It made me have other purposes and other desires. Every vain hope suddenly became worthless to me, and I yearned with an incredible warmth of heart for an immortality of wisdom, and began to arise, that I might return to you. For it was not to sharpen my tongue that I studied that book (which was what I seemed to be buying with my mother's allowances in my nineteenth year, my father having died two years earlier), nor did it persuade me by its style, but by its very subject matter.

How ardent I was then, my God, how ardent to rise above earthly things to you! But I did not know what you would do with me, for with you is wisdom. The love of wisdom is in Greek called "philosophy," and it was this love with which that book inflamed me. There are some who seduce others through philosophy, under a great, alluring and honorable name, coloring and disguising their own errors. And almost all who in Cicero's age and those before him were such seducers, are set forth and censured in that book. There also is made plain that most salutary advice of your Spirit, by your good and devout servant [Paul], *Beware lest any man spoil you through philosophy and vain deceit, after the traditions of men, after the rudiments of the world, and not after Christ. For in him dwells all the fullness of the Godhead bodily.* And since at that time, you know, O Light of my heart, apostolic Scripture was not known to me, I was delighted with that exhortation only insofar that I was strongly roused, kindled and inflamed to love, to seek, to obtain, hold and embrace not this or that sect, but wisdom itself whatever it might be; and the one thing that checked me in my new enthusiasm was that the name of Christ was not in it. For this name, according to your mercy, O Lord, this name of my Savior, your Son, my tender heart had devoutly drunk in even with my mother's milk and had deeply treasured; so whatever omitted that name, though it might be ever so erudite, polished and true, never took complete hold on me.

FIVE

I resolved, therefore, to direct my mind in the Holy Scriptures, so that I might learn what they contained. And behold, I saw something not understood by the proud, not disclosed to the ignorant, but humble as you approach it, sublime as you advance in it, and veiled in mysteries. I was not one of those who could enter into it or submit myself to follow its steps. For I did not feel when I turned to those Scriptures as I do when I speak now. They appeared to me unworthy to be compared to the dignity of Tully; for my inflated pride shrunk from their humble style, and my sharp mind could not pierce their inner meaning. Yet they were such as would grow in your little ones, but I disdained to be a little one. Swollen with pride, I looked on myself as a great one.

SIX

Therefore I fell in with a group of proudly raving men, very carnal and talkative, in whose mouths were the snares of the Devil, lined with a mixture of the syllables of your name and of our Lord Jesus Christ, and of the Holy Spirit, the Paraclete, our Comforter. These names were always in their mouths, but only in sound and the noise of the tongue, for their heart was empty of truth. They cried out "Truth! Truth!" and spoke of it a great deal to me, *yet it was not in them.* They spoke falsehood, not only of you, who in truth are

Truth, but also of the elements of this world, your creation. And I, indeed, ought to have passed by philosophers, even when they spoke the truth concerning those elements, out of love for you, Father, supreme Good, Beauty of all things beautiful. O Truth! Truth! How inwardly did the marrow of my soul pant after you even then, when they frequently and in many ways, in numerous and lengthy books, echoed your name to me, even though it was but an echo! And these were the dishes in which they served to me, hungering as I was for you, the sun and moon, beautiful works of yours, but still your works, not yourself, not even your first works. For your spiritual works came before these physical ones, celestial though they be and shining.

But I hungered and thirsted, not even after those first works, but for you yourself, the Truth, *in whom is no variableness, neither shadow of turning.* Yet they still set before me in those dishes glittering fantasies. It would be better to love the sun itself, which is at least real to our sight, than those illusions which deceive our minds through our eyes. Yet because I supposed them to be you, I fed on them. It was not an eager feeding, because you did not taste to me as you are. For you were not in those empty fictions, and I was not nourished by them, but exhausted instead. Food in our dreams looks very much like our real food, but the sleepers are not nourished by it, because they are asleep. And those fancies were not in any way like you, as you have since revealed yourself to me, for those were all material fantasies, false bodies. The true bodies, celestial or earthly, which we behold with our physical eyes are far more true. The beasts and birds can see them as well as we, and they are far more certain than when we imagine them. But we even imagine them more accurately than we conjecture other vast and infinite bodies which have no existence at all. Those were the empty husks on which I was fed; in truth, though, I was not fed.

But you, my soul's Love, for whom I faint with longing that I might gain strength—you are not those visible bodies, even though they are in heaven; nor are you the invisible ones. For you have created them, and you can create nobler things than they. How far then are you from those fantasies of mine, fantasies of bodies which do not even exist! The images of bodies which do exist are far more real, and even more real are the bodies themselves—yet they are not you. No, nor yet even the soul which is the life of bodies. Better, then, and more certain is the soul of the bodies than the bodies. But you are the Life of the soul, having life in yourself. And you change not, O Life of my soul!

Where then were you to me in that period, and how far from me? I was straying very far from you, kept from the very husks of the swine, whom I was feeding with husks. For how much better are the fables of poets and grammarians than these snares! Verses, poems and "Medea flying" are surely more profitable than these men's five elements, variously depicted, answering to "five caves of darkness," none of which exist, yet slay the believer. For verses and poems I can turn into true food, and though I sang "Medea flying," I did not really believe it; though I heard it sung, I had no faith in it—but those things I did believe. Woe, woe! By what steps was I dragged down to the depths of hell! My God, I confess it to you, who had mercy on me, whom I did not yet confess, that toiling and in turmoil through lack of Truth, I sought after you, not according to the understanding of the mind in which you willed that I should excel the beasts, but according to the sense of the flesh! You were more inward to me than my most inward part; and higher than my highest. I came upon that *bold woman, who is simple and knows nothing*, pictured in Solomon, who sits at the door, saying *Eat the bread of secrets willingly and drink the stolen waters that are sweet*. She seduced me because she found my soul outside her gates, lingering in what was outward and material, and pondering on such food as I had absorbed in that fashion.

SEVEN

Other than this, I did not know what reality was. I was persuaded, as it were, through a sharpness of mind to agree with foolish deceivers when they asked me, "From what source does evil come?" "Is God limited by a bodily shape, and does he have hair and nails?" "Are we to consider those righteous who had many wives at once, and killed men, and sacrificed living animals?" At these questions, in my ignorance, I was much troubled, and departed from the truth though I was making headway toward it; because as yet I did not know that evil was nothing but an absence of good, until at last a thing ceases altogether to be. How could I see this, when my eyes could see only physical bodies and my mind only fantasies? And I did not know God to be a Spirit, not One who has parts extended in length and breadth, or whose being was bulk. For every bulk is less in part than in its entirety; and if it is infinite, it must be less than the space in which it is contained. So it cannot be wholly everywhere, as is a Spirit, as is God. And what that might be in us by which we were like God, and what might rightly in Scripture be said to be "after the image of God," I knew not at all.

Nor did I know that true inward righteousness which does not judge according to custom, but out of the most perfect Law of God Almighty. For though the manners of places and times are adapted to those times and places, that perfect Law in itself is always the same everywhere, not one thing in one place and another in another. According to this, Abraham, Isaac and Jacob, Moses and David were righteous, as well as all those who were commended by the mouth of God. But they were judged unrighteous by foolish men who measured by their own petty standards the manners of the whole human race.

It is as if in an armory, one who was ignorant of what arms were suitable for various parts of the body, were to cover his head with armor designed for the legs, and tried to put a helmet on his feet, complaining that they did not fit. Or, as if on a day when business is publicly stopped in the afternoon, one were angered at not being allowed to keep his shop open because it was lawful for him to be open in the morning. Or when he sees some servant pick up something in his hand which his butler is not allowed to touch, or something is done out of doors which is forbidden in the dining room, he should be angry that in one house and one family, the same thing is not allowed everywhere and to all.

It is exactly the same with those who cannot endure to hear that something was lawful to righteous men in other ages which is not lawful now; or that God, for certain temporal reasons, commanded some to do one thing, and some another, while both obeyed the same righteousness. Yet they see in one man, one day and one house, different things are suitable for different members, and a thing which was formerly lawful, after a certain time to become unlawful—permitted or commanded in one corner, but rightly forbidden and punished in another. Is justice therefore variable and changeable? No, but the times over which it presides are not all alike, because they are temporal. Men, whose days are few upon the earth, cannot harmonize by their own perceptions the causes of former ages and other nations, of which they have had no experience, with those of which they have experience. Though when it concerns the same body, day, or family, they easily see what is fitting for each member, season, part and person. They take exception to what was formerly done, but readily submit to the manners of the present. These things I did not know nor observe then. They were in my plain sight all the time, but I did not see them. I wrote poems in which I could not place every foot everywhere, but in one meter one way, in another another. Even in the same meter, the same foot could not be used everywhere. Yet the art itself, by which I composed, did not have different principles for these different cases, but included them all in one. Still I did not see how that righteousness, which good and holy men obeyed, more excellently and sublimely included in one all those things which God commanded, and never varied; although in varying times it did not prescribe everything at once, but apportioned and required what was proper for each. In my blindness, I blamed the patriarchs, not only where they made use of things as God presently commanded and inspired them to do, but also where they were foreshowing things to come as God was revealing them.

EIGHT

Can it be unrighteous at any time to love God with all one's heart, soul, and mind, and to love one's neighbor as one's self? Therefore, those foul offenses which are against nature are everywhere and at all times detested and punished, such as were those of the Sodomites. Even if all nations were to commit such, they would all stand guilty of the same crime by the law of God, which has not made men in order for them to abuse one another in that way. For even that fellowship which should be between God and us is violated, when that same nature of which he is Author, is polluted by the perversity of lust.

But those offenses which are contrary to the customs of men are to be avoided according to what prevails in different places; so that a thing agreed on and confirmed by the custom or law of any city or nation may not be violated at the lawless pleasure of anyone, be he citizen or stranger. For any part that is not consistent with the whole is offensive. But when God commands anything to be done contrary to the customs or compacts of any people, though it had never been done by them before, it is to be done; and if it has been dropped for a time, it is to be restored; and if never established, it is to be established. For if it is lawful for a king, in the state over which he reigns to command what he himself or anyone before him had heretofore never commanded, and if it is not against the common welfare of the state to obey him (indeed it would be against it if he were not obeyed, for it is a general agreement of human society that princes are to be obeyed), how much more unhesitatingly ought we to obey God in all he commands, the Ruler of all his creatures! For as among the authorities of human society the greater authority is obeyed above the lesser one, so must God be obeyed above all.

In some sins there is a real will to harm another, as in acts of violence (either by harsh words or physical injury); and in either case the deed is done either for the sake of revenge (as one enemy against another), or to gain some desired thing that belongs to another (as the robber to the traveler); or to avoid some evil (as when one person fears another); or through envy (as when a less fortunate person attacks a more prosperous one, or when a prospering one attacks another who is equal to him, whose equality he fears or resents); or for mere pleasure in another's pain (as spectators of gladiators, or deriders and mockers of others). These are the chief iniquities which spring from the lust of the flesh, of the eye, and of power, either singly, or two of them combined, or all of them together. And thus do men live in contradiction to the Three and Seven, that *Psaltery of Ten Strings*, your Ten Commandments, O God most high and most sweet.

But what foul offenses can there be against you, who cannot be defiled? What acts of violence against you who cannot be harmed? But you avenge what men perpetrate against themselves, for when they sin against you, they sin against their own souls, and iniquity lies to itself, by corrupting and perverting their nature which you created and ordained. Or they sin by an immoderate use of things permitted or in a burning desire for things forbidden to that use which is against nature; or when they are found guilty, raging with heart and tongue against you, kicking against the pricks. Or they sin by breaking through the pale of human society, boldly rejoicing in private combinations or divisions, depending on whether they see an object to be gained or wish to take revenge for some offense. These things are done whenever you are forsaken, O Fountain of Life, the only true Creator and Ruler of the universe, and whenever any false thing is selected and loved by a self-willed pride.

So, by a humble piety we return to you; and you cleanse us from our evil habits, and are merciful to the sins of those who confess to you, and *hear the groaning of the prisoner*, and loose us from the chains which we forged for ourselves, if we do not lift up the horns of a pseudo-liberty against you, losing all by coveting more, by loving our own private good more than you, the Good of all.

NINE

Amid all these offenses of infamy, violence, and iniquity are the sins of men who are on the whole making progress. These sins are censured by those who judge right and after the rule of perfection, yet the persons themselves are encouraged in the hope of bearing fruit, like the green blade of growing grain.

And there are some acts that resemble offenses of infamy or violence which are not sins, because they do not offend you, our Lord God, nor human society. When, for example, things that are suitable for the time are provided for the use of life, we do not know whether it involves a lust to possess; or when acts are punished by constituted authority for the sake of correction, we do not know whether the punishment involves a lust for causing pain. Many a deed, then, which in men's sight is disapproved, is approved by your testimony; and many actions praised by men are condemned by you, because the outward appearance of the deed and the mind of the doer, and the unknown circumstance of the moment vary. But when you suddenly command an unusual and unthought-of thing—yes, although you have formerly forbidden it and still for the time hide the reason for your command, even if it is against the ordinance of some society of men, who can doubt that it is to be done? But blessed are they who know your commands! For all kinds of things were done by your servants, either to exhibit something necessary for that time, or to foreshow things to come.

TEN

Being ignorant of these things, I scoffed at your holy servants and prophets. What did I gain by scoffing at them but to be scoffed at by you, being unknowingly and little by little, led on to those follies, so as to believe that a fig tree wept when the fig was plucked, and the tree from which it was picked, its mother, shed milky tears? This fig, nevertheless, having been picked by someone else (thereby incurring the guilt) some [Manichean] saint was then able to eat it without guilt, and mingling it in his bowels, he would have breathed out of it angels. Yes, and there would burst forth particles of divinity at every moan or groan in his prayer, which particles of the most high and true God would have remained bound in that fig if they had not been freed by the teeth or belly of some "elect" saint! And I, wretched one, believed that more mercy was to be shown to the fruits of the earth than to men for whom they were created. For if a hungry person who was not a Manichean were hungry and asked for a bite, any morsel given to him would appear, as it were, condemned to capital punishment.

ELEVEN

And you sent your hand from above and drew out my soul from that profound darkness, because my mother, your faithful one, continued to weep before you on my behalf more than mothers weep over the bodily death of their children. For, by that faith and spirit which she had from you, she saw that I was dead. You heard her, O Lord. You heard her and did not despise her tears which streamed down and watered the ground under her eyes wherever she prayed. Yes, you heard her! For where did that dream come from by which you so comforted her that she allowed me to live with her and eat at the same table in the house (which she had begun to deny me, abhorring and detesting the blasphemy of my error)? She saw herself standing on a certain wooden rule, and a bright youth coming toward her, cheerful and smiling at her, as she grieved, overcome with sorrow. He asked her the cause of her grief and daily tears (not that he needed to be instructed, but in order to instruct her), and she answered that she was lamenting my perdition. He bade her rest contented, and told her to look and observe "that where she was, there was I also." When she looked, she saw me standing by her on the same rule. Where could this have come from, but that your ears were inclined to her heart, O good Almighty? You so care for every one of us as if you cared for us alone, and so for all, as if all were but one!

And it must have come from the same Source, that when she told me about this vision, and I wanted to twist it to mean that she rather should not despair of being one day what I was, she replied without any hesitation, "No! For I was not told, 'Where he is there you will be,' but 'Where you are, there he will be.'" I confess to you, Lord, that to the best of my remembrance (and I have often spoken of this), your answer through my waking mother—that she was not confused by the plausibility of my false interpretation and saw in a moment what was to be seen, and which I certainly had not perceived before she spoke—even then moved me more than the dream itself, by which the happiness of that devout woman, to be realized so long after, was foretold for the alleviation of her present anxiety. For almost nine years passed in which I wallowed in the mire of that deep pit and the darkness of falsehood, often trying to rise, but always dashed down more grievously. And all this time that chaste, godly and sober widow (such as you love), now cheered with hope, yet not relaxing one whit in her weeping and mourning, never ceased at all the hours of her prayers to bewail my case before you. And her *prayers entered into your presence.* Yet you allowed me to be wrapped up and still more wrapped up in that darkness.

TWELVE

You gave her meantime another answer, which I remember. For I pass over much to confess those things that are most important, and I skip over much that I do not remember. You granted her another answer by a priest of yours, a certain bishop brought up in your Church and well versed in your Scriptures. She entreated him to talk with me, refute my errors and teach me good things. This he was in the habit of doing when he found persons ready to receive it. He refused wisely, however, as I afterward came to see, and answered that I was still unteachable, being inflated with the novelty of that heresy [Manicheism], and that I had already confused various inexperienced persons with tricky questions, as my mother had related to him.

"Let him alone awhile," he said. "Just pray to God for him; he will of himself find out by reading what that error is and how great its impiety."

At the same time he told her how he himself, when but a child, had been turned over to the Manicheans by his mother, and had not only read but even copied out almost all their books. But without any argument or proof from anyone, he had come to see how much that sect ought to be avoided, and avoid it he did.

When my mother would not be satisfied with this, but pressed him more urgently with many tears, he agreed to see me and talk with me, a little displeased at her insistence.

"Go your way and God bless you," he said, "for it is not possible that the son of these tears should perish." This answer (as she often mentioned in her conversations with me) she accepted as if it had been spoken from heaven.

BOOK IV

From Age Eighteen to Twenty-seven

ONE

For a period of nine years, from age eighteen to twenty-seven, I lived seduced and seducing, deceived and deceiving, in various forms of unholy desires: openly, by teaching what they call liberal sciences; secretly, by adhering to a false religion.[1] Here proud, there superstitious, everywhere vain! On the one hand I was striving after the emptiness of popular praise, down even to theatrical applause, poetic prizes and competitions for grassy garlands, the follies of theatrical shows and untempered lusts. On the other hand, I desired to be cleansed of these defilements by carrying food to those who were called Elect and Holy, out of which, in the laboratories of their stomachs, they should forge for us angels and gods by whom we might be cleansed. I followed these things and practiced them with my friends who were deceived by me and with me.

Let the arrogant mock me, and such as have not been struck down by you, O my God; but I would still in your praise confess my own shame to you. Bear with me, and give me grace, I pray, to go over the wanderings of former years, and to offer to you the sacrifice of thanksgiving. For without you, what am I to myself, but a guide to my own downfall? Or at my best, what am I but an infant suckled on your milk and feeding on you, O Food that never perishes? But what sort of man is any man, since he is but a man? Let the strong and mighty laugh at me. In my need and helplessness I will confess to you.

TWO

In those years I taught rhetoric, and driven by an inordinate desire for wealth, I offered the art of speaking for sale. Yet you know, Lord, that I preferred honest scholars, as honesty goes, and that I taught them tricks without trickery, not to be used against the life of the guiltless, although sometimes in behalf of the life of the guilty. And from afar, O God, you saw me stumbling in that slippery path and amid much smoke, sending out some sparks of faithfulness which I showed in my guidance of those who *loved vanity and sought after falsehood*. In truth I was their companion.

In those years I had a mistress, not a wife in lawful marriage, but a woman whom I had met following my wayward passion, as void of understanding as I was. I remained faithful to her, and experienced for myself what difference there is between the self-restraint of the marriage covenant made for the sake of raising a family and the bargain of a lustful love, where children are born against their parents' will, although, once born, they may constrain our love.

I remember also, that when I had decided to enter a contest for a theatrical prize, a soothsayer asked me what I would give him to win. Detesting and abhorring such foul mysteries, I answered, "Though the wreath should be made of gold itself, I would not permit a fly to be killed to gain it." For he would have killed a certain living creature to sacrifice, and by that means invite the devils to favor me. I rejected this evil, but not out of a pure love for you, O God of my heart; for I did not know how to love you, not knowing how to conceive of anything beyond a material brightness. And does not a person, sighing after such idle fictions, commit fornication against you, trust in unreality and feed the wind? I would not have him sacrifice to devils for me, but I was sacrificing to them myself by my superstition. What else is it to feed the wind but to feed the devils, that is, by our wanderings to become their pleasure and mockery?

THREE

Those imposters whom they call mathematicians, I consulted without scruple, because they used no sacrifice, and did not pray to any spirit for their divinations. Yet true Christian piety consistently rejects and condemns them, too. For it is a good thing to confess to you and say, "Have mercy on me, heal my soul, for I have sinned against you," and not to abuse your mercy for a license to sin, but to remember the Lord's words, *Behold, you are made whole, sin no more, lest a worse thing come upon you.* All this good advice these men strive to destroy, saying, "The cause of your sin is inevitably determined in heaven," and "This Venus did, or Saturn, or Mars," so that man, indeed, flesh and blood and proud corruption, may be blameless, while the Creator and Ordainer of heaven and the stars is to bear the blame. And who is he but our God, the very Sweetness and Wellspring of righteousness, who *renders to every man according to his works, who will not despise a broken and contrite heart?*

In those days there was a wise man who was proconsul, very learned and well known in medicine, who put the Agonistic wreath with his own hand on my distempered head, though not as a physician. For this disease only you can cure, who *resist the proud and give grace to the humble.* You spoke to me, even by that old man, to heal my soul. For having become acquainted with him, I hung persistently and fixedly on his speech, for though spoken in simple terms, it was vivid, lively, and earnest. When he gathered from our conversations that I was much given to the books of astrology, with the kindlines of a father he advised me to throw them away, and not to waste any care or attention on these vanities. He said that he had studied that art in his earlier years, intending to make it his profession. Since he understood Hippocrates, he could just as easily have understood such a subject as this. Yet he had abandoned it and taken up medicine for one reason only: he found astrology to be utterly false, and as a serious man, he would not get his living by deluding people.

"But you," he said, "you have rhetoric to support yourself by, so you follow this by free choice and not by necessity. That is all the more reason to believe me, who labored to acquire it so perfectly that I could make my living by it alone."

When I had demanded to know then how many true things could be foretold by it, he answered me as best he could that the force of chance, spread through the whole order of things, made this possible. For when a man by chance opened the pages of some poet, who sang and thought of something wholly different, a verse oftentimes fell out that was wondrously suited to the present circumstance. It is not to be wondered at if, out of the soul of man, by some higher but unconscious instinct within it, an answer should be given, not by art but by mere chance, that corresponds to the business and actions of the questioner.

Either from him or through him, you conveyed to me and planted in my memory what I would later examine for myself. But at that time neither he nor my dear friend, Nebridius, a young man singularly good and morally pure, who laughed at the whole subject of divination, could persuade me to forsake it. The authority of the authors still influenced me more greatly, and as yet I had found no certain proof, such as I sought, by which it might be shown beyond all doubt, that what had been accurately forecast by those consulted was the result of chance rather than the art of the stargazers.

FOUR

In those years when I first began to teach rhetoric in my native town, I had acquired a very dear friend of my own age from association in our studies. Like me, he was in the first opening flower of youth. We had grown up together as children and we had been both school-fellows and playmates. But he was not yet my friend as he became later, nor even then as true friendship is; for no friendship can be true unless you are the bond that holds it together, binding it to yourself by that love that is *shed abroad in our hearts by the Holy Spirit who is given to us.* Yet it was too sweet, ripened as it was by the warmth of similar studies; for I had turned him from the true faith, which he had not soundly and thoroughly taken in as a youth, toward those pernicious and superstitious fables which my mother mourned in me. He now went astray with me in these errors, and my soul could not be without him. But you were close on the steps of your fugitives. At once God of vengeance and Fountain of mercies, you turn us to yourself by wonderful means. You took that man from this life after scarcely a year of a friendship that had grown sweet to me above all the sweetness of my life.

Who can sing all your praise which one has felt in himself alone? What did you do then, my God, and how unsearchable are the depths of your judgments! For a long time my friend lay unconscious in a death-sweat, very sick of a fever. Hope of his recovery being lost, he was baptized without his knowledge. Meanwhile, I paid little regard, presuming that his soul would retain what it had received from me, not what was wrought on his unconscious body [by baptism]. But it proved otherwise, for he was revived and restored. Then, as soon as I could speak with him (and I could as soon as he was able, for I never left him, and we hung all too much on each other), I tried to joke with him, thinking that he would jest with me about that baptism which he had received when totally without consciousnes or feeling. But he drew back from me, as from an enemy. In a remarkable and unexpected freedom, he told me that if I wanted to continue to be his friend, to refrain from speaking to him in such a way. I, all confounded and amazed, concealed all my emotions till he should get well and his health strong enough for me to deal with him as I wished.

But he was removed from my madness that he might be saved by you for my comfort. A few days later, during my absence, he had a return of the fever and died.

My heart was utterly darkened by this grief. Whatever I looked at was death. My native country was torture to me, and my father's house a strange unhappiness. Whatever I had shared with my friend became in his absence a frightful torture. My eyes looked for him everywhere in vain. I hated all places because he was not in them. Nor could they now say to me "he will be coming," as they did when he was alive and absent. I became a great puzzle to myself, and asked my soul why it was so sad, and why it troubled me so sorely. But my soul did not have an answer for me. And if I said "Hope in God," it would not obey me, because that most dear friend, whom it had lost, being a man, was better and more real than the imagined deity it was bidden to trust in. Nothing was sweet to me but tears, and they filled the void my friend had left in the affections of my heart.

FIVE

These things are long past, Lord, and time has healed my wound. May I learn from you, who are Truth? May I hold the ear of my heart close to your mouth, that you may tell me why weeping is sweet to the sorrowing? Have you, although present everywhere, cast away our misery far from you? You abide in yourself, while we are tossed about with various trials. And yet, if we did not weep in your ears, we would have no hope left. From where, then, comes the sweet fruit gathered from the bitterness of life, from groans, tears, sighs and laments? Does it sweeten it to hope that you hear?

This is true of prayer, for in it there is a longing to approach you. But is it also true in grief for a lost friend, and in the sorrow which then overwhelmed me? For I neither hoped he should return to life, nor did I ask for this with my tears. I wept and grieved only because I was miserable and had lost my joy. Or is weeping bitter when we have the things we enjoy, only to grow delightful when we lose them?

SIX

But why do I speak of these things? For this is no time to ask questions, but to confess to you. I was wretched, as every one is wretched who is bound by friendship to mortal things. He is torn apart when he loses them, and feels the misery which he was subject to even before he lost them. So it was at that time with me. I wept most bitterly and found my rest in bitterness. Thus I was miserable but I held even that life of misery dearer than my friend. For though I would willingly have changed it, yet I was less willing to part with it than with him; yes, I do not know whether I would have parted with it even for him, as is related (if it is not fiction) of Pylades and Orestes, that they would gladly have died for one another, since not to live together was to them worse than death. But in me there had grown up some kind of feeling wholly contrary to this; for at the same time I hated exceedingly to live and feared to die. I suppose that the more I loved him, the more I hated and feared death, which as a most cruel enemy, had taken him from me. I imagined that it would make a speedy end of all men, since it had such power over him. This is the way it was with me, as I recall.

Behold my heart, O God. Look deep within me and see, for I well remember it, O my Hope, who cleanses me from the impurity of such affections, directing my eyes toward you, and plucking my feet out of the net. For I wondered that others, subject to death, should live, since he whom I loved as if he should never die, was dead. And I wondered yet more that I myself, who was like a second self to him, could still live though he was dead. Well did someone call his friend "half of my soul" for I felt that my soul and his were one soul in two bodies, and therefore my life was a horror to me, because I would not live cut in half. Therefore, perhaps I feared to die lest he whom I loved so much should die completely.

SEVEN

O madness which does not know how to love men as men! O foolish man that I was then, enduring the lot of man with such impatience! I fretted, sighed, wept, tormented myself, and took neither rest nor advice. For I carried about a torn and bleeding soul, tired of being borne by me, yet I could not find anywhere to let it rest. Not in pleasant groves, not in games or music, nor in perfumed gardens, nor in banqueting, nor in the pleasures of the bed and couch—not even in books or poetry did I find rest. All things looked terrible, even the very light itself. Whatever was not him was revolting and hateful. Only in groans and tears did I find a little refreshment, and when I gave these up even for a little time, a huge load of misery weighed me down.

My soul should have been raised to you, O Lord, for you to lighten my burden. I knew it, but was neither willing nor able, for truthfully, when I thought of you, you were not anything solid or substantial to me. My god was not you, yourself, but one of vain imagination and error. If I attempted to lay my load on this god, so that it might rest, it sank into nothingness and came rushing back on me again. I remained an unhappy place to myself, where I could not stay and which I could not leave. For where could my heart flee from my heart? Where could I fly from myself? How could I not follow myself? And yet I fled out of my native country, for my eyes would seek him less where they were not used to seeing him. And so I left Tagaste for Carthage.

EIGHT

Time hastens on. Nor does it roll idly by. Through our senses it works a strange work on the mind. Behold, the moments came and went, day by day, and by coming and going introduced other ideas and other remembrances to my mind. Little by little they patched me up again with my old kind of delights, and to these my sorrow gave way. There followed then, not other griefs, indeed, but the causes for griefs to come. For how could that former grief so easily have reached my inmost soul, but that I had poured out my soul in the dust in loving one who must die as if he would never die? What restored and refreshed me chiefly was the consolation of other friends with whom I had loved him instead of you. And this was a kind of fable, a drawn out lie by whose adulterous contact my soul, which lay itching in my ears, was being defiled. But that fable would not die to me, no matter how often any of my friends might die. There were other things in them which took up my mind; to talk and joke together, to do each other kindnesses by turn, to read pleasant books together; to play the fool or to be serious together; to disagree at times, as a man might do with himself, and by the infrequency of these differences, seasoning our more frequent agreements; sometimes teaching, sometimes learning; longing for the absent with impatience, and welcoming their coming with joy. These and other things like them, proceeding out of the hearts of those that loved and were loved in return, by look, speech, the eyes, and a thousand pleasing gestures, were so much fuel to meld our souls together and out of many to make us one.

NINE

This is what is loved in friends, and loved so much that a man's conscience condemns him if he does not love the person who loves him, looking for nothing but indications of his love. From this comes mourning when one dies, the blackness of sorrow, the soaking of the heart in tears, all sweetness turned into bitterness, and with the loss of the life of the dying, the "death" of the living. Blessed is the man who loves you, and his friends in you, and his enemy for your sake. For he alone loses none dear to him, if all are dear in him, who cannot be lost. And who is that but our God, the God who made heaven and earth, and fills them, even by filling them [with himself], creating them? None lose you but the one who leaves you. And in leaving you, where does he flee but from you well-pleased to you displeased? For where does he not find your law fulfilled in his own punishment? And *your law is truth*, and you are truth yourself.

TEN

Turn us again, O God of hosts; cause your face to shine and we shall be saved. For no matter where the soul of man turns itself, unless it is toward you, it is riveted to sorrows, yes, even though it is attached to beautiful things. Yet such things would be nothing if they were not from you. They rise and set; and by rising, they begin, as it were, to be; and they grow toward their perfection; and perfected, they grow old, and perish. All of them do not grow old, but all of them perish. The more quickly they rise, the more rapidly they hasten toward not being. This is their law. This much you have allowed them, because they are portions of things which do not exist all at the same time, but by following one another in succession, they make up that universe of which they are parts.

In the same way our speech is completed by separate sounds. But it is necessary for one word to pass away when it has sounded its part, so that another may succeed it. Out of all these things let my soul praise you, O God, Creator of all. Yet do not allow my soul to be fastened to these things with love of them through my physical senses. For they tend toward "not being," tearing the soul with pestilent longings, because it longs to be, yet loves to rest in what it loves. But it cannot rest in these things; they do not remain. They fly away, and who can follow them with the senses of the flesh? Yes, who can grasp them, even when they are close by? For the sense of the flesh is slow because it is a fleshly sense, and is limited by the flesh. It is sufficient for the end for which it was made, but it does not suffice to stop things running toward their appointed end. For in your Word, by which they are created, they receive their commission, "This far—and no farther!"

ELEVEN

Do not be foolish, my soul, and do not deaden the ear of your heart with the tumult of your folly. And hear! The Word itself calls you to return to that place of rest where love is not abandoned if it does not first abandon itself. Behold, some things pass away that others may replace them, and so this lower universe is made complete in all its parts. "But do I ever depart?" asks the Word of God. Fix your dwelling there; trust whatsoever you have there, O my soul, for now you are worn out with deceits. Entrust to Truth whatever you have from the Truth, and you will lose nothing; and what is decayed in you will flourish again, and all your diseases will be healed. Your perishable [bodily] parts will be re-formed and renewed, and restored to you again. They will not drag you down to where they themselves are laid, but they will abide with you before God, who continues and abides forever.

Why then, O my soul, be perverse and follow your flesh? Let it turn and follow you instead. Whatever you feel through it is but a part of the whole. Feeling only the parts, you do not know the whole, yet you are delighted by them. But if the senses of the flesh had the capacity for comprehending the whole, and if they had not been justly restricted to parts of the whole, you would wish that all the parts would pass away, so that the whole might better please you. For what we speak, you hear by the same sense of the flesh, and you would not wish each syllable to remain. Rather you want them to fly away so that other syllables may follow and the whole be heard. And so it is ever: when anything is made up of different parts, all of which do not exist together, they would please you more if they could all be perceived at once than they do severally. But far better than these is he who made the whole. He is our God. He does not pass away, and there is no one to take his place.

TWELVE

If physical things please you, then praise God for them, but turn back your love to him who created them, lest in the things that please you, you displease him. If souls please you, love them in God; for in themselves they are changeable, but in him they are firmly established. Without him they pass away and perish. In him, then, let them be loved, and carry along with you to him as many souls as you can, and say to them "Let us love him, let us love him; he made the world and is not far from it. He did not make all things and then leave them, but they are of him and in him. See, there he is wherever truth is loved. He is within the very heart, yet the heart has strayed from him. Return to your heart, O you transgressors, and hold fast to him who made you. Stand with him and you will stand fast. Rest in him and you shall be at rest. Where do you go in these rugged paths? Where do you go?

The good that you love is from him. But it is good and pleasant by being referred to him, and it will justly become bitterness if he is forsaken for it. Why, then, do you still wander in these difficult and toilsome ways? There is no rest where you seek it. Seek what you seek, but it is not where you seek it. You seek a blessed life in the land of death; it is not there. How could there be a blessed life where life itself is not?

"Our true Life came down to this earth, and bore our death and killed it out of the abundance of his own life. Thundering loudly, he called to us to return to him into that secret place from which he came forth to us—coming first into the Virgin's womb, where humanity was joined to him, our mortal flesh, that it might not be forever mortal, and from there, *like a bridegroom coming out of his chamber and rejoicing as a strong man to run a race.* For he did not delay, but ran, calling loudly by words, deeds, death, life, descent, ascension, crying loudly for us to return to him. And he departed from our sight, so that we might return to our heart and find him there. For he departed, and lo, he is here! He would not remain with us, yet he did not leave us; for he went back to that place he never left, because *the world was made by him.* He was in this world, and he *came into the world to save sinners.* My soul confesses to him and he heals it, for it has sinned against him. O you children of men, how long will you be so slow of heart? Even now, after Life has descended to you, will you not ascend and live? But to where will you ascend, since you are already in a high place, and have set your mouth against the heavens? First come down, that you may ascend, and ascend to God. For you have fallen by rising against him."

Tell your friends this, that they may weep in this valley of tears, and so draw them to God with you, because it is by his Spirit that you speak to them this way, if you speak glowing with the fire of love.

THIRTEEN

I did not know these things then, and I loved those lower beauties. I was sinking into the very depths, and I said to my friends, "Do we love anything but what is beautiful? What then is the beautiful? And what is beauty? What is it that attracts and unites us to the things we love? For unless they contain a grace and beauty, they could by no means attract us to them." And I marked and perceived that in the objects themselves there was one beauty by themselves alone, and another that depended on their proper and mutual relationship within the whole, as a part of the body with its whole, or a shoe with a foot, and the like. This consideration came to my mind out of my inmost heart, and I wrote books (two or three, I think)—*De Pulchris et Apto*, "On the Beautiful and the Fitting"; you know how many, O God, but I have forgotten. I do not have them, for they have strayed from me, I know not how.

FOURTEEN

What was it that prompted me, O Lord my God, to dedicate these books to Hierius, an orator of Rome, whom I did not know by sight, but whom I loved for the fame of his learning for which he was well known, and for some of his words I had heard, which pleased me? But he pleased me chiefly because he pleased others, who praised him highly, amazed that a Syrian, first taught in Greek eloquence, should become a wonderful Latin orator and one so learned in philosophy. Thus a man is commended and loved, though we have never seen him. Does this love come into the heart of the hearer from the mouth of the one who praises him? Not at all. But through one who loves, another's love is set ablaze. This is why we love the one commended when we believe that the praise comes from a sincere heart; that is, when the praise is from one who truly loves him.

Thus at that time I loved men on the judgment of others, not upon yours, O my God, in whom no man is deceived. Yet why did I not love them for qualities like those of the renowned charioteer, or the great fighter with beasts in the amphitheater, whose popularity and fame spread far and wide? Although I admired them, I did not care to be like them. I had no desire to be praised and liked as actors are, though I myself praised and loved them. I would have chosen to remain unknown than to be known as they were, and even hated rather than loved as they were. How are these various and different loves distributed in one soul? Why, since we are all equally men, do I love in another what I would hate to be? It does not follow, since a good horse is loved by one who would not choose to be a horse even if he could, that the same may be said of an actor, since we are both sharing the same nature. Man is a great deep, and you number his very hairs, Lord. Not one of them falls without you. And yet the hairs of his head are more easily numbered than are his feelings and the movements of his heart.

But that orator whom I admired so much was the kind of man I wanted to be myself; I strayed through inflated pride, and I was *carried about by every wind*, yet you steered my course, though very secretly. I know very well now and I confess to you with sure confidence that I loved him more for the praise he received from others than for the things for which he was being praised. Because if he had been criticized, and those same men had disapproved of him, and had told the very same things about him with scorn and contempt, I would never have been inspired and drawn to love him. Yet his qualities would have been no different, but only the attitude of those who spoke about him. See how the soul lies helpless and prostrate when it is not yet stayed on the firmness of truth! The gales of speech blow from the breasts of the opinionated, and we are carried this way and that, driven forward and backward; the light is obscured to us, and the truth is not seen. Yet, there it is in front of us.

It was a great concern to me that my style and ideas should be known to that man. If he approved, I would be filled with more admiration for him. But if he disapproved, this vain heart of mine, void of your stability, would have been offended. And yet, I reflected with pleasure *On the Beautiful and the Fitting*, about which I wrote to him, and viewed it and admired it—though no one else joined me in doing so.

FIFTEEN

I did not yet see how this great matter [of the Beautiful and the Fitting] turns upon your wisdom, O Omnipotence, for you alone do great wonders; but my mind ranged through corporeal forms. I defined and distinguished as "fair" that which is so in itself; and I defined as "fitting" that which is beautiful in its relationship and fitness to some other thing, and I supported this by corporeal examples. I turned my attention to the nature of the mind, but the false notions I had of spiritual things prevented me from seeing the truth. Yet the very force of truth did of itself flash into my eyes, but I turned away my thirsty soul from incorporeal substance to line, colors and shapes. Because I could not see these in my mind, I concluded that I could not perceive my mind. And since I loved the peace in virtue and hated the discord in vice, I distinguished a kind of unity in the first and a sort of disunity in the other. I conceived that the rational soul, the nature of truth and the highest good were all included in that unity.[2] In the disunity, unfortunately, I imagined there was some unknown substance of irrational life, and thought the nature of the greatest evil was not only a substance, but had real life, too, and that it did not emanate from you, O my God, of whom are all things. And the first I called a Monad, as if it were a soul without sex. The other I called a Duad—anger, deeds of violence, in deeds of passion and lust—not knowing what I was talking about. For I had not known, nor had I been taught, that evil was not a substance nor was our soul that chief and unchangeable good.

For just as it is in the case of violent deeds, if the emotion of the soul from which the impulse comes is depraved and thrusts itself arrogantly and shamefully, and as it is in acts of passion when the emotion of the soul is unrestrained in its carnal desires—so also, errors and false opinions contaminate our life if the rational soul itself is depraved, as mine was then. I did not know that it must be enlightened by another light to be partaker of truth, since it is not itself the essence of truth. *For you will light my candle, O Lord my God. You will enlighten my darkness. And of your fullness have we all received.* For you are *the true Light who enlightens every one who comes into the world.* In you there is *no variableness, neither shadow of change.*

But though I pressed toward you, I was thrust back from you, so that I might taste of death, for you *resist the proud.* And what was prouder than for me to maintain with a marvelous madness that I myself was by nature what you are? For since I was subject to change (that much was very clear to me, my very desire to become wise being the desire of the worse to change for the better), still I chose to imagine that you were subject to change rather than to see myself not to be what you are. Therefore I was repelled by you, and you resisted my changeable stiff-neckedness. So I went on making mental images of bodily forms. Being flesh, I accused the flesh; and being *a wind that passes away,* I did not return to you, but kept on wandering toward things that have no being, neither in you, nor in me, nor in the body. They were not created for me by your truth, but they were made up out of corporeal things by my vanity. I used to ask your faithful little ones, my fellow citizens (from whom I was in exile, though I did not know it)—and I used to ask flippantly and foolishly, "Why does the soul err if God created it?" But I would not allow anyone to ask me, "Why, then, does God err?" Yet I maintained that your immutable substance was forced to err rather than to confess that my mutable substance had gone astray through its own fault, and now lay in error for its punishment.[3]

I was about twenty-six or twenty-seven years old when I wrote these books, meditating on the corporeal images which clamored in the ears of my heart. These I directed, O sweet Truth, to your inward melody, meditating on "the beautiful and the fitting," longing to stay and listen to you, to rejoice at the Bridegroom's voice, but I could not. By the voices of my own errors I was driven forth, and by the weight of my own pride, I was sinking into the lowest pit. For you did not *make me to hear joy and gladness*, nor did *the bones rejoice* which were not yet humbled.

SIXTEEN

And what did it profit me, that when I was barely twenty years old, a book of Aristotle's entitled *The Ten Categories* fell into my hands? I hung on its very name as something great and divine, since my teacher who taught me rhetoric at Carthage and others who were considered learned, referred to it with cheeks swelling with pride. I read it alone and understood it without the aid of anyone. And of conferring with others, who said that they had scarcely understood it with the aid of able tutors who not only explained it orally, but drew many things in the sand, they could tell me no more about it than I had learned by reading it alone. And the book appeared to me to speak very clearly of substances, such as man; and of his features, such as the figure of a man, the shape and size, height; and of his relationship, whose brother he is; or where placed, or when born; or whether he stands or sits; is shod or armed, or is doing something or having something done to him—and all the other countless things that might be classed under these nine categories—of which I have given some examples, or under that chief category of substance.

What did all this profit me, since it actually hindered me? For imagining that whatsoever existed was included in those ten categories, I tried to understand you, O my God, your wonderful and immutable unity in the same way, as if you were subject to your own greatness or beauty; so that they should exist in you as their subject, as it is in bodies—whereas you are yourself your own greatness and beauty. But a material body is not great or fair because it is a body, since it would not cease being a body if it were smaller or less beautiful. But what I conceived of you was falsehood, not truth—fictions of my misery, not the realities of your blessedness. For you had commanded and it was done in me, that the earth should bring forth briars and thorns to me, and that in the sweat of my brow I should eat my bread.

And what did it profit me that all the books that I could find of the so-called liberal arts I could read and understand by myself, I who was a slave of vile affections? I took delight in them, not knowing him from whom came all that was true or certain in them. For I had my back to the light and my face toward the things enlightened, so even when I discerned things enlightened, my face itself was not enlightened. Whatever was written either on rhetoric or logic, geometry, music, or arithmetic, I understood without any great difficulty and without any instructor, as you know, O Lord my God, because both quickness of understanding and acuteness in discerning were your gifts. Yet I did not give you thanks for them. So they did not serve to my profit but for my harm, since I desired to get so great a share of my substance into my own power. I did not reserve my strength for you, but went away from you into a far country, to waste my substance on harlotry. What good was it to me to have good abilities if I did not employ them to good use? For I did not perceive that those arts were attained with great difficulty even by the studious and talented, until I attempted to explain them to others; and he was considered the most proficient in them who could follow my explanations most easily.

But what did this profit me while I supposed you, O Lord, God, the Truth, to be a vast and bright body, and I a fragment of that body? Perverseness too great! But that is what I was. I do not blush, O my God, to confess before you your mercies toward me, and to call on you, I who did not then blush to profess my blasphemies before men and to bark against you. Of what profit to me was my nimble wit in those sciences and all those knotty volumes which I unraveled without human aid, seeing that I erred so odiously and with such sacrilegious shamelessness in the doctrine of piety? A far slower wit was more profitable to your little ones, since they did not depart from you that in the nest of your Church they might safely become fledged and nourish the wings of their charity by the food of a sound faith.

O Lord our God, under the shadow of your wings let us hope. Protect us, and carry us. You will carry us when we are little, and even down to our gray hairs you will carry us; for when you are our strength, then is it strength indeed; but when it is our own, then it is weakness. Our good lives only with you; when we are averted we are perverted. Let us now, O Lord, return, that we may not be overturned; because with you good lives without any decay, for you are that good. We need not fear that because we fell away from it we will find no place to which we can return; for when we left it, our home, your eternity, did not fall.

BOOK V
At Age Twenty-eight

ONE

Accept the sacrifice of my confessions by the means of my tongue, which you have formed and have prompted to confess to your name. *Heal all my bones* and *let them say, "O Lord, who is like you?"* For he who confesses to you does not inform you what takes place within him, since a closed heart does not shut out your eye, nor can man's hardheartedness repulse your hand. For you dissolve it at will, either in pity or in vengeance, and *nothing can hide itself from your heart*. But let my soul praise you, that it may love you. Let it confess your own mercies before you, that it may praise you. Your whole creation ceases not to praise you—the spirit of every man whose voice is directed to you, all created things, animate and inanimate, by the voice of those who meditate on them, so that our souls may arise to you from their weariness, and leaning on those things which you have created, pass on to you, who made them wonderfully. Refreshment and true strength are there.

TWO

Let the restless and the wicked depart and flee from you. You see them and pierce through the darkness. And behold, everything with them is fair, but they are foul.[1] How have they injured you? In what have they disgraced your government, which is just and perfect from heaven to the lowest earth? Where did they flee when they fled from your presence? Or where do you not find them? They fled so that they might not see you seeing them, and in their blindness might stumble into you, because you forsake nothing that you have made, that the wicked, I say, might stumble upon you, and be justly hurt. Withdrawing themselves from your gentleness, and stumbling at your uprightness, and falling upon their own roughness. In truth they do not know that you, whom no place encompasses, are everywhere, and that you alone are near even to those who remove themselves far from you.

Let them then be turned and seek you, because you have not forsaken your creature as they have forsaken their Creator. Let them be turned and seek you, and behold, you are there in their hearts, in the hearts of those who confess before you and cast themselves upon you, and weep on your bosom after all their stubborn ways. Then you gently wipe away their tears, and they weep the more, and rejoice in their weeping, since you, Lord, not man of flesh and blood, but you, Lord, who made them—now remake and comfort them. And where was I when I was seeking you? And you were there before me, but I had gone away even from myself. I could not find myself, how much less you!

THREE

Let me now lay open before my God my twenty-ninth year. A certain bishop of the Manicheans had then come to Carthage, Faustus by name, a great snare of the devil. Many were entangled by him through the lure of his sweet language. Though I commended his speech, I could not separate myself from the truth I was so eager to learn. I was not so much concerned with the small dish of speech but with the knowledge which this Faustus, so praised among them, might set before me to feed on. His fame had already informed me that he was skilled in all valuable learning, and especially learned in the liberal sciences.

Since I had read and could remember much of the philosophers, I used to compare some of what they had written with those long fables of the Manicheans. What the philosophers taught seemed to me more probable, even though they could only pertain to this lower world. They could by no means find out the Lord of it. For you are great, *O Lord, and regard the lowly, but the proud you know afar off.* You draw near to none but to the contrite in heart, nor are you found by the proud, no, not even if by cunning skill they could count the number of the stars and the sand, and measure the starry regions and trace the courses of the planets. For with their understanding and the capacity which you have given them, the philosophers search out these things. They have found out much. They foretold, many years before, eclipses of the sun and moon, what day and hour and minute. Their calculations did not fail, but it came to pass as they foretold. They wrote down the rules they had found out, and these are read to this day. From them others can foretell in what year, month, day and hour, and at what quarter of its light, the moon or sun will be eclipsed; and so it shall be as it is foretold. Those who do not know this art marvel and are astonished at this, and they who know it rejoice and are exalted. By an ungodly pride, departing from you, forsaking your light, they foretell an eclipse of the sun's light long before it will happen, but they do not see the eclipse of their own light which is already present. For they do not search religiously where their intelligence comes from. And when they find out that you made these things, they do not give themselves to you that you may preserve what you made, nor do they offer to you what they have made themselves. They do not slay their own soaring pride, *as fowls of the air,* nor their own curiosities, by which, like *the fishes of the sea,* they wander over the unknown paths of the abyss. Nor do they curb their own extravagances, like *beasts of the field*; so that you, Lord, you, *a consuming fire*, might burn up those dead cares of theirs and renew the men themselves to immortality.

But they did not know your Word, the way by which you created these things which they number, and those who number them, and the ability to perceive what they number and the understanding by which they can number. They do not know that *of your wisdom there is no number*. But the only Begotten himself is *made unto us wisdom and righteousness and sanctification*, and has been numbered among us, and paid tribute to Caesar. They did not know this way by which they might descend to him from themselves, not that through him they might ascend to him. They did not know this way and fancied themselves exalted among the stars and shining, and lo! they fell to the earth, and *their foolish heart was darkened*. They say many true things concerning the creation; but Truth, the Architect of creation, they do not seek reverently, and therefore do not find him. Or if they find him, knowing him to be God, *they do not glorify him as God, neither are thankful, but become vain in their imaginations and claim themselves to be wise*, attributing to themselves what is yours. At the same time, with a perverse blindness, they attribute to you their own qualities, forging lies about you who are the Truth, and *changing the glory of the incorruptible God into an image made like a corruptible man, and to birds, and four-footed beasts, and creeping things, changing your truth into a lie, and worshiping and serving the creature more than the Creator.*

Yet I did retain many truths from these men concerning the creation, and I saw their theories confirmed by calculations, the succession of seasons, and the visible evidence of the stars. I compared them with the sayings of Manicheus, who in his frenzy had written many books on these subjects, but I did not discover any account of the solstices, or equinoxes, or the eclipses of the greater lights, nor anything of the kind I had learned in the books of secular philosophy. But I was ordered to believe what did not correspond to what had been established by mathematics and by my own sight, but was very different.

FOUR

Yet, Lord God of truth, does the man who knows these things therefore please you? Surely, he is unhappy who knows all these and does not know you; but happy is he who knows you though he may not know these things. And whoever knows both you and them is not happier on account of them, but only on account of you, if knowing you he glorifies you as God, gives thanks, and does not become vain in his thoughts. But he is happier who knows how to own a tree and give thanks to you for the use of it—although he may not know how many feet high it is, or how wide it spreads—than is he who measures it and counts all its branches, but neither owns it nor knows or loves its Creator. Even so, a just man to whom all the world of wealth belongs, and who, as having nothing, yet possesses all things by holding fast to you whom all things serve, though he does not know even the circles of the Great Bear, is doubtless in a better state than one who can measure the heavens, number the stars and weigh the elements, but is forgetful of you *who made all things in number, weight and measure.*

FIVE

But yet who ordered this Manicheus to write on all these things, too, the knowledge of which was not necessary to piety? For you have told man that *the fear of the Lord is wisdom.* Manicheus might have been ignorant of this even if he had had perfect knowledge of these created things; but since he had no knowledge of these things, yet most impudently dared to teach them, it is clear that he had no acquaintance with the fear of the Lord. Even if we have a knowledge of these worldly matters, it is folly to make a profession of them; but confession before you is our duty. It was for this reason that this straying one spoke much of these things, that standing convicted by those who had truly learned them, what understanding he had in other, more difficult matters might be brought into question. For he did not want to be lightly esteemed, but went about trying to persuade men that the Holy Spirit, the Comforter and Enricher of your faithful people, was resident in him with full authority. So when it was discovered that his teaching about the heavens and stars and the movements of the sun and moon was false (although these things do not pertain to the teaching of religion), his sacrilegious presumption would become plain enough, since he spoke of things which not only did he not know, but which were false, and did so with such a flagrant vanity of pride that he would try to attribute them to himself as to a divine person.

For when I hear a Christian brother ignorant of these things, and mistaken on them, I can bear patiently with such a man holding to his opinions. I do not think any ignorance as to the position or character of this material creation can injure him as long as he does not believe anything unworthy of you, O Lord, the Creator of all. But it does injure him if he imagines it to pertain to the essence of divine doctrine, or still holds too strongly to that of which he is ignorant. And yet even such a weakness in the infancy of faith is borne by Charity, our mother, while the new man grows up *into a mature person*, so as not to be *carried about with every wind of doctrine*.

But in Manicheus who thus presumed to be at once the teacher, author, head and leader of all he could induce to believe him, so that all who followed him believed that they followed not a mere man, but your Holy Spirit—who would not judge that, when once convicted of having taught anything false, he should he abhorred and utterly rejected? But I had not yet clearly ascertained whether the changes of longer and shorter days and nights, and day and night itself, with the eclipses of the sun and moon, and whatever else of the kind I had read of in other books, could be harmonized with his words. If by any means they could, I would still have questioned whether his theories were true or not, although I might, on account of his reputed sanctity, have continued to rest my faith upon his authority.

SIX

For almost all those nine years during which, with an unsettled mind, I had been a Manichean disciple, I had been looking forward very eagerly to the coming of this Faustus. For the other members of the sect, whom I had chanced to meet, when unable to answer the questions I raised, always held out to me the coming of this Faustus, when these and greater questions would be most readily and abundantly cleared up in conference with him. When he came then, I found him a man of pleasant speech, who could speak fluently and in better language, but yet he said the very same things the others had said.

But to what avail was a more elegant cupbearer, since he did not offer me the more precious draught for which I thirsted? My ears were already filled with such things, and they did not seem to me more convincing because they were better expressed; nor were they true because they were eloquent; nor the soul wise because the face was handsome and the language eloquent. But they who extolled him to me were not competent judges. They thought he was prudent and wise because he was pleasing in his speech.

I was aware, however, that another kind of people was suspicious even of truth itself, if it came in smooth and flowing language. But you, O my God, had already instructed me in wonderful and secret ways. I believe that it was you who taught me, because it is truth, and there is no teacher of truth besides you, wherever or from whatever direction it may dawn on us! From you, therefore, I had now learned that a thing should not be considered true because it was well spoken; nor untrue because it came from a stammering tongue; neither true because delivered unskillfully, nor untrue because the language was fine. Just as wholesome and unwholesome food may be served either in elegant or plain dishes, so wisdom or folly may come in either elegant or simple language. Either kind of food may be served up in either kind of dish.

That eagerness, then, with which I had waited so long for this man was in truth delighted with his manner and attitude when we conversed, and with the fluent and apt words he used to clothe his ideas. I was delighted then, and with many others (and even more than others) I praised and extolled him. It annoyed me, however, that in the meetings of his hearers I was not allowed to introduce those questions that troubled me in a familiar exchange of discussion with him. When I was able to speak, and began with my friends to engage him in conversation at such times as it was not unbecoming for him to discuss with me, and had mentioned the questions that perplexed me, I found him first utterly ignorant of the liberal sciences except grammar, and even that only in an ordinary way. But because he had read some of Tully's *Orations*, a very few books of Seneca, some things of the poets and the few volumes of his own sect that were written in Latin, and was daily practiced in speaking, he had acquired a certain eloquence which proved more pleasing and enticing under the control of a ready wit and a kind of natural grace. Was it not as I recall it, O Lord my God, Judge of my conscience? My heart and my memory are laid open before you, who at this time directed me by the hidden mystery of your providence, bringing those shameful errors of mine before my eyes, so that I might see them and loathe them.

SEVEN

For after it became clear to me that he was ignorant of those arts in which I had thought he excelled, I began to despair of his clearing up and explaining the difficulties which bothered me. Although he was ignorant of these, he might still have held the truths of godliness if he had not been a Manichean. For their books are filled with lengthy fables about the sky, the stars, the sun and moon, and I had ceased to believe that he was able to show me in any satisfactory way what I so earnestly desired—whether, on comparing these things with the mathematical calculations I had read elsewhere, the accounts given in the books of Manicheus were preferable, or at least as good. When I suggested this to be considered and discussed, he was modest enough to shrink from the burden of it. For he knew that he did not know these things and was not ashamed to acknowledge it. He was not one of those talkative persons, many of whom I had been troubled with, who attempted to teach me these things and said nothing. This man had a heart, and though it was not right toward you, yet it was not altogether false toward himself. He was not altogether ignorant of his own ignorance, and he would not rashly entangle himself in a controversy from which he could neither retreat nor extricate himself gracefully. For that reason I liked him better. The modesty of a candid mind is more beautiful than the acquaintance of the knowledge I desired—and such I found him to be in all the more difficult and subtle questions.

My eagerness for the writings of Manicheus having been blunted, I despaired even more of their other teachers. Since, Faustus, so renowned among them, had turned out as he had in the various things that troubled me, I began to occupy myself with him in the study of literature in which he was greatly interested, and which I, as a professor of rhetoric was teaching young students at Carthage. With him I read either the books he expressed a wish to hear, or those I thought suited to his bent of mind. But all my efforts by which I had purposed to advance in that sect came utterly to an end by my acquaintance with that man. It was not that I separated myself from them altogether, but, finding nothing better, I had decided to content myself with what I had happened on in any way, unless by chance something more desirable should present itself. Thus Faustus, the snare of death to so many, had, without willing nor knowing it, now begun to loosen the snare in which I had been held. For your hands, O my God, in the secret purpose of your providence, did not forsake my soul. Out of my mother's heart's blood a sacrifice was offered to you for me, her tears pouring forth day and night. And you dealt with me in marvelous ways. It was you who did it, O my God: *for the steps of a man are ordered by the Lord, and he shall dispose his way.* For how shall we obtain salvation but from your hand, remaking what it has made?

EIGHT

It was by your dealing with me that I was persuaded to go to Rome to teach there what I had been teaching at Carthage. And how I was persuaded to do this, I will not fail to confess before you, for the profoundest workings of your wisdom and your ever-present mercy to me must be pondered and acknowledged in this also.

I did not wish to go to Rome because greater advantages and higher dignities were guaranteed me by the friends who persuaded me to it (though these things did have an influence over my mind at that time). My chief and almost only reason was that I heard that youths studied there more quietly and were kept under the control of a more rigid discipline, so that they did not impudently rush into the class of a teacher who was not their own whenever they liked, and were not even allowed to enter without his permission.

At Carthage, on the other hand, there reigns a most disgraceful and unruly license among the students. They burst in rudely, and with the wildest gestures they interrupt the order which anyone has established for the good of his scholars. They commit all kinds of outrages with an amazing insensitivity, punishable by law if custom did not support them. That custom shows them to be all the more worthless, because they think that what they do is now lawful, though it will never be lawful by your unchangeable law, and they think they are doing it with impunity. Their very blindness is their punishment, though, and they suffer far worse things than they do themselves. The manners, then, which I would not adopt as a student, I was compelled as a teacher to endure in others; and so I was only too glad to go to a place where all who knew anything about it assured me these things were not done. But you, *my refuge and my portion in the land of the living*, goaded me while I was at Carthage, that I might be torn from it, while you offered me enticements at Rome by which to attract me there, by men who loved this dying life, the one doing insane things, the other promising vain things. To correct my path, you secretly employed their perversity and mine. For those who disturbed my tranquillity were blinded by a shameful madness and those who allured me elsewhere savored of the earth. And I, who hated my real misery in one place sought fictitious happiness in another. You knew, O Lord, why I left one country to go to the other, yet you did not show it either to me or to my mother, who grievously lamented my going and followed me as far as the sea. But I deceived her when she tried desperately to hold me back by force, determined either to keep me back or go with me. I pretended that I had a friend whom I could not leave until he had a favorable wind to set sail. And I lied to my mother (and such a mother) and got away. But you have mercifully pardoned me for this, saving me, so filled with abominable defilements from the waters of the sea, for the water of your grace by which, when I was cleansed, the fountains of my mother's eyes would be dried, the tears with which she daily watered the ground under her face. And yet, refusing to return without me, it was with difficulty that I persuaded her to spend that night in a place not far from our ship, where there was a chapel in memory of the blessed Cyprian. That night I secretly left while she remained praying and weeping.

What was it, O Lord, that she asked of you with so many tears, but that you would not allow me to sail? But you, in the depths of your counsels, and hearing the real purpose of her request, did not grant what she was asking then, in order to make me what she more deeply desired. The wind blew and filled our sails, and the shore disappeared from our sight. The next day she was there, wild with grief, filling your ears with complaints and groans, which you disregarded. All the while, by means of my longings, you were speeding me to the end of all longing; and the earthly part of her love for me was being chastened by the just scourge of sorrow. For she loved to have me with her, as mothers do, but even more than many do, and she did not know what great joy you were preparing for her by my absence. Not knowing this, she wept and mourned, and in her agony showed the inheritance of Eve—seeking in sorrow what in sorrow she had brought forth. And yet, after accusing my treachery and cruelty, she took up her intercessions for me with you again, and returned home, while I went on to Rome.

NINE

When I got to Rome, I was welcomed with the scourge of bodily illness, and I very nearly fell into hell, burdened with all the sins which I had committed against you, myself and others—many and grievous sins—over and above that bondage of original sin by which we all die in Adam. For you had not forgiven me any of these things in Christ, neither had he abolished by his cross the enmity which I had incurred with you by my sins. For how could he by the crucifixion of a phantom, which was all I supposed him to be? The death of my soul then was as real as the death of his flesh seemed unreal to me. And if the death of his flesh was true, the life of my soul was false, since I did not believe it. My fever increased, and I was at the point of death and leaving this world forever. If I had then gone hence, where would I have gone but into the fiery torments my misdeeds deserved in the truth of your Law?

My mother did not know this, yet she prayed for me, far away. And you, present everywhere, heard her where she was, and you had pity on me where I was, that I should regain the health of my body, though still sick in my sacrilegious heart. For in all that danger I did not seek your baptism, and I was better as a boy when I asked for it of my mother's piety, as I have already related and confessed. But I had grown up to my own dishonor, and I madly derided all the purposes of your medicine, which would not have allowed me, even such as I was, to have died a double death. If my mother's heart had been pierced with this wound, it could never have been healed. For I cannot sufficiently express the love she had for me, nor how she labored for me in the spirit with a far keener anguish than when she gave me birth in the flesh.

I cannot conceive then, how she could have been healed if my death in sin had come to pierce the deepest heart of her love. And where then would have been those earnest, frequent and unceasing prayers of hers? You would not, O God of mercies, despise the *contrite and humble heart* of that chaste and prudent widow, so full of deeds of charity, so full of duty and service to your saints, never for a day missing the oblation at your altar both morning and evening, coming to your church, not for idle tattlings and old wives tales, but that she might hear you in your sermons and that you might hear her prayers. Could you—you by whose gift she was such—despise and withhold your help from the tears of such a one, by which she begged you not for gold or silver, nor any changeable or fleeting good, but for the salvation of her son's soul? Never, Lord! Yes, you were at hand, and were hearing and acting in the way which you had determined before that it should be done. Far be it that you should deceive her in your visions and the answers she had from you—some of which I have spoken of, some I have not mentioned—which she had laid up in her faithful heart. Always praying, she pressed these on you as your own signature. For, because *your mercy endures for ever*, you condescend to those whose debts you have pardoned, to become a Debtor yourself by your promises.

TEN

You restored me then from that sickness, and healed the son of your handmaid in his body, that he might live for you, to bestow on him a better and more enduring health. But even then at Rome I joined those deluding and deluded "saints"; not their "hearers" only (it was in the house of one of them that I had fallen sick and had recovered), but also with those whom they call "The Elect." For I still thought that it was not we who sin, but that some other nature sinned within us. And it gratified my pride to be free from blame. When I had committed any evil, I did not confess that I had done it, so that *you might heal my soul because it had sinned against you*, but I loved to excuse it, and to accuse something else (I do not know *what* other thing) which was within me but was not

I, myself. But in truth it was all I, and my ungodliness had divided me against myself; and that sin was all the more incurable because I did not judge myself to be a sinner. It was a loathsome iniquity, O God Omnipotent, that I would rather have you to suffer defeat in me to my destruction than myself to be overcome by you to my salvation.[2] You had not as yet set a watch before my mouth, and a door of safekeeping around my lips, that my heart might not turn aside to wicked speeches, to make excuses for sins with men that work iniquity. Therefore I was still united with their "Elect."

But now, hopeless of becoming proficient in that false doctrine, I held more loosely and carelessly even those things with which I had resolved to rest contented if I could find no better. For I was now half inclined to believe that those philosophers whom they call Academics were wiser than the others, in that they held that we ought to doubt everything, and taught that man cannot comprehend any truth. This is what I thought they taught, as they are commonly held to do, not yet realizing their meaning. I did not hesitate freely and openly to discourage my host from that overconfidence I perceived in him toward those fictions of which the Manichean books are full. Yet I lived in closer friendship with them than with others who were not of this heresy. But I did not defend it with my former eagerness. Still my intimacy with that sect, many of them living secretly in Rome, made me hesitant to seek any other way—especially in your Church, O Lord of heaven and earth, Creator of all things visible and invisible. For they had turned me away from it, and it still seemed very uncouth to believe you to have the form of human flesh, to be bounded by the bodily features of our members. When I wanted to think about my God, I did not know what to think of but a mass of bodies, for I thought that anything other than such a mass was nothing. This was the greatest and almost only cause of my inevitable error.

It followed then, that I also believed evil to be a similar sort of substance, and that it had its own foul and misshapen bulk— whether it was dense (which they called earth), or thin and tenuous, like the air (which they imagine to be some malignant mind creeping through the earth). And because my piety, such as it was, constrained me to believe that the good God never created any evil nature, I conceived two masses, opposed to one another, both infinite, but the evil more contracted, the good more expansive.[3] The other profanities followed from this pernicious beginning. For when my mind tried to revert to the Catholic faith, I was repulsed, because the Catholic faith is not what I thought it to be. It seemed more devout to believe that you, my God (to whom I make confession of your mercies), were infinite on all sides except that side where the mass of evil was opposed to you (there I was compelled to consider you to be finite), than if I should imagine you to be limited on all sides by the form of a human body. And it seemed better to me to believe that no evil had been created by you—which in my ignorance I thought was not only a substance, but a bodily one. This was because I had no conception of the mind except as an extremely thin body, diffused in local spaces. And this seemed better than to believe that the nature of evil, such as I considered it to be, could have emanated from you. And our very Savior himself, your Only Begotten, I believed to have been brought forth, as it were, for our salvation out of the mass of your most shining substance, so as to believe nothing of him but what I was able to imagine in my vanity. I thought, then, that such a nature could not have been born of the Virgin Mary without being mingled with her flesh; and I could not see how that nature which I had thus reasoned to myself, could be mingled without being contaminated. Therefore I was afraid to believe that he was born in the flesh, lest I be forced to believe him to have been contaminated by the flesh. Now your spiritual people will smile blandly and lovingly at me if they read these confessions of mine. Yet this is what I was.

ELEVEN

Furthermore, I thought the things the Manicheans had criticized in your Scriptures could not be defended. Yet truly sometimes I wanted to confer upon these different points with someone very well learned in those books, to find what he thought of them. For the speech of one Elpidius, who had spoken and disputed face to face with the Manicheans, had begun to affect me, even when I was at Carthage. He had produced many arguments from the Scriptures not easy to dispute, and the answers of the Manicheans to them seemed weak to me. They preferred not to give their answers publicly, but only to us in private, that the Scriptures of the New Testament had been tampered with by some unknown hand who wished to engraft the Jewish law on the Christian faith. But they themselves did not produce any uncorrupted copies. Still thinking in terms of corporeal bodies, however, I was held captive, oppressed and to a degree suffocated by the concept of those masses, gasping for the breath of your truth, which I was not able to breathe pure and untainted.

TWELVE

Then I began diligently to practice what I had come to Rome to do—the teaching of rhetoric. First, I gathered in my house some to whom and through whom I had begun to be known. And then I learned that other offenses were committed in Rome to which I had not been exposed in Africa. True, as I had been told, those riotous disruptions of abandoned young men were not practiced here. But I was told that all of a sudden, in order to avoid paying their teacher his fees, a number of them would conspire together and go off to another teacher—breakers of faith, who for the love of money hold justice cheap. My heart hated them, but not with a perfect hatred; for perhaps I hated them more because I was to suffer by them, than because they did things utterly unlawful. Of a truth, such are base persons, and they are unfaithful to you by loving these fleeting mockeries of temporal things and filthy lucre which fouls the hand that grasps it, hugging this passing world and despising you. You abide and call back and forgive the adulterous human soul when it returns to you. I still hate such perverse and crooked persons, though I love them if they can be corrected, so as to prefer the learning they acquire to the money, and to prefer learning of you, O God, the truth and fullness of assured good, the most pure peace. But I disliked them then for my own sake rather than wishing them to become good for your sake.

THIRTEEN

When a message came from Milan to Rome to the prefect of the city requesting a teacher of rhetoric for that city to be sent at public expense, I applied for the job. I did this through those same persons, still intoxicated with Manichean vanities, in order to be freed from those very vanities, though neither they nor I knew it at the time. They recommended that Symmachus, the prefect, test me by a speech on some subject and so send me on.

I went to Milan then, to Ambrose the bishop, known to the whole world as one of the best of men, a devout servant of yours. His eloquent discourse in those times dispensed plentifully the flour of your wheat, the gladness of your oil, and the sober intoxication of your wine to your people. I was unknowingly led to him by you, that knowingly I might be led to you by him. That man of God received me like a father, and as a bishop gave a kindly welcome at my arrival. I began to love him, not at first as a teacher of the truth (which I utterly despaired of finding in your Church), but as a man who was friendly to me. I listened diligently to him as he preached to the people, not with the motive I should have had, but, as it were, testing his eloquence, to see if it truly measured up to its fame or was greater or less than others had claimed for it. I hung on his words intently, but of their meaning I was a careless and scornful spectator. I was delighted with the charm of his speech, though it was less cheerful and soothing in manner than that of Faustus. As to the content, there could be no comparison, however; for Faustus was wandering amid Manichean delusions, while Ambrose was teaching salvation most soundly. But *salvation is far from the wicked*, such as I was then. Yet little by little I was drawing nearer without knowing it.

FOURTEEN

Although I took no pains to learn what he preached, but only to hear how he spoke (for that empty care was all that I had left, despairing of finding a way open for man to you); yet along with the words which I prized, there also came into my mind the ideas which I ignored, for I could not separate them. And while I opened my heart to let in "how eloquently he spoke," there also entered in "how truly he spoke." But this was only by degrees. For the first time these things began to appear to me to be defensible, and the Catholic faith, for which I had thought nothing could be said against the attacks of the Manicheans, I now began to see might be defended without embarrassment. This was especially so after I had heard one or two places of the Old Testament explained, often allegorically, which when I understood them literally, had killed me spiritually.[4] When many of these passages had been explained this way, I came to blame my despair in having believed that no reply could be made to those who hated and scoffed at the Law and the Prophets. Yet I still did not see that the Catholic way was therefore to be held because it could find learned advocates who could defend it adequately and answer objections with some show of reason; nor did I know that what I held was therefore to be condemned, because both sides seemed to me to be equally defensible. The Catholic cause did not appear to me vanquished; but neither did it yet seem victorious.

I proceeded to devote my thoughts to see if I could in any way convict the Manicheans of falsehood by any certain proof. If once I could have conceived of a spiritual substance, all their strongholds would have crumbled and been cast utterly out of my mind. But I could not. As I considered and compared things more and more, concerning the body of this world, the whole of nature which the senses of the flesh can apprehend, I judged that opinions of the philosophers were much more probable. So in what I thought was the manner of the Academics—doubting everything and wavering between all—I settled on this much: that I must leave the Manicheans. I judged that, while I was in such doubt, I could not remain in that sect, since I already preferred some of the philosophers to it. I utterly refused to commit the cure of my sick soul to the philosophers, however, because they were without the saving name of Christ. I determined then, to become a catechumen in the Catholic Church, to which I had been commended by my parents, till something certain should manifest itself to me by which I might steer my course.

BOOK VI

At Age Twenty-nine

ONE

O Hope from my youth, where were you at that period, and where had you gone? Had you not created me and made me different from the beasts of the field and the birds of the air? You had made me wiser than they, yet I walked in dark and slippery places. I sought you outside myself and did not find the God of my heart. I had come into the depths of the sea, and distrusted and despaired of ever discovering the truth. By this time my mother had come to me, strengthened by her piety, following me over sea and land, and trusting you through all danger. In the perils of the sea, she comforted even the sailors who were themselves more used to comforting the passengers who were unfamiliar with the sea when they were frightened. She assured them of a safe arrival, because you had given her this assurance in a vision.

She found me in deadly trouble through my despair of ever finding the truth. But when I had told her that I was now no longer a Manichean, though not yet a Catholic Christian, she was not overjoyed, as at a happy surprise, for she had already been reassured concerning that part of my misery for which she had mourned me as one dead, but also as one who would be raised to you. She had carried me on the bier of her thoughts as one on his way to the grave, so that you might say to the widow's son, *Young man, I tell you, Arise,* and he would revive and begin to speak, and you would deliver him to his mother. Her heart then was not shaken with some tumultuous exultation when she heard that what she had sought of the Lord daily with so many tears was in so great a part already accomplished. For though I had not yet come to the truth, I was rescued from falsehood. But since she was confident that you, who had promised the whole, would one day give the rest, she replied to me most calmly and with a heart full of faith, that she believed in Christ that before she departed this life she would see me a Catholic believer. This much she said to me; but to you, Fountain of mercies, she poured forth more copious prayers and tears, that you would hasten your help and enlighten my darkness. She hurried all the more eagerly to the Church, hanging on the words of Ambrose, praying for the fountain of that water which springs up to everlasting life. For she loved that man as an angel of God, because she knew that I had been brought to the questioning state of faith I was now in by him, and she anticipated most confidently that I would pass through it from sickness to health after the onslaught, as it were, of a sharper "fit" like that which physicians term the "crisis."

TWO

When my mother at one time brought some cakes, bread and wine to the chapels built in memory of the saints, as her custom was in Africa, she was forbidden by the doorkeeper. As soon as she learned that the bishop had forbidden her, she piously and obediently acceded to his wishes. I myself wondered at how readily she blamed her own custom rather than question his prohibition. For drinking had not taken hold of her spirit, nor did the love of wine provoke her to hatred of the truth, as it does to too many men and women who revolt at a lesson of sobriety as much as drunken men would revolt at a drink of water. But when she had brought her basket with the accustomed festival-food, to be but tasted by herself and then given away, she never allowed herself more than one small cup of wine, diluted according to her own temperate palate, which she would taste out of courtesy. And if there were many chapels of departed saints to be honored in that way, she would carry around that same one cup and use it everywhere, which was not only made very watery, but became unpleasantly warmed by being carried about; she would distribute this to those about her in small sips, for she sought devotion, not pleasure. As soon, then, as she found this custom had been forbidden even to those who would use it with moderation, by that famous preacher and most pious prelate, lest it should become an occasion of excess to the drunken, and because these festivals in honor of the dead so greatly resembled the superstition of pagans, she most willingly abstained from it. In place of a basket filled with fruits of the earth, she learned to bring to these chapels of the martyrs a heart filled with more purified prayers. Thus she gave all she could to the poor, that in this way, the communion of the Lord's Body might be rightly celebrated where, after the example of his suffering, the martyrs had been sacrificed and crowned.

But yet it seems to me, O Lord my God, and my heart is known to you concerning it, that perhaps she would not have yielded so readily to relinquishing this custom if it had been forbidden by someone else whom she did not love as she loved Ambrose, whom she loved most dearly for the sake of my salvation. And he loved her, too, for her most religious way of life, for she frequented the church in good works, so *fervent in spirit*. He would often, when he saw me, burst forth in her praises, congratulating me that I had such a mother, little knowing what a son she had in me. For I doubted all these things and thought that the way of life could not be discovered.

THREE

Nor did I yet groan in my prayers, that you would help me, but my spirit was wholly intent on knowledge and eager to argue. I counted Ambrose himself a happy man, as the world counts happiness, because he was held in honor by such great personages. Only his celibacy seemed to me a painful burden. I could not guess, nor had I experienced what hope he carried within him, what struggles he had against the temptations which beset his high place, or what comfort in adversities and what sweet joys your Bread had for the hidden mouth of his heart as it fed on it. Nor did he know the heat of my desires nor the depth of my danger. I could not ask of him what I needed to as I would have liked, because I was kept from talking with him by the crowds of busy people to whose weaknesses he devoted himself. The small periods of time when he was not engaged with these, he used either to refresh his body with necessary sustenance or his mind with reading. But when he was reading, his eye glided over the pages and his mind searched out the meaning, but his voice and tongue were silent.

Often when we had come (for no man was forbidden to enter, nor was it his practice to have anyone announced to him), we saw him reading this way to himself, and never any other way. Having long sat in silence (for who would dare interrupt one so intent?) we were inclined to leave, concluding that in the few moments he had free from the demands of others' business, he was unwilling to be distracted from the renewal of his mind. Perhaps he feared that if the author he was reading expressed himself vaguely, some attentive and perplexed hearer might want him to explain it, or to discuss some of the harder questions; so he could not get through as many volumes as he desired if he spent this time otherwise. Also, the preservation of his voice, which was very easily made hoarse, may have been the real reason for his reading to himself. But whatever his reason for doing so, certainly in such a man, it was a good one. In any case, I had no opportunity of inquiring from that holy spokesman of yours what was in his heart, unless the question could be answered briefly. But those surgings in me to be poured out to him would require his full leisure and never found it. I heard him, indeed, every Lord's day, *rightly dividing the Word of Truth* among the people, and I was more and more convinced that all those knots of crafty calumnies which our deceivers had knit against the holy books could be unraveled. And when I finally understood that the words "Man created in the image of God" were not understood by your spiritual sons (whom you have begotten anew of the Catholic mother through grace) to mean that they believed you to be limited by a human shape—although what the nature of a spiritual substance could be I did not have the faintest or dimmest notion—I blushed with joy that for so many years I had barked, not against the Catholic faith, but against the fictions of carnal imaginations. I had been so rash and impious in this that I had condemned ignorantly what I ought to have learned. For you, most high and most near, most hidden yet most present, do not have limbs, some larger, some smaller, but are wholly everywhere, yet nowhere in space. You are not of such bodily shape, yet you made man after your own image; and behold, he is confined in space from head to foot.

FOUR

Not understanding then, how this image of yours could have existence, I should have knocked and expressed my doubt as to how it was to be believed instead of insultingly opposing it as if it were believed. The more sharply doubts as to what to hold for certain gnawed at my heart, the more ashamed I became that I had been deluded and deceived so long by the promise of certainties, and that with childish error and rashness I had talked long and foolishly about so many uncertainties as if they were true. For it had not yet become clear to me that they were completely false. However, I was certain that they were uncertain, and that I had formerly held them to be certain, when with a blind contentiousness, I had accused your Catholic Church. Though I had not yet discovered that it teaches the truth, I knew at least that it did not teach that of which I had so vehemently accused her. So I was confounded and converted. I rejoiced, O my God, that the one Church, the Body of your only Son, wherein the name of Christ had been put upon me as an infant, had no taste for these infantile trifles. Furthermore I found that she did not in her sound teaching maintain any tenet that would confine you, the Creator of all, in space, however great or large, yet bounded on all sides by a human form.

I rejoiced, too, that the old Scriptures of the Law and the Prophets were set before me, to be studied no longer with that eye to which they had seemed absurd previously, when I reviled your saints for thinking what they did not actually think. With delight I often heard Ambrose say in his sermons to the people, as though he were earnestly commending it as a rule of interpretation, *"The letter kills, but the spirit gives life."* And he would then draw aside the mystic veil, laying open spiritually what according to the letter seemed to teach something unsound. His teaching thus had nothing that offended me, though I did not know yet whether or not it was true. For I kept my heart from assenting to anything, fearing to fall headlong; but by hanging in suspense, I was in worse shape. For I wanted to be as certain of invisible things as I was that seven and three are ten. For I was not so mad as to think that even this could not be known for sure; but I wanted to have other things as clear as this, whether they were corporeal things, which were not present to my senses, or spiritual ones, which I did not know how to conceive, except corporeally.

By believing, I might have been cured, so that the eyesight of my soul being made clear, I might have been led to your truth, which abides forever and fails in nothing. But as it happens that he who has tried a bad physician fears to trust himself to a good one, so it was with my soul, which could only be healed by believing. For fear that it should believe falsehoods again, it refused to be cured. Thus I resisted your hands, who prepared the medicines of faith for us and applied them to the diseases of the whole world, and gave them such great power.

FIVE

From this time, then, being led to prefer Catholic doctrine, I felt that the Church acted more modestly and honestly when she required things to be believed which could not be proved—whether they could be proved only to some people, or could not be proved at all—whereas, among the Manicheans, our credulity was mocked by a promise of sure knowledge, and then so many of the most fantastic and absurd things were forced on us to be believed because they could not be proved. After that, O Lord, little by little, with a most gentle and merciful hand, drawing and calming my heart, you persuaded me to consider the innumerable things I believed which I had never seen nor was present when they happened. These include many things in secular history, the numerous reports of places and cities which I had not seen; so many things told me by friends, by doctors, and by others, that if we did not believe, we should do nothing at all in this life. Finally, I thought of how firmly I believed that I was born of particular parents, which I could not know, but had taken on hearsay. Taking all this into consideration, you persuaded me that it was not those who believe your Books, which you have established with such great authority among nearly all nations, but those who did not believe them who were to be faulted; and that those men were not to be listened to who say to me, "How do you know that those Books have been given to mankind by the Spirit of the one true and most true God?" For this very thing was above all to be believed, since no argument of all that multitude of blasphemous questionings which I had read in the self-contradicting philosophers could wring from me the belief that you are—though what you are I did not know—and that the government of human affairs belongs to you.

This much I believed, sometimes more strongly than others. Yet I always believed both that you are and that you have a care for us, though I was ignorant of how to think of your substance and of what way led, or led back, to you. Since we then were too weak to discover truth by our unaided reason, and since for this very cause we needed the authority of Holy Writ, I had now begun to believe that you would never have given such excellency of authority to Scripture in all lands if you had not willed yourself to be sought and believed in through them. For those things in the Scripture whose strange meanings used to offend me, now that many of them were satisfactorily explained, I ascribed to the depth of the mysteries; and the authority of the Bible seemed to me all the more venerable and worthy of religious belief in that while it was open to all to read, it reserved the majesty of its mysteries within its deeper meaning. Stooping to all in the great plainness of its language and simplicity of style, it yet calls forth the most intense application of serious minds. In this way it might receive all in its open bosom, and through narrow passages carry over some few toward you—yet many more than if it did not stand on such a height of authority, or draw multitudes within its bosom by its holy humility. I continued to think on these things, and you were with me. I sighed, and you heard me. I vacillated and you guided me. I roamed through the broad way of the world, but you did not forsake me.

SIX

I longed for honors, money, marriage, and you laughed at me. In these desires I underwent most bitter crosses, but in this you were too gracious to me to allow anything to grow sweet to me which was not yourself. Behold my heart, O Lord, for it is your will that I remember all this and confess it before you. Let my soul hold fast to you, now that you have freed it from the tenacious hold of death. How wretched it was! And you touched the wound on the quick, so that forsaking all else, it might be converted to you, who are above all, and without whom all things would be nothing, that it might be converted and healed.

How miserable I was, and how you dealt with me, to make me feel my misery on that day when I was preparing to recite an oration eulogizing the Emperor! In it I was to utter many a lie, and to be applauded by those who knew I was lying. My heart was very troubled with a sense of guilt and boiling with the fever of consuming thoughts. For, while walking along one of the streets of Milan, I observed a poor beggar. I suppose he had just eaten—he was joking and joyous. I sighed and spoke to the friends around me about the sorrows that our ambitions entail. For by such efforts as those in which I was then laboring, dragging along the burden of my own unhappiness, and making it worse by dragging it with me, I only sought the joyousness that beggar had, but possibly might never attain it. What he had gotten by means of a few coins begged from others, the joy of a temporary happiness—I was scheming for by many a torturous twisting and turning. To be sure, his joy was not true joy. Yet with all my ambitions I was seeking one even more untrue. For he was joyous, while I was anxious. He was free from care, I full of fears. But if anyone should have asked me, would I rather be merry or fearful, I would answer, merry. Again, if he had asked if I would rather be such as the beggar was than as I was then, I would have chosen myself, though beset with cares and fears—out of perversity. But would this be wise and reasonable? For I ought not to prefer myself to him because I was more learned than he, since I had no joy in it, but only sought to please others by it. In this way you broke my bones with the rod of your correction.

Away with those from my soul, then, who say to it, "It makes a difference where a man's joy comes from. That beggar was glad in drunkenness; you longed to rejoice in glory." What glory, O Lord? Glory which is not in you is no true glory; and it overthrew my soul more than his false joy. For he would digest his drunkenness that night, but I had slept and risen again with mine, and was to sleep again and again, to rise with it, how many days! It does indeed make a difference where a man's joy comes from. I know it, and the joy of a faithful hope lies far beyond such vanity. Yes, he was beyond me then. Truly he was happier, not only because he was thoroughly drenched in mirth, while I was torn to pieces with cares, but also because by giving good wishes he had obtained wine, and I was seeking empty praise by lying. I said much to this effect to my good friends, and I often noticed in them what I was feeling then, that when it went badly with me, I grieved and doubled the ill. And if any prosperity smiled on me, I loathed to seize it, for almost before I could grasp it, it flew away.

SEVEN

We who were living as friends together bemoaned these things, but I talked of it mainly and most intimately with Alypius and Nebridius. Alypius came from the same town as myself, his parents being of the highest rank there. He was younger than I, and had studied under me, first when I taught in our hometown, and later at Carthage. He thought a great deal of me, because I seemed kind and learned to him, and I loved him for his innate love of virtue, which was remarkable in one of his years. Yet the whirlpool of Carthaginian customs had drawn him into the madness of the gladiatorial games. Among them these frivolous spectacles are followed passionately. When he first became embroiled in this wretched addiction, I had a public school and was teaching rhetoric there. Because of some ill feeling between his father and me, he was not attending my classes. Seeing how fatally he was doting upon the Circus, I was deeply grieved that he seemed about to throw away his great promise, if, indeed, he had not already done so. Yet I had no means of advising or reclaiming him with any sort of constraint, either by the kindness of a friend or with the authority of a teacher. For I assumed he thought of me as his father did. But he did not. He put aside his father's will in the matter and began to greet me, coming sometimes into my classroom to listen a little and then leaving.

I had put out of my mind any thought that I could deal with him to prevent the undoing of so good a mind through a blind and headstrong passion for vain pastimes. But surely you, Lord, who guide the course of all you have created, had not forgotten him who was to be one day among your children, a bishop in your Church; and so that his amendment might plainly be attributed to you, you brought it about through me without my knowing it. For as I sat one day in my usual place with my students before me, he came in, greeted me, sat down, and turned his attention to what I was saying. By chance I was dealing with a certain passage, when a simile borrowed from the Circensian games occurred to me, as apt to make what I wanted to convey plainer and more pleasant, seasoned with a biting jibe at those whom that madness had enthralled. You know, O God, that I was not thinking then of curing Alypius of that plague. But he took it to himself and thought that I said it simply for his sake. What another would have taken as an occasion of offense with me, that right-minded young man took as a reason to be offended at himself and to love me more warmly. You said long ago and it is written in your Book, *Rebuke a wise man and he will love you.* I had not rebuked him, but you make use of all people, with or without their knowledge, to that purpose which you know. You made burning coals out of my heart and tongue, to set on fire and heal the hopeful mind of that young man thus languishing. Let him be silent in your praises who does not meditate on your mercies, which from my inmost soul I confess before you. For after that speech, Alypius rushed out of that deep pit in which he had been willfully plunged, blinded with its wretched pastimes. He roused his mind with resolute self-control. As a result, all the filth of the Circensian games fell away from him, and he never returned to them again.

Upon this he prevailed upon his reluctant father to let him become my pupil. He gave way, and consented. Alypius, beginning to hear me again, became involved in the same superstition as I was, loving in the Manicheans that show of continence which he believed was true and unfeigned. But it was a senseles and seducing continence, ensnaring precious souls who were not able as yet to reach the height of virtue, and were easily beguiled with the veneer of what was but a shadowy and counterfeit virtue.

EIGHT

Pursuing the worldly course which his parents had urged him to follow, he had gone to Rome before me to study law. There he was carried away with an incredible passion for the gladiatorial shows. For, while at first he utterly detested such spectacles, one day by chance he met several of his acquaintances and fellow-students coming from dinner. With a friendly violence, they forced him along with them into the amphitheater, he resisting and vehemently protesting, "Though you may drag my body into that place and set me down, can you force me to turn my mind or my eyes to those shows? I shall then be absent though present, and shall overcome both you and them." Hearing this, they led him on, nevertheless, possibly wanting to test him, whether he could do as he said. When they got there and had taken such seats as they could find, the whole place became excited with the inhuman sport. He closed his eyes and forbade his mind to roam abroad after such evil. Would that he had shut his ears also! For in the fight, when one fell, a mighty cry of the whole crowd stirred him strongly. Overcome by curiosity, as if ready to despise and rise above whatever it might be, even when seen, he opened his eyes, and was struck with a deeper wound in his soul than the gladiator whom he had wanted to see had received in his body. Thus he fell more miserably than the one whose fall had occasioned the great noise. That noise, entering through his ears and unlocking his eyes, struck and beat down his soul, which was bold rather than resolute, and weaker because it had presumed on itself when it ought to have relied on you. For as soon as he saw that blood, he drank down a sort of savageness with it. Nor did he turn away, but fixed his eyes, drinking in madness unawares, was delighted with the guilty fight and drunk with that bloody pastime.

He was now no longer the man who had come in, but was one of the crowd he had come into—and a true companion of those who had brought him. Why say more? He looked, shouted, was excited, and carried away with him the madness which would stimulate him not only to return with those who first drew him there, but even without them, yes, and to draw in others. Yet from all this you plucked him with a most strong and most merciful hand, and taught him to place his confidence not in himself, but in you. But this was later.

NINE

All this was being stored up in his memory to be a medicine later on. So, too, was the following incident that happened when he was studying under me at Carthage. At noonday he was meditating in the marketplace on what he had to recite (as scholars used to do). You allowed him to be apprehended by the officers of the marketplace as a thief. I think you allowed it for no other reason than that he, who would later prove to be so great a man, should begin to learn that in judging cases, man should not readily be condemned by man with reckless credulity.

As he was walking up and down by himself before the judgment-seat, with his notebook and pen, a young man, one of the scholars—the real thief—secretly carrying a hatchet, unseen by Alypius, got in as far as the lead gratings which protect the silversmiths' shops. He began to cut away the lead, but the noise of the hatchet roused the silversmiths below, and they sent men to take whomever they should find into custody. But the thief, hearing their voices, ran away, leaving his hatchet, fearing to be caught with it. Alypius now, who had not seen him enter, noticed him leaving, and saw how fast he made off. Wanting to know more of what was going on, he entered the place, and finding the hatchet, he stood wondering and considering it, when behold, those who had been sent caught him alone, hatchet in hand. They seized him, dragged him away, and gathering the tenants in the marketplace together, boasted of having captured a notorious thief. Then he was led away to appear before the judge.

But this was the end of his lesson. For immediately, O Lord, you came to the aid of his innocence, of which you were the only witness. For as he was being led away to prison or punishment, they were met by a certain architect who had charge of the public buildings. They were especially glad to see him, for he used to suspect them of stealing the goods that disappeared out of the marketplace, as though they could at last show him who the real thief was. This man had seen Alypius often at a certain senator's house, where he often called to pay his respects. Recognizing him at once, he took him aside by the hand and asked the occasion of such a great calamity, heard the whole matter, and commanded the rabble present (who were causing a great tumult with their shouts and threats) to go with him. It happened that they passed the house of the young man who had committed the theft, and in front of the door was a boy young enough to be likely to disclose the whole story, not sensing any harm to his master. Alypius remembered that this boy was with the thief in the marketplace, and told the architect. Showing the hatchet to the boy, he asked him whose it was. "Ours," he said immediately; and being questioned further, he disclosed everything. Thus the crime was transferred to that house, and the crowd, which had been hurling insults at Alypius, was shamed. And he who would one day be a preacher of your Word and a judge of numerous cases in your Church went away better experienced and instructed.

TEN

I found Alypius at Rome and we became close friends. He went with me to Milan, so that he might still be with me to practice something of the law he had studied more to please his parents than himself. He had already sat as assessor three terms with an honesty which made others wonder. On the other hand, he wondered at others who could prefer gold to honesty. His character was tested, not only with the bait of covetousness, but with the goad of fear. At Rome he was assessor to the Count of the Italian Treasury. There was at that time a very powerful senator to whose favors many stood indebted, and who was feared by many. He wanted a thing granted him that was forbidden by the laws, such as his power usually achieved. Alypius resisted him. With all his heart he refused his proffered bribes. Threats were made, but he trampled them under his feet. All the while, people were astonished at so rare a spirit which neither desired the friendship nor feared the enmity of one so powerful and so widely known for the innumerable means he had of doing good or evil. And the very judge for whom Alypius worked as councilor, although also unwilling that the thing should be done, did not dare openly refuse this senator, but put the matter off on Alypius, claiming that he would not allow him to do as the senator wished. And in truth, if the judge had tried to do it, Alypius would have left his court.

There was one thing in the way of learning by which he was very nearly seduced, that he might have books copied for him at praetorian prices. Thinking about the justice of the case, however, he changed his mind for the better, considering equity that hindered him more valuable than the power that permitted him to do it. These are little things, but *he who is faithful in little is also faithful in much.* Nor can that possibly be in vain which proceeded out of the mouth of your Truth, *If you have not been faithful in the unrighteous mammon, who will commit to your trust the true riches? And if you have not been faithful in that which is another man's, who shall give you that which is your own?* This is the man he was who was so close a friend and wavered in purpose as I did, as to what course of life he should take.

Nebridius also had left his native country near Carthage, and Carthage itself, where he used to live. He had left behind his fine family estate, his house and his mother who would not follow him. He had come to Milan for no other reason but that he might live with me in an ardent search after truth and wisdom. Like me he sighed, like me he wavered, an ardent seeker after true life and a very acute examiner of the most difficult questions. There we were—three needy mouths sighing out their poverty to one another, waiting upon you that you might *give them their food in due season*. And in all the bitterness which by your mercy followed our worldly affairs, and in all the darkness that met us when we sought to know the reason for these things, we said, "How long shall these things be?" We often said this, but saying it, did not forsake these affairs, for as yet we had discovered nothing certain which we might embrace when we forsook these.

ELEVEN

I wondered at length, anxiously reviewing how much time had passed since my nineteenth year, when I had first begun to burn with a desire for wisdom, resolving to abandon all empty hopes and vain desires when I had found it. Now I was in my thirtieth year, stuck in the same mire, greedy to enjoy fleeting pleasure, saying to myself, "Tomorrow I shall find wisdom; and it will appear plainly, and I shall grasp it. Behold, Faustus will come and explain everything! O you great men, you Academicians, is it true, then, that nothing certain can be attained to guide one's life?"

"Not let me search more diligently and not despair. Look! Things in the ecclesiastical books which once seemed absurd do not appear so now, but may be honestly understood in other ways. I will take my stand where my parents placed me as a child until the clear truth be discovered.

"But where shall it be sought, and when? Ambrose has no free time. I have no leisure to read. Where shall I find the books? When and from where can I procure them? From whom could I borrow them? Let times be set, certain hours for the health of my soul. A great hope has dawned on us that the Catholic faith does not teach what I thought and vainly accused it of teaching. Her learned ones hold it an abomination to believe that God is limited by the form of a human body. Do I doubt that I should knock, in order that the rest may be opened? My mornings are taken up with my scholars; what do I do with the rest of the day? Why do we not set about this? But when, then, could we visit our great friends, whose favors we need? When could I prepare the lessons the scholars pay for? When could we refresh ourselves and relax our minds from the pressure of work?

"Perish everything! Dismiss these empty vanities! I will betake myself to the one search for truth! Life is miserable, death is uncertain. If it steals on me of a sudden, in what state shall I depart hence, and where shall I learn what I have neglected here? Or rather, shall I not suffer the punishment of this negligence? What if death itself should cut off and completely put an end, along with thought itself, to all feeling and care? This too must be examined. But God forbid that it should be so! It is not an empty thing. It is not without reason that the lofty authority of the Christian faith has overspread the whole world. Never would such and so great a thing have been wrought by God for us if with the death of the body the life of the soul came to an end. Why, then, do I delay to abandon worldly hopes and give myself wholly to seek God and the blessed life?

"But wait! Worldly things are pleasant. They have some sweetness—and no little sweetness it is. I must not lightly give them up, for it would be embarrassing to return to them again. Look how easy it is now to obtain some position of honor, and what more could I want? I have a store of influential friends. If nothing else comes along, at least a governorship may be offered me and a wife with some money so she would not be an added expense. And so I would have reached the height of my desires. Many great men, and most worthy of imitation, have applied themselves to the study of wisdom in the state of marriage."

While I talked over these things, and these winds shifted and drove my heart this way and that, time passed on. But I delayed to turn to the Lord. From day to day, I postponed to live in you, but I did not postpone daily to die in myself. Loving a happy life, I feared to seek it in its own place, but sought it by fleeing from it. I thought I should be too miserable if I could not be enfolded in a woman's arms. And I did not think of your mercy as a healing medicine for that infirmity, not having tried it. As for continence, I supposed it to be in our own power (though in myself I did not find that power), being so foolish as not to know what is written, that none can be continent unles you grant it. Certainly you would have given it if with heartfelt groaning I had beset your ears, and with a firm faith had cast my care upon you.

TWELVE

It was actually Alypius who kept me from marrying. He alleged that if I did, we could by no means live together with the leisure of seeking the wisdom we had long desired. He himself was even then so chaste that it was wonderful—all the more so, too, since in his early youth he had erred on the path, but he had felt remorse and revulsion at it, and from then on had lived in complete continence. I opposed him with the examples of married men who had cherished wisdom and found favor with God, retaining their friends and loving them faithfully. But I fell far short of their greatness of spirit and was enslaved with the disease of the flesh. Its deadly sweetness dragged my chain along, dreading to be loosed, and as if it pressed my wound, rejected his good persuasions as if it were the hand of one who would unchain me. Moreover, the serpent spoke to Alypius himself through me, weaving and laying pleasurable snares in his path, in which his virtuous and free feet might become entangled.

For he wondered that I, whom he esteemed so greatly, should be stuck so fast in the grip of that pleasure as to affirm whenever we discussed it that I could never lead a single life. I urged in my defense, when I saw him wonder, that there was a great difference between his momentary and furtive experience of that life (which he hardly remembered and could so easily despise) and my continued acquaintance with it. It needed only the honorable name of marriage to be added, and he would not then be astonished at my inability to abandon that way of life. Then he began also to want to be married, not as being overcome with lust for such pleasure, but from curiosity. For he wanted to know, he said, what it was without which my life—which seemed so pleasant to him—should seem to be no life at all but a punishment. His mind, free from that chain, was astounded at my slavery, and through that amazement went on to a desire to try it. From the desire, he was going on to the trial itself, and thence, he might have sunk into that bondage which at present he wondered at. For he was willing to make *a covenant with death*, and *he who loves danger shall fall in it*. Whatever honor there is in the state of a well-ordered married life and the bringing up of children had but slight interest to us. As for myself, it was for the most part trying to satisfy an insatiable lust; but Alypius was about to be led captive by curiosity. Thus we remained until you, O most High, not forsaking our lowliness, had mercy on our misery and came to our aid by wonderful and secret ways.

THIRTEEN

Active efforts were made to get me a wife. I wooed. I was engaged, largely through my mother's efforts, because once married, I was to be baptized, and she rejoiced that I was daily becoming more disposed to it. She observed that her desires and your promises were being fulfilled in my faith. Then by my own request and her own desires, she besought you daily that you would show her something concerning my future marriage by a vision, but you would not. She saw, indeed, certain meaningles fantasies, such as the human spirit, preoccupied with such things, can conjure up. She told these to me, but not with the usual confidence she displayed when you showed her anything. For she could, she declared, discern between your revelations and the dreams of her own soul, through a certain feeling which she could not put into words. Yet the matter was pressed on, and a maiden asked in marriage. She was two years under the marriageable age.[2] But since she was pleasing, I waited for her.

FOURTEEN

Many of us friends, conferring about and detesting the turbulent vexations of human life, had almost decided to seek a life of peace, apart from the bustle of men. This was to be obtained by bringing together whatever we might severally procure and make one household of it all; so that through the sincerity of our friendship nothing should belong especially to any one of us, and the whole to all.[3] We thought there might be some ten persons in this group, some of whom were very rich, especially Romanianus, our townsman, a close friend of mine from childhood. Grave business matters had brought him up to Court, and he was the most eager of us all for this project. His voice carried great weight in commanding it, because his ample estate far exceeded any of the rest. We had resolved also that two officers should be chosen each year to provide everything necessary, while the rest were to be left undisturbed. But when we began to consider whether the wives, which some of us already had, and others hoped to have, would permit this, all that plan, which was being so well framed, came to pieces in our hands and was utterly wrecked and cast aside. Then we fell again into sighs and groans, following the broad and beaten ways of the world. Many thoughts were in our hearts, but *your counsel stands forever*. Out of your counsel, you laughed at ours, and prepared your own, purposing *to give us food in due season* and *to open your hand, and to fill our souls with blessing.*

FIFTEEN

Meanwhile my sins were being multiplied. My mistress was torn from my side as a hindrance to my marriage. My heart, which clung to her, was torn, wounded and bleeding. She returned to Africa, vowing to you never to know another man, leaving with me my natural son by her.[4] But unhappy as I was, I could not imitate her resolve. Impatient of delay, since it would be two years before I could obtain the one I sought, not being so much a lover of marriage as a slave to lust, I procured another mistress, not a wife, of course. In this way, by its enslavement to a lasting habit, my soul's disease was nourished and kept vigorous, or even increased until I should reach the realm of marriage. Nor was that wound of my heart caused by the separation from my former mistress yet healed; but after inflammation and most acute pain, it festered and the pain became numbed, but more hopeless.

SIXTEEN

To you, be praise, to you be glory, O Fountain of mercies! As I became more miserable, you were drawing nearer. Your right hand was continually ready to pluck me out of the mire and to cleanse me, but I did not know it. Nothing called me back from a yet deeper gulf of carnal pleasures but the fear of death and of your judgment to come, which amid all my changes of opinion never left my breast. In a dispute with my friends, Alypius and Nebridius, on the nature of good and evil, I held that Epicurus would have, to my mind, won the argument if I had not believed that there remained a life for the soul after death and a place of requital according to men's deserts, which Epicurus did not believe.

"Supposing us to be immortal and to be living in the enjoyment of perpetual bodily pleasure without fear of losing it, why should we not be happy, or what else should we seek?" I asked, not knowing that this very thing was at the heart of my misery. Being sunk and blinded as I was, I could not discern that light of excellence and beauty which is to be embraced for its own sake. The carnal eye cannot see it, but it is seen by the inner man. Nor did I even consider how it was that I talked with pleasure on such foul subjects with my friends, while at the same time, I could not be happy without these friends, even in the midst of the greatest abundance of carnal pleasures. Yet I loved these friends for their own sakes and I felt that I was loved by them for my own sake.

O crooked paths! Woe to the audacious soul which hoped that by forsaking you it could gain some better thing! Tossed up and down, upon its back, its sides, and its belly, it found only discomfort, for you alone are rest. And behold, you are near, to deliver us from our wretched wanderings and place us in your way. You comfort us and say, "Run. I will carry you. Yes, I will bring you through and even there I will carry you."

BOOK VII

At Age Thirty

ONE

My evil and abominable youth was now dead, and I was passing into early manhood.[1] As I increased in years, I grew more defiled in vanity, for I could not conceive of any substance but such as I saw with my own eyes. I did not think of you, O God, under the form of a human body. From the time I began to hear anything of philosophy, I had always avoided this, and I rejoiced to have found the same rejection in the faith of our spiritual mother, your Catholic Church. But I did not know how else to think of you. As a man, and such as I was, I sought to conceive of you as the sovereign, only true God. In my inmost soul I believed you to be incorruptible, inviolable and unchangeable; because though I did not know whence or how, yet I saw most plainly and felt sure that what can be corrupted must be inferior to the incorruptible. What could not be violated I preferred unhesitatingly to what could receive injury and I deemed the unchangeable to be better than that which is changeable. My heart passionately cried out against all my mental constructs, and with one blow I sought to drive away from my mind's eye all that unclean troop which buzzed around it.

But alas! In the twinkling of an eye, they gathered again thickly about me, flew against my face, and clouded my vision; so that, though I did not think of you under the form of a human body, yet I was forced to conceive of you as being something corporeal in space, either infused into the world or diffused infinitely outside it—a Being that was incorruptible, inviolable and unchangeable. I preferred this to one that was corruptible, and violable, and changeable. For whatever I conceived to be deprived of this space seemed to me to be nothing, yes, altogether nothing, not even a void. If a body were taken out of its place and the place should remain empty of any body at all, of earth and water, air and the heavens, yet it would remain an empty space, a spacious nothing, as it were.

Being thus totally materialistically minded, not clear even to myself, so that whatever was not extended over certain spaces, either diffused or massed together or puffed out, or whatever did not or could not receive some of these dimensions, I thought was altogether nothing. For my heart then ranged over such forms as I could see with my eyes. I did not yet understand that this very observation by which I formed those same images was invisible to the eye, and yet my mind could not have formed them if it had not itself been some great thing. In the same way I tried to conceive of you, Life of my life, as vast, extending through infinite spaces, penetrating on every side the whole mass of the universe, and extending beyond it in every direction through immeasurable, boundless space. Thus the earth would have you, the heavens would have you, all things could have you, and they would have their limits within you, but you as having no limits. For as the body of the air which is above the earth does not hinder the light of the sun from passing through it, penetrating it, not by bursting or by cutting, but by filling it wholly, so I imagined the body of the heavens, air and sea, and of the earth, too, as being pervious to you, so that all its parts, the greatest and the smallest, admitted your presence and by an invisible inspiration you governed everything you have created, both inwardly and outwardly. This is what I conjectured, because I was unable to think of anything else, for this was false. If this were true, then a greater part of the earth would in that case contain a greater part of you, and a smaller one, less of you. And all things would be full of you in such a way that the body of an elephant would contain more of you than that of a sparrow, since it is larger and takes up more room. Thus you would make parts of you present to the several parts of the world in fragments, large pieces to the large, little pieces to the small.

You are not like this, but you had not yet enlightened my darkness.

TWO

It was sufficient for me, Lord, to oppose those deceived deceivers, those dumb prattlers (dumb, since your word did not sound forth from them), to use the argument Nebridius used to propound while we were still at Carthage. All of us who heard it were disturbed by it at the time. It went like this: "What could that supposed kingdom of darkness, which the Manicheans consider a mass opposed to you, have done to God if he refused to fight with it?" If they answered that it would have done God some hurt, then God would be subject to injury and corruption. But if they said that it could do God no hurt, then there was no reason why God should fight against it. But they held, it was this very fighting that involved some part of you. Some members or offspring of your very substance were intermingled with opposing powers and natures not created by you, and were corrupted and deteriorated to such an extent by them as to be turned from happiness to misery and to need assistance in order to be delivered and purified. This offspring of your substance, they taught, is the soul which, enslaved, defiled and corrupted as it is, can be relieved by your Word free, pure and whole. But Nebridius argued, "In that case, the Word itself is then corruptible, because it was of one and the same substance as the soul." And if they affirmed that your essential Being (that is, your substance) is incorruptible, then all these sayings of theirs were false and deplorable. But if they said that you are corruptible, then that very statement showed itself to be false and to be abhorred. This argument of Nebridius was an adequate one, then, against those who deserved to be vomited forth from the surfeited stomach, since it gave them no escape from this dilemma without horrible blasphemy of heart and tongue, thinking and speaking such things of you.

THREE

But although I held and was fully persuaded, O Lord, the true God, who made not only our souls, but our bodies, and not only our souls and bodies, but all beings and all things, that you were incorruptible and unchangeable, and in no part mutable, yet I did not understand clearly and without difficulty the cause of evil. Whatever it was, I perceived that it must be understood so as not to force me to believe the unchanging God to be changeable, lest I should become the very evil I was seeking to understand. I tried to understand it then, free from anxiety, sure of untruthfulness of what the Manicheans asserted, whom I shunned with my whole heart; for I saw that by seeking the origin of evil, they were filled with evil themselves, in that they preferred to think that your Substance suffered evil than that their own committed it.

So I directed my attention to discern what I had now heard—that free will was the cause of our doing evil, and your righteous judgment the cause of our suffering it. But I could not clearly discern it. When I tried to draw the eye of my mind out of that deep pit, I was plunged into it again. And as often as I tried, I was thrown back again. But this raised me a little toward your light, in that I knew now that I had a will as well as that I had life. When I was willing or was unwilling to do something, I was very certain that it was none but myself who was willing or unwilling. Immediately I perceived that the cause of my sin lay there.

But what I did against my will, I saw that I suffered rather than did, and that I judged not to be my fault, but my punishment. However, since I believed you to be most just, I quickly confessed that I was being justly punished.

But again I asked, "Who made me? Did not my God who is not only good, but Goodness itself? How did I come then to will to do evil and to be unwilling to do good, so that I am justly punished in this way? Who put this in me and implanted in me this *root of bitterness*, since I was completely made by my most sweet God? If the devil were the author, where did the devil himself come from? And if he was a good angel who became a devil by his own perverse will, where, again, did that evil will in him come from, seeing the whole nature of angels was made altogether good by that most good Creator?"

By these thoughts I was again sunk down and stifled. Yet I was not plunged into that hell of error (where no man confesses to you) to think that you suffer evil, rather than that men do it.

FOUR

I was struggling to discover answers to other difficulties, having already found out that the incorruptible must be better than the corruptible. Whatever you were, I acknowledged you to be incorruptible. For no one ever was nor ever shall be able to conceive of anything better than you, who are the highest and best Good. But since the incorruptible is most surely and certainly to be preferred to the corruptible (as I now preferred it), then if you were not incorruptible, it would have been possible for me to conceive of something better than my God. To the corruptible, I saw that I should seek you there, and learn from there the origin of evil, that is, where the corruption comes from by which your substance cannot be profaned. For corruption truly in no way contaminates our God, by no will, by no necessity, by no unforeseen chance, because he is God, and what he wills is good, and he himself is that Good. But to be corrupted is not good, nor are you compelled to do anything against your will, since your will is not greater than your power. But it would be greater if you yourself were greater than yourself. For the will and power of God is God himself. And what can be unforeseen by you, who know all things? Nor is there any sort of nature that you do not know. And why should we give any more reasons why that substance which is God cannot be corruptible, since if it were so, it could not be God?

FIVE

I kept seeking the origin of evil. I sought in an evil way, but did not see the evil in my very search. I now set before the eye of my mind the whole creation, whatever we can see in it—the sea, earth, air, stars, trees, living creatures, and whatever we cannot see, such as the firmament of heaven, all the angels, and all the spiritual inhabitants of heaven. My imagination placed all these, as if they were bodies, each in its own place. I made one huge mass of your creatures, differentiated according to the kinds of bodies—some of them real bodies, some of them what I imagined spirits to be. I made this mass huge—not as it was, which I could not know, but as large as I thought sufficient, yet finite in every way. But I imagined you, O Lord, as surrounding it on every side and penetrating it through and through, though in every way infinite. It was as if there were a sea everywhere, and on every side through unmeasured space, nothing but an infinite sea; and it contained within it some sponge, huge, but finite, so that every part of the sponge would be filled with that immeasurable sea.

This is the way I conceived your creation to be, finite itself, filled with you, the Infinite. And I said, "Behold God, and behold what he has created! And God is good, yes, most mightily and incomparably better than all these; but yet he, the Good, created them good. See how he encircles and fills them. Where then is evil, and from where does it come, and how did it creep in? What is its root and what is its seed? Or, if it has no being at all, why then do we fear and avoid what has no being? Or if we fear it needlessly, then surely that very fear is evil, by which the heart is pricked and tormented—yes, and so much greater an evil, if we have nothing to fear, and yet do fear! Therefore, either the evil we fear exists, or our fear is evil.

"But then, where does it come from, seeing that God, the Good, has created all these things good? He indeed, the greatest and chief Good, has created all these lesser goods, but both Creator and created are all good. Whence then is evil? Or was there some evil matter out of which he made and formed and ordered it, yet left something in it which he did not convert into good? If so, why? Did he lack the power to turn and change the whole lump, so that no evil should remain in it, seeing that he is omnipotent?

"Finally, why would he make anything at all of it, and not rather by that same Omnipotence cause it not to be at all? Or could it indeed exist contrary to his will? Or, if it were from eternity, why did he allow it to be so through the infinite reaches of time in the past, and why was he pleased after so long a time to make something out of it? Or, if he wished suddenly to act, the Almighty should rather have acted so that this evil matter should not exist at all, and so that he alone should be the whole, true, highest and infinite Good. Or if it was not good that he who was good should not also be the Framer and Creator of what was good, then having taken away and annihilated that evil matter, he might form good matter out of which to create all things. For he would not be omnipotent if he could not create something good without the aid of that matter which he himself had not created."

These thoughts turned over and over in my miserable heart, overwhelmed and gnawed at by the fear that I should die before I had found the truth. Yet the faith of your Christ, our Lord and Savior, as it was held in the Catholic Church, was firmly fixed in my heart, although yet unformed in many points and diverging from the rule of right doctrine. Yet my mind did not utterly leave it, but drank in more and more of it every day.

SIX

By this time I had rejected the false divinations and blasphemous absurdities of the astrologers. Let your own mercies, out of my very inmost soul, confess this also before you, O my God. For who else calls us back from the death of all errors except the Life which cannot die and the wisdom which, needing no light, enlightens the minds that need it, by which the universe is directed, even down to the fluttering leaves of the trees? You alone made provision to cure my obstinacy with which I struggled with Vindicianus, an acute old man, and Nebridius, a young man of remarkable talents. Vindicianus vigorously declared and Nebridius, though with some doubtfulness, often maintained that no such art existed by which to foresee future things, but that men's guesses were like a sort of lottery, and that out of many things which they predicted, some actually did happen without the predictors actually knowing that they would; and that they had merely stumbled on these things by their numerous guesses.

You provided me with a friend, then, who was a fairly frequent consulter of astrologers, but not deeply versed in their lore. He was, as I said, one who consulted them out of curiosity, and yet he knew something which he said he had heard from his father. He did not know, however, how far his story would go in overthrowing my estimation of that art. This man, then, Firminius by name, a man of liberal education and well learned in rhetoric, asked me, his friend, to interpret, according to his so-called constellations, some affairs of his in which his worldly hopes had risen. Although I had now begun to lean toward Nebridius' opinion, I did not altogether refuse to speculate about the matter and to tell him what came into my mind, undecided though it was. But I added that I was now almost persuaded that these were but empty and ridiculous follies.

Upon this he told me that his father had been very interested in astrological books, and had a friend as interested in them as himself. With joint study and consultation, they had fanned the flame of their affections for these follies, so that they would observe the moments when the dumb animals about their houses gave birth to their young, and then observed the relative position of the heavens, to gather fresh proofs of this so-called art. He said, moreover, that his father had told him that when his mother was about to give birth to him [Firminius], a female slave of that friend of his father's was also pregnant at the same time. This could not be unnoticed by her master, who took care with the most exact diligence to know the births even of his puppies. And so they did their calculations (one for his wife and the other for his servant), with the most careful observation, calculating the days, hours, and minutes. It happened that both were delivered at the same moment, so that each had precisely the same horoscope, down to the minutest points, heir and slave alike. For as soon as the women began to be in labor, each man notified the other what was happening in their respective homes, and had messengers ready to send to one another as soon as they had notice of the actual birth. Each had provided for this in his own house, and the messengers of the respective parties met, he said, at such an equal distance from either house that neither of them could make out any difference in the position of the stars or any other minutest points. And yet Firminius, born in a high estate in his parents' house, ran his course through the more prosperous ways of this world, increased in wealth and rose to honors; whereas that slave continued to serve his masters with no relaxation of his yoke, as Firminius, who knew him, told me.

Upon hearing and believing these things, in view of the character of the narrator, all my resistance gave way. First, I tried to reclaim Firminius himself from that curiosity by telling him that upon inspecting his constellations, I ought, if I were to predict truly, to have seen in them parents eminent among their neighbors, a noble family in its own city, high birth, good education, liberal learning. But if that servant had consulted me upon the same constellations, since they were his also (again, if it were accurate), I should see in them a most abject lineage, a slavish condition, and everything else utterly at variance with the former. Thus looking at the same constellations, if I spoke the truth, I would have spoken different things to each; or if I spoke the same, I would have spoken falsely. From this it was to be gathered most certainly that whatever was foretold accurately upon consideration of these constellations was not by art, but by chance. And whatever was foretold inaccurately was not from lack of skill in the art, but the error of chance.

Approaching the subject from this side, I began to consider other similar situations, so that none of those fools who followed such an occupation (whom I longed to attack and confute with ridicule), might argue against me that either Firminius had informed me falsely, or his father him. So I turned my thoughts to those who are born twins, who for the most part, emerge from the womb so close to each other that the small interval between them—however much influence they claim for it as an actual fact—cannot be noted by human observation, or be accurately expressed in those figures the astrologer examines in order to predict accurately. Yet they cannot be true: for looking into the same figures, he must have predicted the same things concerning Esau and Jacob, while on the contrary the same did not happen to them. He must therefore speak falsely. If he is to speak accurately, then looking into the same figures, he must not give the same answer. Any accurate answer, then, is not by art then, but by chance. For you, O Lord, most righteous Ruler of the universe, while the consulters and the consulted know it not, can so act upon them both by your hidden inspiration that the consulter hears out of the unsearchable depth of your righteous judgment what he ought to hear according to the secret deservings of his soul. Let no man say to you "What is this?" or "Why is that?" Let him not say it, let him not say it, for he is but man.

SEVEN

And now, O my Helper, you had loosed me from those fetters. But still I sought, "Whence is evil?" and found no answer. But you did not allow me to be carried away from, by any fluctuations of thought, the faith by which I still believed both that you are and that your substance is unchangeable, and that you care for and would judge men, and that in Christ, your Son, our Lord, and in the Holy Scriptures, which the authority of your Catholic Church pressed upon me, you had planned the way of man's salvation to that life which is to come after this death.

With these things safe and immovably settled in my mind, I eagerly sought the origin of evil. What torments did my travailing heart endure! What sighs, O my God! Yet even there your ears were open and I did not know it. When in stillness I sought earnestly, those silent contritions of my soul were loud cries to your mercy. No man knew, but you alone knew what I endured. How little of it did my tongue utter to the ears of my closest friends! Did the whole tumult of my soul, for which neither time nor words was sufficient, reach them? Yet it all went into your ears, all that I roared out from the groanings of my heart. And my desire was before you, and the light of my eyes failed me;[2] for that light was within, and I was looking without. Nor was that light in space, but my attention was directed to things contained in space. I found there no resting place, nor did they receive me in such a way that I could say, "It is enough. It is well." Nor did they let me turn back to where it might be well enough with me. For I was superior to these things, but inferior to you. You are my true joy when I am subjected to you, and when you have subjected to me what you created beneath me. And this was the happy mean and middle way of my safety, that I should remain in your image and by serving you have dominion over the body. But when I lifted myself proudly against you and *ran against the Lord, even against his neck, with the thick studs of my buckler*, even these inferior things were placed above me, and pressed me down, so that nowhere was there any respite or relief. They met my sight on all sides crowds and troops, and their images appeared to my thoughts unsought as I was returning to you, as if to say to me, "Where are you going, unworthy and defiled one?" All these things had grown out of my wound, for you humble the proud like one that is wounded, and through my own inflated pride, I was separated from you. Yes, my eyes were swelled shut by my pride-bloated face.

EIGHT

But you, Lord, abide forever. Yet you are not angry with us forever, because you have pity on our dust and ashes. It was pleasing in your sight to reform my deformities, and you disturbed me by inward goads to make me dissatisfied until you were revealed to my inward sight. Thus, by the secret hand of your remedy my swelling was reduced, and the disordered and bedimmed sight of my mind was made whole from day to day by the stinging anointings of healthful sorrows.

NINE

First of all, willing to show me how you *resist the proud but give grace to the humble*, and with what great mercy you have shown men the way of humility, in that your *Word was made flesh and dwelt among men*, you procured for me, by means of one puffed up with the most monstrous pride, certain books of the Platonists, translated from Greek into Latin.[3] In them I read, not indeed in the very words, but with exactly the same meaning, enforced by many and various reasonings, that *In the beginning was the Word, and the Word was with God, and the Word was God; the same was in the beginning with God; all things were made by him, and without him was nothing made; that which was made by him is life, and the life was the light of men, and the light shines in darkness, and the darkness comprehended it not.* And that the soul of man, though it bears witness to the light, yet itself is not that light; but the Word of God, being God, *is that true light that lightens every man that comes into the world.* And that *he was in the world, and the world was made by him, but the world knew him not.* But I did not read there that *he came to his own and his own received him not.* But as *many as received him, to them he gave power to become the sons of God, as many as believed in his name.*

In the same way I read there that God the Word was born not of flesh, nor of blood, nor of the will of the flesh, but of God. But that *the Word was made flesh and dwelt among us*, I did not read there. For I discovered in those books that it was said in many and different ways that the Son was in the form of the Father, and *did not think it robbery to be equal with God*, because he was naturally the same substance. But I did not read there that *he emptied himself and took upon him the form of a servant, and was made man; and being found in the likeness of man, he humbled himself and became obedient unto death, even the death of the cross. Therefore God has highly exalted him* from the dead *and bestowed on him the name which is above every name, that at the name of Jesus every knee should bow, in heaven and on earth and under the earth, and every tongue confess that Jesus Christ is Lord, to the glory of God the Father.*

I read there that before all time, and above all times, your only-begotten Son remains unchangeably co-eternal with you, and that of *his fullness* souls receive, that they may be blessed; and that by participation in that wisdom which remains in them they are renewed that they may be wise. But I did not read that *in due time he died for the ungodly*; and that *you spared not your only Son, but delivered him up for us all*. For *you hide these things from the wise and reveal them to babes*, so that they *who labor and are heavy laden might come to him, and he refresh them, because he is meek and lowly in heart; and he directs the meek in righteousness, and he teaches his ways to the gentle, taking note of our lowliness and troubles, and forgiving all our sins*. But such as are puffed up with the elation of some would-be sublimer learning do not hear him saying, *Learn of me; for I am meek and lowly in heart, and you shall find rest to your souls*. Although *they knew God, they did not honor him as God or give thanks to him, but they became futile in their thinking and their senseless minds were darkened. Claiming to be wise, they became fools.*

Moreover, I read there that they had *exchanged the glory of your immortal nature for images resembling mortal man or birds or animals or reptiles*—namely, into that Egyptian food for which Esau lost his birthright; so that your firstborn people worshiped the head of a four-footed beast instead of you, turning back in heart toward Egypt, and prostrating your image (their own soul) before the image *of an ox that eats hay*. I found these things there, but I did not feed on them. For it pleased you, O Lord, to take away the reproach of his lesser status from Jacob, that the elder should serve the younger; and you have called the Gentiles into your inheritance. And I had come to you from among the Gentiles, and I strained after that gold which you willed your people to take from Egypt, since wherever it was, it was yours. And to the Athenians you said by your apostle that in you *we live, and move, and have our being*, as one of their own poets had said. And certainly these books came from there [Athens]. But I did not set my mind on the idols of Egypt, whom they served with your gold, *changing the truth of God into a lie, and worshiping and serving the creature more than the Creator.*[4]

TEN

Being warned by these writers to return to myself, I entered into my inward soul, guided by you. And I was able to do it because you had become my Helper. I entered and with the eye of my soul (such as it was), I saw beyond my soul, beyond my mind, the Unchangeable Light. It was not the ordinary light which all flesh can look upon, nor as it were, a greater one of the same kind, as though the brightness of ordinary light were intensified many times and would fill up all things with its brilliance. This light was not that kind, but far different from all these. Nor was it above my mind as oil is above water, or as heaven is above earth. But it was above because it made me, and I was below it because I was made by it, he who knows the truth, knows what that Light is; and he who knows it, knows eternity. Love knows it.

O eternal Truth, and true Love, and beloved Eternity! You are my God; to you I sigh both night and day. When I first knew you, you lifted me up, that I might see that there was something for me to see, and that I was not yet ready to see it. Streaming forth your beams of light upon me most intensely, you dazzled the weakness of my sight, and I trembled with love and awe. I realized that I was far from you, in the region of dissimilarity, as if I heard your voice from on high, saying, "I am the food of grown men; grow and you shall feed on Me; you shall not change Me, like the food of your flesh, into what you are, but you shall be changed into what I am." And I learned that *you correct man for his iniquity, and you made my soul consume away as though eaten by a spider.* And I said, "Is Truth, then, nothing at all, since it is not spread out through finite or infinite space?" And you cried to me from afar, "Yes, truly I AM THAT I AM." And I heard, as the heart hears and had no room to doubt I would rather have doubted that I was alive than that Truth is, which is *clearly seen, being understood by the things that are made.*

ELEVEN

And I viewed the other things below you, and perceived that they neither totally *are*, nor totally *are not.* For they exist because they are from you; but they do not exist independently, because they are not what you are.[5] For that truly is, which remains unchangeable. *So it is good for me to hold fast unto God;* for if I do not remain in him, I cannot remain in myself. But he remaining in himself, renews all things. And you are the Lord my God; *I have no good apart from you.*

TWELVE

And it was made clear to me that all things which undergo corruption are (in themselves) good. If they were supremely good, they could not be corrupted, but neither could they be corrupted unless they were good. If they were supremely good, they would be incorruptible. If they were not good at all, there would be nothing in them to be corrupted. For corruption injures, but unless it could diminish goodness, it could not harm. Either, then, corruption does not injure (which cannot be); or, what is most certain of all, all that is corrupted is deprived of some good. But if they are deprived of all good, they will cease to be. For if they could be, and now can be corrupted no longer, they would be better than before, because they would remain incorruptible. And what could be more monstrous than to affirm that things are made better by losing all their goodness? Therefore, if they were deprived of all good, they would no longer exist. So long as they are, then, they are good; therefore, whatever is, is good. Evil then, the origin of which I sought, is not a substance at all. For if it were a substance, it would be good. For either it would be an incorruptible substance, and so a chief good, or a corruptible substance, which could not be corrupted unless it were good. I perceived therefore, and it was shown to me, that you made all things good, and that there is no substance at all which you did not make. And it is because you have not made all things equal that each individual thing is called good, and all things together are called not only good, but very good, for our God has made all things very good.[6]

THIRTEEN

To you evil is nothing whatsoever: yes, not only to you, but also to your creation as a whole, because there is nothing outside it which could break in and mar that order which you have appointed for it. But in the parts of it, some things, because they are not in harmony with others, are considered evil. Yet those same things harmonize with others and are good, and in themselves are good. All these things which do not harmonize together, still harmonize with that lower part of creation which we call the earth, which has its own cloudy and windy sky harmonizing with it. Far be it from me, then, to say, "These things should not be." For if I saw nothing but these, I would indeed long for better; but even for these alone I should praise you, for that you are to be praised is shown from the *earth, dragons, and all deeps, fire, hail, snow, ice and stormy wind, which fulfill your word; mountains and all hills, fruit trees and all cedars; beasts and all cattle, creeping things and flying fowls; kings of the earth and all peoples; princes and all judges of the earth; young men and maidens, old men and young,* praise your name! And when from the heavens, O our God, these praise you, then *all your angels praise you in the heights, and all your hosts, sun and moon, all stars and light, the Heaven of heavens, and the waters that are above the heavens, praise your name.* I did not now long for better things, because I considered them all, and with a sounder judgment I realized that while the things above were better than those below, all things together were better than those above would be by themselves alone.

FOURTEEN

There is no wholeness in those who are displeased with any part of your creation, no more than there was in me when I was displeased with so many things that you had made. And because my soul did not dare to be displeased with my God, I preferred not to account that which displeased me as yours. From this I had accepted the notion of two substances (one evil, one good), and I found no rest, but kept talking idly. Turning from that error, I had made for myself a god which occupied infinite measures of all space, and thought that it was you, and placed this god in my heart. But again, it had become the temple of its own idol, an abomination to you. But after you had eased the pain of my mind, unknown to me, and closed my eyes that they should not behold vanity, I ceased from myself a little, and my madness was lulled to sleep; and I awoke in you, and saw you to be infinite in a different way; but that sight did not come from the flesh.

FIFTEEN

I looked back at other things, and I saw that they owed their being to you; and were all bounded in you; but in a different way, not as being in space, but because you contain all things in the hand of your truth; and all things are true insofar as they have being. There is no falsehood, unless what is not is thought to be. And I saw that all things harmonized, not only with their places, but with their seasons. And that you, who alone are eternal, did not begin to work after innumerable eons of time had passed, for all periods of time, past and future, do not come to pass nor pass away, except through you working and abiding.

SIXTEEN

I understood, and had thought nothing of it, that the same bread which is distasteful to a sick palate is pleasant to a healthy one; that light is offensive to sore eyes, but delightful to sound ones. Your righteousness displeases the wicked; but so do the vipers and smaller worms; yet you created these good, suiting them in with the lower parts of your creation, with which the wicked themselves are well suited, and even more so, the more unlike you they become. But they fit in with the superior creatures as they become more like you. And I asked what iniquity was, and found that it was not a substance at all, but the perversion of the will, turned away from you, O God, the Supreme Substance, toward these lower things, throwing away one's inner self and swelling up outwardly.

SEVENTEEN

And I wondered that I now loved you and not an imaginary fantasy instead of you. Yet I did not deserve to enjoy my God, but I was transported to you by your beauty, and soon torn away from you by my own weight, sinking with sorrow into inferior things. This weight was carnal habit. Yet there remained with me a remembrance of you, and I did not doubt at all that there was One to whom I might cleave, but felt that I was not yet one who could cleave to you. For the corrupted body pressed down the soul, and the earthly dwelling weighs down the mind that thinks upon many things. I was most sure that your *invisible works from the creation of the world are clearly seen, being understood by the things that are made, even your eternal power and Godhead.* Examining the origin of my admiration for the beauty of the bodies, heavenly and earthly, I sought to understand what aided me in making correct judgments of things mutable, saying, "This should be thus, this not." I was discovering, as I said, that in my sound judgments, when I did make them, I had touched the unchangeable and true eternity of Truth, above my changeable mind.

And thus by degrees, I passed from physical bodies to the soul which perceives them through the bodily senses, and thence to its inward faculty to which the bodily senses report outward things. The faculties of animals reach this far. And from there, again I passed on to the reasoning faculty, to which is referred whatever is received from the senses of the body to be judged. This reasoning faculty, finding itself to be a changeable thing in me, aroused itself to the limit of its own understanding and led my thoughts away from the tyranny of habit. My reason withdrew from the multitudes of contradictory mental images so that it might discover what that light was with which it was being bathed. Then, without a shadow of doubt, it cried out that "the unchangeable was to be preferred to the changeable," and from that it knew the Unchangeable, because unless it knew the unchangeable, it could have had no sure ground to prefer it to the changeable. Thus with the flash of one trembling glance, it arrived at That Which Is. And then I saw that your *invisible nature is clearly perceived in the things that are made*. But I could not steady my gaze on this revelation. My infirmity was beaten back again, and I returned again to my old habits, taking along with me only a loving memory of this insight, and a longing for what I had, as it were, caught the fragrance of, but was not yet able to eat.

EIGHTEEN

Then I looked for a way to obtain enough strength to enjoy you, but did not find it until I embraced that *Mediator between God and men, the man Christ Jesus, who is over all, blessed forever.* He was calling to me, saying, *I am the Way, the Truth and the Life,* mingling that Food which I was unable to receive with my flesh. For *the Word was made flesh* so that your wisdom by which you created all things, might provide milk for our infant state. I did not know Jesus to be my God. Though humbled, I did not yet grasp the humble One, nor did I yet recognize what his weakness was designed to teach. For your Word, the eternal Truth, exalted above your highest creatures, raises up those who are subject to himself. In this lower world, he built for himself a lowly habitation of our clay, by which he intended to bring down from themselves such as would be subjected to him, and bring them over to himself, reducing their swollen pride and increasing their love; so that they might go on no further in self-confidence but rather consent to become weak, seeing the Deity before their feet, made weak by taking on our mortality; and wearied, might cast themselves down on him, so that rising again, he might lift them up.

NINETEEN

But I thought differently, thinking only of my Lord Christ as of a man of excellent wisdom to whom no one could be compared. Being miraculously born of a virgin, he seemed to have attained his great height of authority in this way, to be an example of despising temporal things to obtain immortality, through God's care for us. But what mystery there was in *The Word was made flesh*, I could not even imagine. This I had learned from what is delivered to us in Scripture about him, however, that he ate, drank, slept, walked, rejoiced in spirit, was sorrowful, preached; that flesh alone did not adhere to your Word except with a human soul and mind. All who know the unchangeableness of your Word know this. I now knew as well as I could, and I did not doubt it at all.

For to move the limbs of the body by will at one time, and at another to remain still; at one moment to be moved by some emotion, at another not; now to deliver wise sayings through human speech, now to keep silence—all these belong to the soul and mind which are subject to change. And if these things were falsely written about him, all the rest would be in danger of being labeled false. There would not remain in those Scriptures any saving faith for mankind. But since they were written truthfully, I acknowledged Christ to be a perfect and complete man—not the body of a man only, nor only a feeling soul without a rational one with the body as well, but true man. This very man was to be preferred above all others, not only as being a form of Truth, but because of the great excellence of his human nature and his more perfect participation in the divine wisdom.

But Alypius thought that Catholics believed God to be so clothed with flesh that there was no soul at all in Christ, and he did not think that a human mind was ascribed to him. And because he was fully persuaded that the actions recorded about him could have been performed only by a vital and rational creature, he moved more slowly toward the Christian faith. But understanding afterward that this was the error of the Apollinarian heretics, he rejoiced in the Catholic faith and accepted it. But I admit that it was only some time later that I learned how in that sentence, *The Word was made flesh,* Catholic doctrine is distinguished from the falsehood of Photinus.[7] For the rejection of the truth by heretics makes the tenets of your Church and sound doctrine stand out more clearly. *For there must also be heresies, that they who are approved may be made manifest among the weak.*

TWENTY

Having read those books of the Platonists and having been taught by them to search for the incorporeal Truth, I saw that *your invisible things are understood by the things that are made,* and though I was foiled in this attempt to attain to the incorporeal truth, I perceived what the truth was which the darkness of my mind would not permit me to contemplate. I was assured that you are, and that you are infinite, yet not diffused in space, finite or infinite; and that you truly are the same forever, varying neither in part or motion; and that all other things are from you, as is proved by the fact that they *are* at all.

Of these things I was assured, yet too weak in faith to enjoy you. I chattered as one well skilled; but if I had not sought your way in Christ our Savior, I would have proved not skilled but killed. For now, filled with my own punishment, I had begun to wish to appear wise. Yet I did not mourn, but rather was puffed up with knowledge. Where was that charity which builds upon the *foundation* of humility, which is Christ Jesus? Or when would these books of the philosophers teach me that? I believe you willed that I should become acquainted with them before I studied your Scriptures, so that it might be imprinted on my memory how I was affected by them; and that afterward, having been subdued through your books, and my wounds having been touched by your healing fingers, I might discern and distinguish the difference between presumption and confession, between those on the one hand who see where they are to go, yet do not see the way, and on the other, the Way which leads us not only to behold the beatific country, but to dwell in it. For if I had first been formed in your Holy Scriptures, and if you had grown sweet to me in the familiar use of them, and I had then fallen upon these other volumes, they might perhaps have led me away from the solid ground of piety. Or if I had stood firm in that wholesome disposition which I had gained from Scripture, I might have thought that it could also have been obtained from the study of those books alone.

TWENTY-ONE

Most eagerly, then, I seized that venerable writing of your Spirit, and especially upon the Apostle Paul.[8] Those difficulties vanished away in which he at one time seemed to me to contradict himself, and the text of his discourse had not seemed to agree with the testimonies of the Law and the Prophets. And that pure Word now seemed to me to have but one Face, and I learned to rejoice with trembling. So I began, and I found that whatever truth I had read in those other books was declared here amid the praises of your grace; so that whoever sees it *may not glory as if he had not received*, not only *what* he sees, but also the power of seeing (for *what has he, which he has not received?*). And I found that he may not only be taught to *see* you, who are ever the same, but also being healed, may take hold of you; and that he who cannot see you from afar, may still walk on the way by which he may reach, behold and posses you. For, though a man is *delighted with the law of God after the inner man*, what shall he do with that *other law in his members which wars against the law of his mind and brings him into captivity to the law of sin which is in his members?* For *you are righteous, O Lord,* but *we have sinned and committed iniquity, and have done wickedly.* Your hand has grown heavy upon us, and we are justly delivered over to that ancient sinner, the governor of death who persuaded our will to be like his will, whereby he did not abide in your truth. What shall wretched man do? *Who shall deliver him from the body of this death*, but only your grace, *through Jesus Christ our Lord*, whom you have begotten co-eternal and formed in the beginning of your ways?[9] *In him the prince of this world found nothing worthy of death.* Yet he killed him, and *the handwriting which was against us was blotted out.*

The Platonic writings did not contain this. Their pages do not express this kind of piety—the tears of confession, your sacrifice, a troubled spirit, *a broken and contrite heart*, the salvation of your people, the espoused City, the promise of the Holy Spirit, the chalice of our redemption. No man sings there, *Shall not my soul be submitted to God? For from him comes my salvation; for he is my God and my salvation, my defender: I shall never be moved.* No one there hears him calling, *Come unto me, all who labor.* They scorn to learn of him, *because he is meek and lowly in heart*; for *you have hidden these things from the wise and prudent, and have revealed them unto babes.* For it is one thing, from the wooded mountain-top, to view the land of peace, and fail to find the way to it—to attempt impassible ways in vain, beset by fugitives and deserters and opposed by their captain, the Lion and the Dragon; it is quite another thing to keep on the way that leads thither, guarded by the hosts of the heavenly King, where those who have deserted the heavenly army cannot rob us—indeed they shun the way as torment itself. These things sank wonderfully into my heart when I read that *least of your apostles*, and meditated upon your works, and trembled.

BOOK VIII

At Age Thirty-one

ONE

O my God, let me remember and confess with gratitude to you your mercies bestowed on me. Let my bones be steeped in your love, and let them say to you, *Who is like you, O Lord? You have broken my bonds; I will offer to you the sacrifice of thanksgiving.* I shall declare how you have broken them; and all who worship you, when they hear these things, shall say, *Blessed be the Lord in heaven and earth; great and wonderful is his name.*

Your words had fastened themselves in my heart, and I was surrounded by you on all sides. I was now certain of your eternal life, though I had seen it *through a glass darkly.* Yet I no longer doubted that there was an incorruptible substance from which all other substance came. I no longer desired to be more certain of you, but to be more steadfast in you.

As for my temporal life, all things were wavering, and my heart had to be purged from the old leaven. The Way, the Savior himself, pleased me well, but as yet I shrank from going through the narrowness of that Way. Then you put into my mind, and it seemed good to me, to go to Simplicianus, who seemed to me a faithful servant of yours. Your grace shone in him. I had heard also that from his very youth he had lived in complete devotion to you. Now he was advanced in years, and because of his great age, spent in such zeal in following your ways, I thought it likely that he had learned much from his experience, and so he had. Out of that store of experience I hoped that he would advise me, as I set my anxieties before him, which way would be most fitting for one afflicted as I was to walk in your paths.

For I saw that the church was full, with one going this way, and another that. But I was not happy to lead a secular life; indeed, since my hopes of honor and wealth no longer spurred me on, it was a very grievous burden to undergo so heavy a servitude. For, compared to your sweetness and the beauty of your house which I loved, those things no longer delighted me. But I was still tenaciously held by the love of women, nor did the apostle forbid me to marry, although he exhorted me to something better, wishing all men to be as he was himself. But I, being weak, chose the more indulgent place; and because of this alone, was tossed up and down in indecision, faint and wasted with withering cares, because I would be constrained in other matters contrary to my desires if I obligated myself to undertake a married life, to which I was so much completely bound I had heard from the mouth of Truth, that *there are some who have made themselves eunuchs for the sake of the kingdom of heaven*; but, he says, *Let him who can receive it receive it.* Surely all men who do not have the knowledge of God are vain, and could not, out of the good things that are seen, find him out who is good. But I was no longer in that vanity. I had surmounted it, and by the united witness of your whole creation had found you, our Creator, and your Word—God with you—by whom you created all things. But there is another kind of impiety, that of men who when *they knew God, did not glorify him as God, neither were thankful.* Into this I had fallen, but *your right hand upheld me*, and took me from it, and you placed me where I might recover. For you have said to mankind, *Behold the fear of the Lord is wisdom*, and again, *Do not desire to seem wise, because professing themselves to be wise they become fools.* But I had now found the goodly pearl, which, selling all that I had, I ought to have bought. But I hesitated.

TWO

I went to Simplicianus, then, the spiritual father of Ambrose (at that time bishop of Milan), who loved him as truly as a father. I told him the windings of my wanderings. But when I mentioned that I had read certain books of the Platonists, which had been translated into Latin by Victorinus, formerly Professor of Rhetoric at Rome (who died a Christian, as I had been told), Simplicianus expressed his joy that I had not fallen upon the writings of other philosophers which were full of fallacies and deceits, *after the rudiments of this world*. The Platonists, on the other hand, in many ways led to the belief in God and his Word. Then to exhort me to the humility of Christ, *hidden from the wise and revealed to babes*, he spoke of Victorinus himself, whom he had known most intimately while he was at Rome. I will not hold back what he told me about him, for it contains great praise of your grace which ought to be acknowledged to you. He told me that Victorinus had been highly skilled in the liberal arts, had read very many philosophical writings, had read them with discrimination, and had been the teacher of many noble senators. As a memorial of his distinction as a teacher, a statue of him had been placed in the Roman Forum (which men of this world esteem a high honor). Up to that time he had been a worshiper of idols and a participant in the sacrilegious rites to which almost all the nobility of Rome were given. He had inspired the people in their love of *The barking deity, Anubis, and all the motley crew of monster gods who stood in arms 'gainst Neptune, Venus, Minerva, and the steel-clad Mars.*

Rome, with its gods, once conquered them, but now worshiped them, and all this the aged Victorinus had defended with thundering eloquence for many years. But now he did not blush to be the child of your Christ, a newborn babe at your baptismal font, bowing his neck to the yoke of humility, and subduing his pride to the reproach of the cross.

O Lord, Lord, who bowed the heavens and came down, touched the mountains and they smoked, by what means did you convey yourself to that heart? He used to read the Holy Scriptures, as Simplicianus said, and most studiously sought after and searched into all the Christian writings. To Simplicianus he said, not openly, but privately, as to a friend, "Please understand that I am already a Christian." Simplicianus answered, "I will not believe it, nor will I rank you among Christians until I see you in the Church of Christ." The other, in banter, replied, "Then do walls make Christians?" And he often repeated that he was already a Christian. But Simplicianus as often made the same answer, and the jest about "walls" was repeated by the other again. For he was fearful of offending his friends, proud demon-worshipers, fearing a storm of enmity might fall heavily on him from the height of their Babylonian dignity, as from cedars of Lebanon, which the Lord had not yet broken down. But when he had gathered strength by reading and diligent inquiry, and began to fear being denied by Christ before the holy angels if he now should be afraid to confess him before men, he began to feel himself guilty of a great offense in being ashamed of the sacraments of the humility of your Word, when he had not been ashamed of the sacrilegious rites of those proud demons, whose pride he had imitated and whose rites he had adopted. He became bold-faced against vanity and shame-faced toward the truth. Suddenly and unexpectedly, he said to Simplicianus, as he himself told me, "Let us go to the Church, for I wish to become a Christian." Simplicianus, unable to contain himself for joy, went with him. And having been admitted to the first sacramental instructions and become a catechumen, not long afterward gave in his name that he might be regenerated by baptism, to the wonder of Rome and the joy of the Church. The proud beheld and were enraged; they gnashed their teeth and melted away! But the Lord God was the hope of your servant, and he paid no regard to their vanities and lying madness.

Finally, the hour came to make his profession of faith, which at Rome, they who are about to approach this grace deliver a set of words committed to memory from an elevated place in the sight of all the faithful. The presbyters offered Victorinus the chance to make his profession more privately. This was often done to those who were likely to be put off by their timidity. But Victorinus chose rather to profess his salvation in the presence of the holy multitude. For it was not salvation that he taught in rhetoric, and yet he had publicly professed that. How much less then should he dread your meek flock when proclaiming your Word, when he had not feared a mad multitude when proclaiming his own words!

So then, when he went up to make his profession, everyone, as they recognized him, whispered his name to one another, with the voice of congratulations. And who was there who did not know him? A low murmur ran through all the mouths of the rejoicing multitude, "Victorinus! Victorinus!" The sudden burst of rapture at the sight of him was followed by a sudden hush that they might hear him. He proclaimed the true faith with great boldness, and all desired to draw him into their very heart. Indeed, they took him there in their love and joy and received him with their hands.

THREE

Good God, what takes place in man that he rejoices more at the salvation of a soul despaired of and freed from greater peril, than if there had always been hope for him, or the danger had been less? For you also, O merciful Father, *rejoice more over one sinner who repents than over ninety-nine righteous persons that need no repentance.* And with much joyfulness we hear about the sheep which has strayed and is brought back upon the Shepherd's shoulders while the angels rejoice; and how the coin is restored to your treasury while the neighbors rejoice with the woman who found it. And the joy of the solemn service of your house brings tears to our eyes when we hear the story of your younger son, that *he was dead, and is alive again; had been lost, and is found.* For you rejoice in us and in your holy angels, holy through holy love. For you are ever the same, and you know in the same way all things which do not remain the same, nor are they eternal.

What, then, goes on in the soul when it is more delighted at finding or recovering the things it loves, than if they had never been lost? Yes, and other things witness to the same; and all things are full of witnesses, crying out, "So it is." The conquering commander triumphs; yet he would not have conquered if he had not fought; and the greater the danger there was in the battle, the more joy in the triumph. The storm tosses the sailors, threatens shipwreck, and every one grows pale with the threat of death; the sky and sea become calm and they rejoice as greatly as they had feared much. A friend is sick, and his pulse indicates danger; all who desire his safety are sick at heart over him. He recovers, though not as yet able to walk with his former strength; yet there is more joy than there was earlier, when he walked sound and strong. Yes, the very pleasures of human life we acquire with difficulties—not only those which rush upon us unexpectedly and against our wills, but those which are voluntary and planned. There is no pleasure in eating and drinking unless the pinching of hunger and thirst go before. Drunkards eat certain salty meats to create a painful thirst, and the drink brings pleasure as it allays it. It is also customary that the promised bride not be given too quickly, so that the husband may not value her any less, whom as his betrothed he had longed for.

This law holds true in base and dishonorable pleasure and in that pleasure also which is permitted and lawful; in the sincerity of honest friendship; in him who was dead and lived again; had been lost and was found. Everywhere the greater joy is ushered in by the greater pain. What does this mean, O Lord my God, when you are an everlasting joy to your own Self, and some things about you are ever rejoicing in you? What does it mean that this portion of creation ebbs and flows this way, alternately displeased and reconciled? Is this their allotted measure? Is this all you have assigned to them, that from the highest heavens to the lowest depth of earth, from the beginning of the world to the end of the ages, from the angel to the worm, from the first motion to the last, you set each in its place and appoint each in its proper season—everything good in its own way? Woe is me! How high you are in the highest, and how deep in the deepest! You never depart from us, and yet we—how hardly we return to you!

FOUR

Up, Lord, and act! Stir us up, and recall us; kindle and draw us; inflame, grow sweet to us; let us love you, let us run after you. Do not many people return to you out of a deeper hell of blindness than Victorinus? They approach and are enlightened, receiving that Light which they who receive, receive power from you to become your sons. But even though they are less well-known, they who know them rejoice for them. Yet when many rejoice together, the joy of each one is fuller, being kindled and inflamed by one another. Again, because those who are widely known influence many toward salvation, and lead the way for many to follow, those who went before them rejoice greatly in them, because they do not rejoice over them alone. But let it never be that in your tabernacle the persons of the rich should be more welcome than the poor, or the noble more than the humble; seeing rather that you have *chosen the weak things of the world to confound the strong; and the base things of the world, and the things which are despised, and those things that are not, that you might bring to nought the things that are.* And it was *the least of your apostles,* by whose tongue you sounded forth these words. Yet when Paulus the proconsul, his pride conquered by the apostle's words, was made to pass under the easy yoke of your Christ and became a provincial of the great King, this apostle was pleased to be called Paul instead of his former name, Saul, in testimony of so great a victory.[1] For it is a greater victory over the enemy in one in whom he has more hold and by whom he has hold of more people. But he has more hold of the proud through their concern about position, and through them, he controls more people by their authority. Therefore, the more the heart of Victorinus was esteemed by the world, which the devil had held as an impregnable possession, and the greater the value set on his tongue, the mighty and keen weapon he had used to slay so many, so much more greatly should your children rejoice, seeing that our King had bound the strong man. And they saw his weapons taken from him and cleansed, and made fit for your honor, and made *profitable to the Lord for every good work.*

FIVE

Now when that man of yours, Simplicianus, told me that about Victorinus, I burned with eagerness to imitate him; and it was for this very purpose that he had related it. But when he had added, also, that in the days of the Emperor Julian, a law was made forbidding Christians to teach literature and rhetoric, and that Victorinus, in obedience to this law, chose to give over the language school rather than your Word, by which you make eloquent the tongues of the dumb, he appeared to me not only brave but happy, having thus found an opportunity to serve you alone. This was the very thing I was sighing for, bound as I was, not by the irons of another person, but by my own iron will. The enemy held my will, and by it had made a chain for me and bound me. For from a perverse will comes lust; and lust yielded to, becomes habit; and habit not resisted, becomes necessity. By these links, as it were, joined together as in a chain, a hard bondage held me enthralled. But that new will which had begun to develop in me, to serve you freely and to wish to enjoy you, O my God, my only certain Joy, was not yet able to overcome my former long-established willfulness. Thus my two wills, the new and the old, the carnal and the spiritual, struggled within me, and by their discord, undid my soul.

Thus I came to understand by my own experience what I had read, that *the flesh struggles against the spirit, and the spirit against the flesh.* I experienced both; but more now of that which I approved in myself than of that which I disapproved. For of this last, it was now rather not myself, because in much of it I endured unwillingly rather than acted willingly. Yet it was by my own action that habit had obtained this power of warring against me. I had come willingly to the place I now willed not to be. And who has any right to speak against it, when just punishment follows the sinner? Nor did I now have any longer my former plea, that I hesitated as yet to be above the world and serve you because I was not altogether certain of the truth. For by now I was indeed certain. But, still in slavery to the earth, I refused to be your soldier, and feared as much to be freed of all the encumbrances as I ought to have feared to be weighed down with them.

Thus I was held down with the baggage of this world as pleasantly as one often is in sleep; and the thoughts in which I meditated on you were like the efforts of one who wants to wake up, yet is still overcome with heavy drowsiness and falls asleep again. Since no one wants to sleep forever, and in sober judgment, waking is better, yet a man, for the most part, feeling that heavy lethargy in all his limbs, delays to shake off sleep, and though half-displeased, yet, even after it is time to rise, yields to it with pleasure. In the same way I was assured that it would be much better for me to give myself up to your charity than to yield myself to my own lust. But though the former course satisfied and convinced me, the latter still pleased me and held me in fetters. Nor had I any answer to make to you when you called me: *Awake, O sleeper, and rise from the dead, and Christ shall give you light.* And when you showed me on all sides that what you said was true, convicted by the truth, I had nothing at all to answer, but only those dull and drowsy words, "Soon, soon; leave me a little while." But "soon, soon" had no present, and my "little while" went on for a long while. In vain I delighted *in your law in the inner man while another law in my members warred against the law of my mind and brought me into captivity to the law of sin which is in my members.* For the law of sin is the violence of habit, by which the mind is drawn and held, even against its will. Yet it deserves this, because it willingly fell into it. Who then would *deliver me from the body of this death,* but your grace alone, *through Jesus Christ our Lord?*

SIX

And now I will declare and confess to your name, O Lord, my Helper and Redeemer, how you delivered me out of the bonds of carnal desire by which I was bound most firmly, and out of slavery to worldly things. Amid increasing anxiety I was doing my usual business, and daily sighing to you. I attended Church whenever I was free from the business under the burden of which I groaned. Alypius was with me, now free from his legal office after his third term as Assessor, and awaiting clients to whom to sell his counsel, as I sold the skill of speaking (if indeed teaching can impart it). To please us, Nebridius had consented to teach under Verecundus, a citizen and a grammarian of Milan and an intimate friend of us all, who had urgently requested and by right of friendship challenged from our group the faithful aid he needed. Nebridius was not drawn to do this by any desire of gain, for he might have made much more from his education if he had chosen to do so, but as a most kind and gentle friend he would not let our request go unanswered. But he did it all very discreetly, taking care not to become known to those personages considered great by the world; thus he avoided distraction of mind, wanting to leave himself free to seek, or read, or hear something concerning wisdom.

On a certain day, then, when Nebridius was away—for some reason I cannot recall—a man named Ponticianus came to see Alypius and me. He was an African who held high office in the emperor's court. What he wanted of us I do not know, but we sat down to converse, and it happened that he observed a book on the table. He opened it, and to his surprise found it to be the Epistles of the Apostle Paul. He had thought it would be one of those books which I was wearing myself out in teaching. Looking at me with a smile, he expressed his joy and wonder that he had suddenly found this book, and this only, before my eyes. For he was a baptized Christian, and often bowed himself before you, our God, in the Church, in constant and daily prayer. Then when I told him that I studied these Scriptures with much care, we fell into conversation about Antony, the Egyptian monk, whose name was held in high regard by your people, though up to that time not familiar to us. When he learned this, he dwelt more on that subject, amazed at our ignorance of one so famous. And we also were amazed, hearing of your wonderful works done in the true faith and Catholic Church, in times so recent—almost in our own—and so fully attested. We all wondered—we that they were so great, and he, that we knew nothing about them.

From this, his conversation turned to the large numbers in the monasteries, and their holy ways, a sweet smelling savor to you, and of the fruitful deserts of the wilderness, of which we knew nothing. There was a monastery at Milan, full of good brothers, just outside the city walls, under the protection of Ambrose, but we did not know it. He went on with his talk, and we listened intently and in silence. He then told us how one afternoon at Trier, when the Emperor was taken up with the Circensian games, he [Ponticianus] and three friends went out to walk in gardens near the city walls. There, as they happened to walk in pairs, one of them went apart with him, while the other two wandered by themselves; these in their wanderings came on a certain cottage inhabited by some of your servants, *poor in spirit*, of whom *is the kingdom of heaven*, and there they found a little book containing the life of Antony. One of them began to read it, admire it, and was inflamed by it. As he read, he began to consider taking up such a life and giving up his worldly service to serve you. He and his companion were two of those they call "Agents for Public Affairs."

Suddenly filled with holy love and a sober sense of shame, angry with himself, he looked at his friend and said, "Tell me, please, what do we gain by all these labors of ours? What are we aiming at? What do we serve for? Can our hopes in court rise higher than to be the Emperor's favorites? And in such a position, what is there that is not fragile and full of dangers? And by how many perils will we arrive at even greater peril? And when will we arrive there? But if I desire to become a friend of God, I can do so at once!" So he said. And in the pangs of travail with new life, he turned his eyes again on the book and read on, and was inwardly changed, as you saw. His mind was divested of the world, as soon became evident. For as he read, and the waves of his heart rolled up and down, he stormed at himself a while. Then he saw and resolved on a better course, and now having become yours, he said to his friend, "Now I have broken loose from those false hopes, and am determined to serve God. From this hour, in this place, I enter that service. If you will not imitate me, don't oppose me." His friend answered that he would stick with him, to partake of so glorious a reward, so glorious a service. So both of them, now being yours, were building a tower at the necessary cost—forsaking all they had and following you.

Then Ponticianus and the friend who was with him, who had been walking in other parts of the garden, came in search of them to the same place. On finding them, they reminded them to return, as the day was declining. But the others, relating their resolution and purpose and how the resolve had begun and had become confirmed in them, begged them not to molest them if they would not join them. Ponticianus and his friend, though not changed from their former state, nevertheless (as he told us) bewailed themselves and piously congratulated their friends and commended themselves to their prayers. So with hearts lingering on the earth, they went away to the palace. But the other two, fixing their hearts on heaven, remained in the cottage. Both of them were engaged to be married. Their affianced brides, when they heard of this, also dedicated their virginity to you.

SEVEN

Such was the story of Ponticianus; but you, O Lord, were focusing it on myself while he was speaking, taking me from behind my own back, where I had placed myself, being unwilling to look at myself. And you set me before my own face so that I might see how foul I was, how crooked and sordid, how bespotted and ulcerous. I looked and loathed myself, but I could find nowhere to flee from myself. If I tried to turn my eyes from myself, Ponticianus went on with his story, and you again set me face to face with myself and thrust me before my eyes, that I might discover my iniquity and hate it. I had known it, but acted as though I did not see it—winked at it and forgot it.

But now, the more ardently I loved those whose wholesome affections I heard about, men who had given themselves up wholly to you to be healed, the more I abhorred myself compared to them. For many years (perhaps twelve) had gone by since my nineteenth year, when I was stirred to an earnest love of wisdom on reading Cicero's *Hortensius*. Yet I was still delaying to reject mere worldly happiness to devote myself to search out that of which not only the finding, but the very search itself was preferable to the treasures and kingdoms of this world, though already found, and to the pleasures of the body, though spread around me at my will. But I, wretched young man, most wretched, even in the very earliest days of my youth, had prayed to you for chastity in this way: "Give me chastity and continency, but not yet." For I was afraid that you would hear me too soon and too soon deliver me from the disease of lust which I wished to have satisfied rather than extinguished. And I had wandered through crooked ways in a sacrilegious superstition, not indeed assured of it, but preferring it to the truth which I did not seek religiously, but rather opposed maliciously.

I had thought that I delayed rejecting my worldly hopes from day to day and following only you because there did not appear any sure way by which to direct my course. But now the day had come in which I was to be laid bare to myself and my conscience was to upbraid me. "Where are you now, my tongue? You said that you did not like to cast off the baggage of vanity for uncertain truth. Now truth is certain, yet that burden still oppresses you, while they who have neither worn themselves out with seeking it, nor for ten years and more have been thinking about it, have had their shoulders unburdened and received wings to fly away."

Thus I was inwardly consumed and confused with horrible shame while Ponticianus was speaking. Having finished his tale and the business he came for, he went his way. And I into myself. What did I say that was not against myself? With what scourges of condemnation did I not lash my soul, that it might follow me, striving to go after you! Yet it drew back; it refused, but did not excuse itself. All arguments were exhausted and confuted. There remained a silent shrinking away. My soul feared as it would fear death, to be restrained from the continuation of that habit by which it was actually wasting away to death.

EIGHT

In the midst of this great battle in my heart which I had strongly raised up against my soul, troubled in mind and countenance, I turned upon Alypius. "What is wrong with us?" I exclaimed. "What is it? What did you hear? The unlearned start up and take heaven by force; and we, with all our learning, but lacking heart, wallow in flesh and blood! Are we ashamed to follow because others have gone before us, and not ashamed instead that we are not following?"

I uttered some such words as these, and in my excitement, I flung myself away from him, while he stood looking at me in astonished silence. For it was not my usual tone, and my forehead, my cheeks, eyes, color, the tone of my voice—all expressed my emotion more than the words.

A little garden lay outside our lodging, which we had the use of, as we did of the whole house, for the owner of the house, our landlord, was not living there. The tumult of my breast drove me there, where no man might interfere with the raging battle in which I had become engaged with myself. How it should end, you knew, but I did not. But I was mad to be whole and dying to live, knowing what an evil thing I was, and not knowing what good thing I was shortly to become. I retired then into the garden, with Alypius on my steps. His presence was no bar to my privacy. How could he forsake me when I was in such a state? We sat down as far away from the house as possible. I was troubled in spirit, most vehemently angry with myself that I had not entered your will and covenant, O my God, which all my bones cried out to me to enter, praising it to the skies. We do not enter that will by ships or chariots or feet, nor even by going as far as I had come from the house to that place where we were sitting. For not only to go, but to enter your will was nothing else but to will to enter, resolutely and completely—not to swagger and sway about with a changeable and half-divided will, struggling with itself, one part sinking while another rose up.

Finally, in the fever of my irresolution, I made many of those motions with my body that men sometimes would like to, but cannot, because they do not have the limbs or whose limbs are bound or weakened with infirmity, or are hindered in any other way. Thus, if I tore my hair, beat my forehead, or if, locking my fingers together, I clasped my knee, I did this because I willed it. But I might have willed, and not done it if the power of motion in my limbs had not responded. So many things I did where to will was not the same as having the power, and I did not do what I longed incomparably more to do. But if I had willed thoroughly I could have done it, for then I would have the power to do it. In these things power is one with the will, and to will is to do. Yet it was not done. My body more easily obeyed the slightest wish of my mind in moving its limbs at its direction, than the soul obeyed itself, to carry out this its strong will, which could only be accomplished within the will alone.

NINE

Where does this monstrous condition come from? And why is it? Let your mercy shine on me that I may inquire if the obscurity of man's punishments and the darkest contritions of the sons of Adam may possibly offer me an answer. Where does this monstrous condition come from and why is it? The mind commands the body, and it obeys instantly. The mind commands itself and is resisted. The mind commands the hand to be moved, and such readiness is there that you can hardly distinguish the command from its fulfillment. Yet the mind is mind, the hand is body. The mind commands the mind to will, and yet, though it is itself that commands, it does not obey. Where does this monstrous condition come from and why is it? I repeat: it commands itself to will and would not command unless it willed; yet what it commands is not done. But it does not will completely. Therefore it does not command completely. For so far as it wills it commands, and so far as the thing commanded is not done it does not will. For the will commands that there be a will. But it does not command entirely; therefore what it commands does not come about. If the will were whole, it would not even command it to be, because it would already be. So it is not strange partly to will and partly to be unwilling, but it is actually an infirmity of the mind, that it cannot wholly rise, borne up by truth, but is weighed down by habit. In short, there are two wills, because one is not whole, and one has what the other lacks.

TEN

Let them perish from your presence, O God, as *vain talkers and seducers* of the soul perish, who, because they see two wills, claim that there are two natures in us, one good, the other evil. They themselves are truly evil when they hold these evil opinions, and they shall become good when they hold the truth and assent to the truth, so your apostle may say to them, *you were once darkness, but now you are light in the Lord.* They, wishing to be light (not *in the Lord,* but in themselves, imagining the nature of the soul to be the same as God), become more gross darkness. Through their dreadful arrogance they went farther from you, *the true Light that enlightens every one who comes into the world.* Take heed what you say, and blush for shame. *Draw near to him* and be *enlightened, and your faces shall not be ashamed.*

Deliberating upon serving the Lord my God at that time, as I had long purposed, it was I who willed, I who was unwilling. It was I, even I myself. I neither willed entirely, nor was entirely unwilling. I was therefore at war with myself and torn apart by myself. And this destruction befell me against my will, yet it did not show the presence of another mind, but the punishment of my own. *Therefore it is no longer I who do it, but sin that dwells in me*; the punishment of a sin more freely committed, in that I was a son of Adam.

For if there are as many contrary natures as there are conflicting wills, there would now be not only two, but many. If a man deliberates, whether he should go to their meeting or to the theater, the Manicheans cry out, "Behold! here are two natures: one good drawing this way; the other bad, draws back that way. For from where else does this hesitation between conflicting wills come?" But I say that both are bad: that which draws him toward them is as bad as that which draws toward the theater. But they believe that the will is good which inclines toward them. Suppose one of us should deliberate, and in the battle of his two wills be in a quandary, whether to go to the theater or to our church. Would not these Manicheans also be in a quandary as to what to answer? For either they must confess (which they would not like to do) that the will which leads to our church is good, or they must suppose two evil natures and two evil minds in conflict within one man, instead of seeing the truth: that in deliberation, one mind fluctuates between conflicting wills.

Let them no longer say when they see two conflicting wills in one man, that the conflict is between two contrary natures, between two opposing substances, from two opposing principles, one good, and the other bad. For you, O true God, thus disprove, check and convince them by facts: for instance, when one deliberates whether he should kill a man by poison or by the sword; whether he should seize this or that estate of another's when he cannot seize both; whether he should purchase pleasure by extravagance or keep his money by stinginess; whether he should go to the Circus or to the theater, if both are open on the same day, or make a third choice to rob another's house if he has opportunity; or, even a fourth one, to commit adultery, if at the same time he has the opportunity. All these, concurring at the same point of time, and all being equally desired, but impossible to do at the same time, tear the mind amid the four or even more conflicting wills. But they do not indicate that there are many different substances.

So it is also in wills which are good. For I ask them, is it good to take pleasure in reading the Apostle, or good to take pleasure in a Psalm, or good to discourse on the Gospel? They will answer to each, "It is good." What then, if all give equal pleasure and all are offered at the same time? Do not different wills distract the mind while one deliberates which he would rather choose? Yet all of them are good and are at variance until one is chosen, toward which the whole united will may move which was previously divided into several parts. Thus, also, when eternity delights us and the pleasure of temporal good holds us down below, it is the same soul which wills neither way with an entire will; and therefore it is torn asunder with grievous perplexities, because its love of truth first shows one way to be preferable, while its habits keep it bound to the other.

ELEVEN

Thus I was soul-sick and tormented, accusing myself much more severely than I usually did, tossing and turning myself in my chain, till it should be utterly broken, for what held me now was slight indeed. And you, O Lord, pressed upon me inwardly with severe mercy, redoubling the lashes of fear and shame, lest I should give way again and that slight remaining tie, not being broken, should recover its strength and bind me more strongly. For I said to myself, "Let it be done now, let it be done now!" And as I spoke, I all but made a firm resolve. I almost did it, but did it not. Yet I did not sink back to my old condition, but kept my position close enough to get my breath. I tried again, and came very near reaching the point of resolve, then lacked even a little less, and then I all but touched and grasped it. Yet I still did not quite make it, nor touch it, nor lay hold of it, hesitating to die to death and to live to life. The worse, to which I had become habituated, prevailed more with me than the better which I had not tried. And the very moment in which I was to become another man—the nearer it approached me, the greater horror it struck in me. Yet it did not strike me utterly back nor turn me away, but held me in suspense.

The very toys of toys and vanities of vanities, my old mistresses, still held me. They plucked my fleshly garment and whispered softly, "Are you going to part with us? From that moment shall we never be with you any more forever? And from that moment will this or that never be lawful for you forever?" What did they suggest by those words "this or that"? What was it which they suggested, O my God? Let your mercy turn it away from the mind of your servant! What defilements they suggested! What shame! But now I did not hear them half so loudly, for they did not show themselves openly to contradict me, but muttered, as it were, behind my back, furtively plucking at me as I was leaving, to make me look back on them. Yet they did delay me, so that I hesitated to burst and shake myself free from them, and to leap over to where I was called to be. An unruly habit kept saying to me, "Do you think that you can live without them?"

But now it was saying this very faintly. For on that side to which I had set my face, where I was trembling to go, the chaste dignity of Continence appeared to me—serene, not unduly cheerful, honestly bidding me to come and doubt nothing. She extended her holy hands to receive and embrace me, replete with multitudes of good examples. There were so many young men and maidens here—a multitude of youth and of every age, grave widows and aged virgins; and Continence herself in all, not barren, but a fruitful mother of children of joys by you, her Spouse, O Lord. And she smiled on me with an encouraging mockery, as if to say, "Can you not do what these youths, what these maidens can? Or can any of them do it of themselves, and not rather in the Lord their God? The Lord their God gave me to them. Why do you stand in your own strength and thus not stand at all? Cast yourself fearlessly upon him; he will receive you and will heal you."

And I blushed exceedingly at having listened to the muttering of those toys and hung in indecision. And she again seemed to say, "Stop your ears against your unclean members, that they may be mortified. They tell you of delights, but not as does the law of the Lord your God." This conflict in my heart was self against self only. But Alypius, sitting close by my side in silence, waited the outcome of my unusual emotion.

TWELVE

When my searching reflection had dredged up from the secret depths of my soul all my misery and piled it up in the sight of my heart, a mighty storm arose, bringing a great shower of tears. To give full vent to them, I rose and left Alypius. Complete solitude seemed to me more appropriate for the business of weeping, so I retired so far that even his presence could not be a hindrance to me. He understood this, for I suppose I had said something in which the tone of my voice appeared choked with weeping as I had risen up. So he stayed alone where we had been sitting, still completely astonished. I threw myself down, I know not how, under a certain fig tree, giving full vent to my tears. The streams of my eyes gushed out, an acceptable sacrifice to you. It was not in these words, yet to this purpose that I spoke much to you: *But you, O Lord, how long? How long, Lord? Will you be angry for ever? Remember not our former iniquities against us!* For I felt that I was still held by them. I sent up these sorrowful cries, "How long? How long? Tomorrow and tomorrow? Why not now? Why is there not an end to my uncleanness this very hour?"

I was speaking this way and weeping in the most bitter contrition of my heart, when suddenly I heard from a neighboring house a voice, as of a boy or girl, I know not which—chanting repeatedly, "Take up and read. Take up and read." My facial expression changed instantly, and I began to think most earnestly whether children were in the habit of playing any kind of game with such words. I could not remember ever having heard anything like it. So checking the torrent of my tears, I got up, interpreting it to be nothing other than a command from God to open the Book and to read the first chapter I should find. For I heard of Antony, that when he came in during the reading of these words in the Gospel, *Go, sell all you have and give to the poor, and you shall have treasure in heaven; and come, follow me*, he had received these words as addressed to himself, and by such an oracle was immediately converted to you.

So I quickly returned to the place where Alypius was sitting, where I had laid the volume of the Apostle when I arose from there. I grabbed it, opened it, and in silence read the paragraph on which my eyes first fell: *Not in reveling and drunkenness, not in debauchery and licentiousness, not in strife and envying, but put on the Lord Jesus Christ, and make no provision for the flesh to gratify its desires.* I read no further, nor did I need to. For instantly, at the end of this sentence, by a light, as it were, of serenity infused into my heart, all the darkness of doubt vanished away.

Closing the book, and putting my finger between the pages, I told Alypius about it with a calm countenance. He asked to look at what I had read. I showed him, and he read on even further than I had (I did not know what followed). There it was written, *receive him that is weak in the faith,* which he applied to himself and showed it to me. He was strengthened by this admonition and by a good resolution and purpose, very much in accord with his character (in which he was far different from me and far better), without any restless delay, he joined me.

Then we went, then, in to my mother and told her, relating in order how it took place. She leapt for joy, exulted, and praised you, *who are able to do more than we ask or think.* For she perceived that you had given her more for me than she had been praying for by her pitiful and most sorrowful groanings. For you converted me to yourself, so that I sought neither wife nor any other hope of this world—standing on that rule of faith on which you had showed me to her in a vision so many years before. And you turned her grief into a much more plentiful gladness than she had desired, and in a much dearer and purer way than she used to crave when she asked for grandchildren of my body.

BOOK IX

At Age Thirty-two

ONE

O Lord, I am your servant; I am your servant and the son of your handmaid. You have loosed my bonds. I will offer to you the sacrifice of praise. Let my heart and my tongue praise you; yes, let all my bones say, "Lord, who is like you?" Let them speak like this, and answering, say to my soul, "I am your salvation."

Who am I, what kind of man am I? Rather what evil am I not, either in my deeds or in my words or in my will? But you, Lord, are good and merciful, and your right hand regarded the depth of my death, and from the bottom of my heart you emptied that abyss of corruption. And your whole gift was to cancel what I willed, and to will instead what you willed. But where, through all those years, was my free will, and out of what low and deep recess was it called forth in a moment, so that I submitted my neck to your easy yoke, and my shoulders to your light burden, O Christ Jesus, my Helper and my Redeemer?

How sweet it became to me at once to give up those sweetnesses I had feared to be parted from! You cast them forth from me, O true and highest Sweetness. And you yourself entered, sweeter than all pleasure (though not to flesh and blood); brighter than all light (but more hidden than all depths); more sublime than all honor (except to those who are high in their own imaginations). Now my soul was freed from the gnawing urge to seek and get, to wallow in filth, and to scratch off the itch of lust. And my newborn tongue spoke freely to you, O Lord my God, my Brightness, my Riches and my Health.

TWO

I decided in your sight not to end the service of my tongue in the "speech-market" abruptly, but to withdraw gently. I did not want the young who did not study your law nor your peace to buy ammunition for their madness at my mouth any longer. Happily, it was only a very few days until the Vacation of the Vintage, and I resolved to wait them out, and then take my leave in a regular way, so that having been purchased by you I should no longer sell myself. Our purpose then was known to you, but it was not known to men other than our own friends, for we had agreed among ourselves not to publish it to anyone. In our ascent from the *valley of tears*, and singing that *song of degrees*, you had given us *sharp arrows and burning coals* against whatever deceitful tongue would have thwarted us by pretending to advise us, and any who would have devoured us out of love, as people devour the food they love.

You had pierced our hearts with your love, and we carried your words in our very depths. The examples of your servants whom you had changed from blackness to shining brightness, and from death to life, were so crowded into our consciousness, so kindled and set afire our sluggishness that all the blasts of deceitful tongues from gainsayers could only inflame us more fiercely rather than extinguish us.

Nevertheless, though our vow and purpose might have found some to commend it, for your Name's sake, which you have hallowed throughout the earth, it seemed like ostentation not to wait for the vacation which was so close. To quit a public profession which was known to all before the time of vintage as I wanted to do, so that all, looking on this act of mine, and observing how near it was to vacation time, would talk a great deal about me, as if I wanted to appear to be some great person. And what purpose would it serve that people should discuss and argue about my motives, so that our good should be labeled evil? Furthermore, that very summer, my lungs began to weaken from too much literary labor, and I could draw deep breaths only with difficulty. The pain in my chest showed that they were injured and I was unable to talk too loud or too long. This had troubled me so much that I was almost constrained of necessity to lay down the burden of teaching, or at least to take some time off to see if I could recover. But when I had fully settled on the decision to give myself to leisure in order to meditate on your ways, you know, O God, that I was glad to have this secondary, legitimate excuse which might lessen the offense to those parents who for the sake of their sons would never have allowed me to have the freedom of your sons.

Full of such joy, then, I endured that interval of time. It may have been some twenty days, yet they were endured manfully. I say endured, because the desire for financial gain which had undergirded this heavy business in part for me, had left me, and I remained alone, and would have been overwhelmed if patience had not taken its place. Perhaps some of my brethren, your servants, may say that I sinned in this, that with a heart fully set on your service, I should not allow myself to remain even one hour in teaching lies. I would not argue the point. But have you not, O most merciful Lord, pardoned and remitted this sin also, with my other most horrible and deadly sins, in the holy water [of baptism]?

THREE

Verecundus was filled with anxiety at our new happiness, for being held back by bonds, which most firmly bound him, he saw that he would be separated from us. For he himself was not yet a Christian, though his wife was one of the faithful. Yet it was on this account more than any other chain, he was kept back and hindered from the journey which we had now undertaken. For he would not, he said, be a Christian on any terms other than on those that were impossible. He did courteously invite us to remain at his summer house, however, as long as we desired. You, O Lord, shall reward him in the resurrection of the just, seeing you have already given him the lot of the righteous. For, in our absence at Rome, he was seized with bodily sickness and died, after becoming a Christian during that time and being made one of the faithful. Thus you had mercy not only on him, but on us also, lest remembering the great kindness of our friend toward us, and unable to number him among your flock, we had been tortured with intolerable sorrow. Thanks be to you, our God; we are yours. Your exhortations, consolations and faithful promises assure us that you will repay Verecundus for his country-house of Cassiacum, where we rested in you from the fever of the world. With the eternal freshness of your paradise, you have forgiven him his earthly sins in that rich mountain, that mountain which flows with milk, your own mountain.

He was troubled at that time, however, but Nebridius, on the other hand, rejoiced. For although he, too, was not yet a Christian and had fallen into the pit of that most pernicious error of believing that the flesh of your Son was a mere phantom, yet, emerging from that error, he began to believe as we did, though he had not yet received any sacraments of your Church, but was a most ardent searcher after truth. Not long after our conversion and regeneration of your baptism, he, too, became a faithful member of the Catholic Church, serving you in perfect chastity and continence among his people in Africa. His whole family became Christians through him. Then you released him from the flesh and now he lives in Abraham's bosom. Whatever that may be which is meant by "Abraham's bosom," Nebridius, my dear friend, is your child by adoption, Lord, no longer only a son of a freed man. [Augustine refers to himself as a freed man.] That is where he lives. For what other place is there for such a soul? There he lives, about which he asked so much of me, poor, inexperienced man that I was. He no longer puts his spiritual ear to my mouth, but his spiritual mouth to your fountain and drinks as much as he can receive, wisdom in proportion to his thirst, endlessly happy. But I do not think that he is so inebriated with it as to forget me, since he drinks of you, Lord, who are mindful of us.

There we were then, trying to console the unhappy Verecundus, who grieved as much as friendship allowed, that our conversion was of such sort. We exhorted him to be faithful in his state of marriage and we waited for Nebridius to follow us, which he was so near to doing. And so those days finally came to an end, although long and many they seemed because of my desire for the ease of liberty in which I could sing to you from my inmost depths, *My heart has said to you, I have sought your face; your face, O Lord, will I seek.*

FOUR

Then the day came in which I was indeed to be freed of my professorship in rhetoric, from which I was already freed in my thoughts. And it was done. You rescued my tongue from the place where you had already rescued my heart. And I blessed you, as I retired with all my friends to the villa. My books bear witness to what I did there in writing, now engaged in your service, though still, in this interim as it were, still under the influence of the school of pride. My books show how I debated with others, how I argued with myself alone before you, and how I argued with Nebridius, who was absent. And when shall I have time to rehearse all your great benefits toward me at that time, especially when hurrying on to tell of still greater mercies?

My memory calls me back, and I find pleasure in confessing to you, Lord, the inward goads by which you tamed me; how you humbled me, bringing down the mountains and hills of my high imaginations, straightening my crookedness and smoothing my rough ways; and how you subdued the brother of my heart, Alypius, to the name of your only begotten Son, our Lord and Savior Jesus Christ, a name he would not allow to be inserted into our writings at first. For he wanted them to savor the lofty cedars of the schools, which the Lord has broken down, rather than carry the odor of the wholesome herbs of the Church, antidotes to the bites of serpents.

Oh, in what accents I spoke to you, my God, when I read the Psalms of David! Those faithful songs and sounds of devotion, permit no swelling pride. I was yet a catechumen and novice in your love, resting at that villa with Alypius, also a catechumen. My mother was staying with us—in a woman's garb but with masculine faith, with the tranquillity of age, motherly love and Christian piety. What cries I raised to you in those Psalms! I was on fire toward you, and eager to proclaim them, if possible, to the whole world, against the pride of the human race. They are sung through the whole world, nor can *anyone hide himself from your heat*. I was vehement, bitter and indignant at the Manicheans! And yet I pitied them because they did not know your sacraments, those medicines [of the soul], and were madly set against the very antidote which might have healed them of their madness. How I wished they had been somewhere near me, and without my knowing they were there, could have seen my face and heard my words when I read the fourth Psalm in that time of leisure, and could have seen what that Psalm did within me! *When I called upon you, you heard me, O God of my righteousness; in tribulation you have enlarged me. Have mercy on me, O Lord, and hear my prayer.* I wish they could have heard what I said on those words, without my knowing that they heard it, lest they should think I spoke it for their sakes! Of course I would not have said the same things nor have spoken in the same way if I had known that they heard and saw me; and they would not have received them as they would if they knew that I simply spoke them by and for myself before you, out of the natural feelings of my soul.

I trembled with fear, and again was warm with hope and joy in your mercy, O Father. All this came forth from my eyes and my voice when your good Spirit addressed us, saying, *O you sons of men, how long will you be slow of heart, how long will you lose vanity and seek after falsehood?* And you, Lord, had already glorified your holy One, raising him from the dead and setting him at your right hand, that thence he should send forth his promise from on high, the Paraclete, the Spirit of Truth. He had already sent him, but I did not know it. He had sent him because he was now magnified, risen from the dead and having ascended into heaven. For till then, the Spirit was not yet given, because Jesus was not yet glorified.

And the prophet cries out, *How long, slow of heart? Why do you love vanity and seek after falsehood? Know this, that the Lord has magnified his holy One.* He cries out, *How long?* He cries out, *Know this.* Not knowing, I had long loved vanity and sought after falsehood. Therefore I heard and trembled, because it was spoken to those such as I remember myself to have been. For in those phantoms [or fantasies] which I had held for truths, there was vanity and falsehood. I spoke aloud many things earnestly and forcibly, in the bitterness of my remembrance, which I wish that they who yet love vanity and seek after falsehood might have heard. They might perchance have been troubled and have vomited it up; and you would hear them when they cried to you; for by a true death in the flesh he died for us, *who now intercedes for us with you.*

I read further, *Be angry and sin not.* And I was greatly moved, O my God; for I had now learned to be angry at myself for things past, that I might not sin in time to come. Yes! to be justly angry; for it was not another nature of dark spirits that sinned for me, as they hold who are not angry at themselves. They *store up wrath against the day of wrath* and the revelation of your just judgment. Nor did I find my good outside of me, in that sun seen with the eyes of my flesh. They who would find their joy from outward things soon become vain and waste themselves on the visible and temporal things, and in their starving thoughts they lick at their very shadows. Oh, that they were worn out with their famine, and would say, *Who will show us any good?* Then we would say, *The light of your countenance is beaming on us.* For we are not that *light which enlightens every man*, but we are enlightened by you, that having *been darkness*, we may be *light in you*. Oh, that they could see the Eternal and internal! Having tasted it I was grieved that I could not show it to them, while they brought me their heart in their eyes, eyes roving everywhere but to you, while they kept saying, *Who will show us any good?* There where I was alone in my chamber, where I was inwardly pricked, where I had sacrificed, slaying my old man and commencing the purpose of a new life, putting my trust in you—there you had begun to grow sweet to me, and had put gladness in my heart. And I cried out as I read this aloud, and discovered it inside myself. I did not wish to have worldly goods multiplied, wasting time and being wasted by time. For I had found in your eternal simplicity, other *corn and wine and oil.*

The next verse brought a loud cry from my heart: *O in peace!* O for that very thing! O how he says, *I will lay me down and sleep!* For who shall hinder us, when the saying that is written comes to pass, *Death is swallowed up in victory?* And you are most surely the

Selfsame, for you do not change. In you is the rest which forgets all toil, for there is no other besides you, nor are we to seek those other things which are not what you are. *But you, Lord, only have made me dwell in hope.*

All these things I read, and was enkindled, but what to do with those deaf and dead [Manicheans] I could not discover, for I myself had been one of them, a pestilent member, a blind disputer against those very Scriptures which are honeyed with the honey of heaven and luminous with your own light. Now I was consumed with zeal against the enemies of these Scriptures.

When shall I recall all that passed in those holidays? I have not forgotten them. I will not pass over the severity of your scourge and the wonderful swiftness of your mercy. You tormented me then with a toothache. When it reached such intensity that I could not speak, it came into my mind to ask my friends to pray for me to you, the God of all manner of health. And I wrote this on wax and gave it to them to read. Presently, as soon as we had knelt in humble devotion, the pain disappeared. But what pain? How did it go away? I confess I was afraid, O Lord, my God, for I had never experienced anything like it from my infancy. And the power of your smile of approval impressed me deeply, and rejoicing in faith, I praised your name. But that faith did not allow me to be at ease about my past sins, which were not yet remitted through Baptism.

FIVE

When the vintage vacation was over, I gave notice to the Milanese to provide their scholars with another teacher of rhetoric, both because I had made a choice to serve you and because my difficulty in breathing and the pain in my chest made it impossible to continue the professorship. By letters I notified your bishop, the saintly man, Ambrose, of my former errors and my present desires, asking his advice as to which of your Scriptures I should read to prepare myself to receive so great a grace. He recommended Isaiah the Prophet, because, I think, he foretells the Gospel and the calling of the Gentiles more clearly than the others. But I did not understand the first part, and imagining the rest to be like it, laid it aside to be taken up later on, when better practiced in our Lord's own words.

SIX

When the time arrived to submit my name for baptism, we left the country and returned to Milan. Alypius also decided to be born again in you at the same time. He was already so clothed with the humility becoming your sacraments, and being such a valiant subduer of his body that he could walk the frozen Italian ground with his bare feet. We also took along with us Adeodatus, my son after the flesh, born of my sin. You had made him excellently. He was not quite fifteen, but in wit surpassed many grave and learned men. I acknowledge your gifts, O Lord my God, Creator of all, and you are able to reshape our deformities. For I had no part in that boy but sin. If I brought him up in your discipline, it was you, none else, who inspired me to do it. I acknowledge to you your gifts. There is a book of ours entitled *The Master*. It is a dialogue between Adeodatus and myself. You know that all that is ascribed to the persons conversing with me were his own ideas—in his sixteenth year. I found much else even more admirable in him. His talent filled me with awe. And who but you could be the maker of such wonders? You took his life from this earth while he was still young, and now I remember him without anxiety, fearing nothing for his childhood or youth, nor for his whole self. We took him, as our contemporary in grace, to be brought up in your discipline, and when we were baptized, all anxiety for our past life vanished from us.

I was not satisfied in those days with the wondrous sweetness of contemplating the depth of your counsels concerning the salvation of the human race. Your hymns and canticles made me weep, touched to the quick by the voices of your sweet-sounding Church! The voices flowed into my ears and the truth distilled in my heart; from there the feelings of my devotion overflowed, tears ran down, and I was happy in them.

S E V E N

The Church of Milan had not long been employing this kind of consolation and exhortation, with the brethren singing together with great zeal in harmony of voice and heart. Not much more than a year earlier, Justina, mother to the child Emperor, Valentinian, had persecuted your servant Ambrose in favor of her heresy, to which she had been seduced by the Arians. The devout people kept watch in the Church, ready to die with their bishop, your servant. My mother, your handmaid, took a leading part in these anxieties and watchings, and had lived in prayer. We, not yet thawed by the heat of your Spirit, still were stirred up by the sight of the stunned and troubled city. It was then that hymns and psalms, chanted in the manner of the Eastern Churches, began to be sung, to keep the people from being worn out through the tedium of lamentation. From that day to this the custom has been retained and has been imitated in almost all congregations throughout other parts of the world.

Then in a vision you revealed to your renowned bishop where the bodies of Gervasius and Protasius, the martyrs, lay hidden, which you had preserved incorrupt for so many years in your secret storehouse so that you might produce them at the right time to suppress the fury of a woman—an empress at that! For when they were discovered and exhumed, and transferred to Ambrose's basilica with due honor, not only were people cured who were vexed with unclean spirits—the demons themselves confessing who they were—but also a certain man who had been blind for many years, a citizen well known to the city. Inquiring and hearing the reason for the people's tumultuous joy, he sprang up and asked his guide to lead him to the place. Arriving there, he begged to be allowed to touch with his handkerchief the bier of your saints, *whose death is precious in your sight.* When he had done this, he put the handkerchief to his eyes, and they were immediately opened. From this the fame spread, your praises glowed and shone, and from this time the mind of the enemy, though not converted to the soundness of faith, was at least restrained from her persecuting fury. Thanks to you, O my God. From where and to what end have you thus directed my memory, that I should confess these things, too, to you? For great as they are, I had completely forgotten them. And yet then, when the odor of your ointment was so fragrant, did we not eagerly seek you? That is why I wept all the more as your hymns were sung, having sighed for you, and at last breathing in you, as far as the breath can enter into this "house of grass" of ours.

EIGHT

It is you, O Lord, who make men of one mind to dwell in a house. Associated with us was Euodius, a young man from our home city, an officer of the court who had been converted to you earlier. Having been baptized and having resigned from secular service, he had prepared himself for your service. We had agreed to dwell together in our holy purpose, and seeking where we might most usefully serve you, were returning to Africa. We had gone as far as Ostia, when my mother departed this life.

I omit much, for I hasten toward much more. Receive my confessions and thanksgiving, O my God, for innumerable things on which I am silent. But I will not leave whatever my soul brings forth concerning your handmaid who brought me forth, both in her flesh, that I might be born to this temporal light, and in her heart, that I might be born to eternal light. I would not speak of her gifts, but of yours in her; for she neither created herself nor educated herself. You created her. Nor did her father or mother know what a person should come from them. It was the scepter of your Christ, the discipline of your only-begotten Son, that trained her in the house of one of your faithful ones, a good member of your Church. Yet she did not so much credit her mother's diligence for her good discipline as that of a certain very aged maidservant who had cared for her father in his infancy. For this reason, and because of her great age and excellent character, she was greatly respected by the heads of that Christian home, and she was given charge of her master's daughters. She gave diligent care to this task, restraining them when necessary with a holy severity and teaching them with sober wisdom. For except at those hours in which they were fed very temperately at their parents' table, she would not allow them to drink even water, though parched with thirst. In this way she took precaution against an evil custom, adding this wholesome advice: "You drink water now, because you are not able to drink wine. But when you come to be married and are made mistresses of cellars and cupboards, you will scorn water, but the custom of drinking will remain." By this kind of instruction and the authority she had, she curbed the greediness of childhood and molded their very thirst to such excellent moderation that they no longer craved what they should not have.

Yet, as your handmaid told me, her son, a love of wine had stolen upon her. When, as was custom, she was sent by her parents to draw wine out of the barrel, before she poured it into the flagon, she sipped a little with the edge of her lips. Her instinctive feelings kept her from taking more. She did this, not out of any desire of drink, but out of the exuberance of youth which boils over in mirthful sportiveness and is usually kept in check by the seriousness of their elders. Thus, by adding to that little sip, daily sips (for whoever disregards little things shall fall little by little), she had fallen into such a habit as to drink greedily her little cup almost brimfull of wine. Where then was that discreet old woman and her most earnest prohibition? Would anything avail against our secret diseases if your healing hand, O Lord, did not watch over us? Father, mother, and guardians absent, you are present, who made us, called us, and who work something toward the salvation of our souls by those set over us. What did you do then, O my God? How did you cure her? How did you heal her? Did you not bring out of another soul a hard, sharp taunt, like a lancet out of your secret armory, and remove all that putrefaction with one touch? For a maidservant with whom she used to go to the cellar got into a falling out with her little mistress, as often happens, and when she was alone with her, taunted her about the fault with a most bitter insult, calling her a drunkard. With this taunt, stung to the quick, my mother saw the foulness of her fault and immediately condemned it and forsook it. Just as flattering friends pervert, so reproachful enemies often correct. Yet you, Lord, repay them for what they intend, not for what you do with their reproaches. That slave in her anger sought to trouble her young mistress, not to amend her. She did it in private, either by chance, or out of fear that she would be blamed for not disclosing it earlier. But you, Lord, Governor of all things in heaven and on earth, who turn the deepest currents to your purposes, and rule the turbulent tides of the ages, heal one soul by the very unhealthiness of another. So no one, seeing this, should credit it to his own power when another person, whom he wished to see reformed, is changed through a word of his.

NINE

She was thus modestly and soberly brought up and made subject by you to her parents, rather than by her parents to you. As soon as she was of marriageable age, she was given to a husband, whom she served as her lord. She did her best to win him to you, preaching you to him by her way of life, by which you made her beautiful in his eyes, reverently amiable, and even admirable. And she so endured his infidelities as never to quarrel with her husband about it. For she looked for your mercy on him, that believing in you, he might be made chaste. But besides this, he was hot tempered, both in affection and in anger, and she had learned not to resist an angry husband, either in deed or word. Only when he was soothed and tranquil, and in a mood to receive it, would she give an account of her actions, if by chance he had been angry without reason. In a word, while many wives who had more gentle husbands bore even in their faces marks of blows and would blame their husbands' action in private conversation, my mother would blame their tongues, giving them, as if in jest, this earnest advice: that from the day they heard the marriage contracts read to them, they should consider them instruments whereby they were made servants; and so remembering their condition, they should not set themselves up against their lords. When the others, knowing what a moody husband she endured, marveled that it had never been heard nor in any way suggested that Patricius had beaten his wife, or that there had been any domestic difference between them, even for one day, and confidentially asked the reason, she taught them her rule as I have given it. Those wives who observed it found help and thanked her. Those who did not observe it found no relief and suffered.

Her mother-in-law also, became angry at her through the whisperings of evil servants. But she was so overcome by my mother's persevering endurance and meekness that of her own accord she told her son about the meddling tongues who were disturbing the domestic peace between her and her daughter-in-law, asking him to correct them. In keeping with his mother's wishes, and with a view to the good order of his household and the harmony of its members, he had those who were guilty corrected with stripes. At the same time, his mother promised to do the same to any who should speak ill of her daughter-in-law to her to please her, and none now daring to do so, they lived together with a remarkable sweetness and mutual kindness.

You bestowed another great gift on that good handmaid of yours, my God, my Mercy, in whose womb you created me. Between any disagreeing and discordant parties, where she was able, she showed herself such a peacemaker that when she had heard from both sides of a controversy—such bitter things as growing and unresolved feelings are apt to belch forth, when to a present friend the rawest enmities are breathed out by an acid tongue against an absent enemy—she would never disclose anything about the one to the other but that which might lead to their reconciliation. I might think this a small good if I did not know to my grief the incredible number of persons who, through some horrible and widespread contagion of sin, not only disclose to persons mutually angered things that were said in anger, but even add things that were never said at all. It is no great thing for a humane person not to foment or increase ill will by ill words, but rather he should endeavor by good words to quench it. Such a person was she. You yourself were her most inward Teacher, instructing her in the school of her heart.

Finally, toward the very end of his earthly life, she won her own husband to you. Never did she complain after he became a Christian of what she had endured from him before he was a believer. She was also a servant to your ministers. Any of them who knew her, praised, honored and loved you in her; for through the witness of the fruit of a holy life, they perceived your presence in her heart. She had been the wife of one man, had honored her parents, had governed her household piously, was well known for her good works, had brought up her children, travailing in labor with them whenever she saw them swerving from you. Finally (since you allow your servants to speak of your favor), as though she had been mother to us all, she took care of all of us your servants, O Lord, before she fell asleep in you. We lived united together, having received the grace of your baptism, and she served us, as though she had been the daughter of us all.

TEN

As the day approached on which she was to depart this life (a day you well knew, but we did not) it happened, I believe by your secret arrangement, that she and I stood alone, leaning in a certain window which looked into the garden of the house where we were staying at Ostia. There, removed from the noise of men, we were resting ourselves from the fatigue of a long journey, in preparation for the sea voyage. We were talking together by ourselves very pleasantly, and *forgetting those things which are behind, and reaching forth to those things which are before*, we were discussing in the presence of the Truth which you are, what the nature of the eternal life of the saints was to be, *which eye has not seen, nor ear heard, nor has it entered into the heart of man*. But yet we thirsted with the mouth of our hearts after those heavenly streams of your fountain, the fountain of life which is with you, so that being sprinkled from that fountain as freely as we could receive, we might in some way meditate on so high a mystery.

And our conversation brought us to that point, that the very highest delight of the earthly senses, in the very purest material light was, in comparison to the sweetness of that eternal life, not only not worthy to be compared with it, but not even worthy of mention. Our hearts were lifted to an even more ardent love toward that very Life, and by degrees we passed through all things bodily, even the very heavens, from whence sun and moon and stars shine upon the earth; yes, we were soaring even higher, by inward thought and discourse, admiring your works; and we came to our own minds, and went beyond them, that we might arrive at that region of never-failing plenty, where you feed Israel forever with the food of truth, and where life is that very Wisdom by whom all these things are made, both things that have been and things that shall be. Wisdom is not created, however, but is what it always has been and ever shall be. Yes, rather, *was* or *will be* are not in it, but only *is*, because it is eternal. For *was* and *will be* are not eternal. And while we were talking and longing after Wisdom, we barely touched it with the whole effort of our heart; and we sighed and left bound there the firstfruits of the Spirit, and returned to the sound of language again, where the word spoken has a beginning and an end. And what is like your Word, our Lord, who continues in himself without becoming old and who makes all things new?

We were saying then: Let the tumult of the flesh be hushed; let the images of the earth be hushed, and the waters and the air; hushed also be the poles of heaven, yes, let the very soul be hushed to itself, and so by not thinking on self, rise above itself. Hushed be all dreams and imaginary revelations, every tongue and every sign, and whatever exists only in transitions, if those things can be hushed which say, "We did not make ourselves, but he made us who abides forever." Let them too be hushed, having roused only our ears to him who made them, and let him alone speak, not by them, but by himself, that we may hear his Word, not through any tongue of flesh, nor through an angel's voice, nor the sound of thunder, nor in the dark riddle of a similitude, but by himself, whom we love in these things apart from them.

As the two of us strained ourselves, and in swift thought touched on that eternal Wisdom which abides over all, we said, "If this could be continued on, and other visions of a far different kind be taken away, while this one ravished, absorbed and wrapped up its beholder amidst these inward joys, so that life were forever like that one moment of understanding which we now sighed after, would this not be, *Enter into your Master's joy*? And when shall that be? We will be when we rise again. But *shall we* not *all be changed*?"

I was saying such things (even if not in these same words and same manner). Yet, Lord, you know that on that day when we were speaking of these things, the world with all its delights became, as we talked, contemptible to us. My mother said, "Son, for my own part, I have no further delight in anything in this life. What I am doing here any longer, and to what end I am here, I do not know, now that my hopes in this world are accomplished. There was one thing for which I desired to linger for a while in this life, that I might see you a Catholic Christian before I died. My God has done this for me more abundantly, in that I now see you despising earthly happiness to become his servant. So why do I linger?"

ELEVEN

What answer I made her, I do not remember. It was scarcely five days, however—not much more—until she fell sick with a fever. In that sickness one day she fainted and was unconscious for a while. We hurried to her, but she was soon brought back to her senses, and looking at me and my brother standing by her, asked us, "Where was I?" Then, looking fixedly at us, speechless in our grief, she said, "You shall bury your mother here." I held my peace, and kept myself from weeping, but my brother said something, wishing for her, as the happier lot that she might die in her own land, not in a strange place. At this, with an anxious look, she restrained him with her eyes because he was still concerned about such things, and looking at me, said, "See how he talks!" Then she said to us both, "Lay this body anywhere; do not let the care for that trouble you in any way. My only request is this: remember me at the Lord's altar wherever you are." Having expressed this wish in such words as she could, she fell silent, being in great pain with her increasing sickness.

But I rejoiced, considering your gifts, O God unseen, which you pour into the hearts of your faithful ones, from whence wondrous fruits spring up. I gave thanks to you, remembering what I had known before, how careful and anxious she had always been as to the place of her burial. She had provided and prepared such a place for herself, by the body of her husband. Because they had lived in great harmony together, she wished—so little can the human mind embrace divine things—to have this addition to that happiness, and to have it remembered among men, that after her pilgrimage beyond the seas, that which was earthly of this united pair would be united beneath the same earth. I did not know when this vain desire began to diminish in her through the fullness of your goodness, but I rejoiced that it was so. Indeed in our conversation by the window, when she said, "What am I doing here any longer?" there appeared no desire of dying in her own country. I heard afterward, too, that while we were at Ostia, in my absence one day she was talking with some of my friends about her contempt of this life and the blessings of death; and they were amazed at such courage which you had given to a woman. When they asked whether she were not afraid to leave her body so far from her own city, she replied, "Nothing is far to God. I do not fear that at the end of the world he should fail to know whence to raise me up."

On the ninth day of her illness, and the fifty-sixth year of her age, and in the thirty-third of mine, that devout and holy soul was set free from the body.

TWELVE

I closed her eyes; and a mighty sorrow flooded my heart, overflowing into tears. My eyes, at the same time, by the violent command of my mind, drank up their fountain wholly dry; and woe was me in such a strife! But when she breathed her last, the boy Adeodatus burst out into a loud lament. But then, checked by us all, he held his peace. In the same way a childish feeling in me, seeking its outlet in weeping, was checked and silenced. For we thought it was not fitting to solemnize that funeral with tearful laments and groanings, as though she were unhappy or altogether dead, when in fact she was neither unhappy in her death, nor altogether dead. Of this we were assured on good grounds: the testimony of her good life and her unfeigned faith.

What was it, then, which grievously pained me within, but a fresh wound, wrought through the sudden tearing apart of our most pleasant and cherished habit of living together? I rejoiced indeed in one testimony during her last sickness, when, mixing her endearments with my acts of duty, she called me "dutiful," and remarked with great affection that she had never heard any harsh or reproachful sound uttered by my mouth against her. But yet, O God, what comparison is there between the honor I paid her and her service to me? Deprived of such great comfort in her, my soul was wounded and the life torn apart as it were, hers and mine, which had been made but one.

After the boy had been restrained from weeping, Euodius took up the Psalter and began to sing the Psalm, *I will sing of mercy and judgment to you, O Lord*, and the whole household joined in. Hearing what we were doing, many of the brethren and pious women came together, and while they whose office it was made the body ready for burial according to custom, I stayed in another part of the house with those who thought it was not right to leave me, talking upon something appropriate to the time. By this balm of truth, my torment known to you, was assuaged, which they, listening attentively, did not realize was there, thinking me to be without all feeling of sorrow. But before you, where none of them could hear, I blamed the weakness of my feelings, and stopped my flood of grief a little, but it rose again like a tide, yet not so as to make me burst out in tears or change my facial expression. Still I knew what I was keeping down in my heart. But being very unhappy that these human feelings had such power over me, which in the due course and appointment of our natural condition must needs happen, I grieved with new grief for my grief, and was thus worn down by a double sorrow.

When the body was carried to the burial, we went and returned without tears. I did not weep during those prayers which we poured forth to you when the sacrifice of our redemption was offered for her as her body was placed by the grave, as the custom there is before it was actually buried.[1] Yet the whole day I was secretly very sad, and I prayed to you with a troubled mind as best I could, to heal my sorrow, yet you did not; I believe you were impressing on my memory, by this one instance, how strong the bond of all habit is, even on a soul which now feeds upon the Word without deception. It also seemed good to me to go and bathe, having heard that the bath had its name (*balneum*) from the Greek *Balaneion*, because it drives sadness from the mind. And this also I confess to your mercy, Father of the fatherless: that I bathed and was the same as before I bathed. For the bitterness of sorrow could not be assuaged by bathing. But when I slept and woke up again, I found my grief not a little softened. As I lay alone on my bed, I remembered those true verses of Ambrose. Truly you are

> *Deus, creator omnium,*
> *Polique rector, vestiens*
> *Diem decora lumine,*
> *Noctem sopora gratia.*

Artus solutes ut quies
Reddat laboris usui,
Mentesque jessas allevet,
Luctusque solvat anxios.

God, creator of all,
And ruler of the height,
Who, clothing day in light
Gives slumber in the night.

When our limbs new vigor gain
From rest, new labors to sustain,
Our minds are eased of weary grief,
And anxious hearts find their relief.

And then, little by little, I recovered my former thoughts of your handmaid, her holy manner of life toward you, her holy tenderness and care toward us, of which I was suddenly deprived. And I found comfort in weeping in your sight for her and for myself, in her behalf and my own. And I gave way to the tears I had been holding back, refreshing my heart with them, and it found rest in them, for it was in your ears, not in those of men who would have interpreted my weeping scornfully. But now in writing I confess it to you. Read it now, whoever will, and interpret it however he will. And if he finds sin in that I wept over my mother for a brief part of an hour, the mother who was dead and gone from me, who had wept for me for many years that I might live in your eyes, let him not deride me. Rather, if he be one of great charity, let him weep for my sins to you, the Father of all the family of your Anointed One.

THIRTEEN

Now that my heart is healed from that wound, restored again to its normal feeling, I pour out to you, our God, a far different kind of tears on behalf of your handmaid, flowing from a spirit broken by the thoughts of the dangers of every soul that dies in Adam. For although she had been quickened in Christ, before her release from the flesh, and had lived to the praise of your name in her faith and manner of life, yet I do not dare to say that from the time you regenerated her in baptism, no word ever came forth from her mouth against your commandments. Your Son, the Truth, has said, *Whoever shall say to his brother, "You fool!" shall be in danger of hell fire.* And woe even to the commendable life of men, if you should examine it without regard to your mercy! But because you are not extreme in inquiring after sins, we confidently hope to find some place with you. But whoever adds up his real merits before you, what does he add up to you but your own gifts? Oh that men would know themselves to be but men, and that he *who glories would glory in the Lord*!

Thus, O my Praise and my Life, God of my heart, laying aside for a while her good works, for which I give thanks to you with joy, I now beseech you on behalf of the sins of my mother. Hear me, I pray, by the Healer of our wounds, who hung upon the tree and now sits at your right hand to make intercession for us to you. I know that she dealt mercifully, and from her heart forgave her debtors their debts. Forgive her debts also, whatever she may have contracted in so many years since the waters of salvation. Forgive her, Lord, forgive, I pray; enter not into judgment with her. Let your mercy be exalted above your justice, since your words are true, and you have promised mercy to the merciful. You have made the merciful what they are, and *on those whom you will, you have mercy; and on those whom you will, you have compassion.*

And I believe you have already done what I ask; but accept the freewill offerings of my mouth, Lord. For when the day of her death was at hand, she took no thought to have her body sumptuously wrapped or embalmed with spices, she did not desire a choice monument, nor to be buried in her own land. These things she did not command us, but asked only to have her name remembered at your altar, which she had served without the omission of a single day, and where she knew that holy Sacrifice was offered by which *the handwriting that was against us is blotted out*, that Sacrifice through which the enemy was defeated. When he summed up our [human] offenses and sought what lay to our charge, he found nothing against him in whom we are conquerors. Who shall restore to him his innocent blood? Who will repay him the price with which he bought us and so take us from him? Through the sacrament of our redemption your handmaid bound her soul by the bond of faith. Let none sever her from your protection: let neither the lion nor the dragon interpose himself by force or fraud. For she will not answer that she owes nothing, lest she be convicted and seized by the crafty accuser. Rather, she will answer that her sins are forgiven by him to whom none can repay that price, which he, who owed nothing, paid for us.

May she then rest in peace with her only husband whom she obeyed, bringing forth fruit to you with patience, that she might win him also to you. And inspire, O Lord my God, inspire your servants, my brothers, your sons, my teachers, whom I serve with voice and heart and pen, that as many as shall read these confessions may remember at your altar, Monica, your handmaid, with Patricius, her husband, by whose bodies you brought me into this life, I know not how.[2] May they remember with devout affection my parents in this transitory light, my brother and sister under you, our Father in our Catholic mother [the Church], my fellow citizens in that eternal Jerusalem for which your pilgrim people sigh in their pilgrimage from birth even until they return to it. So may my mother's last request of me be fulfilled even more abundantly through these confessions of mine than through my prayers alone, by means of the prayers of many.[3]

BOOK X

The Examined Life

ONE

Let me know you, Lord, who know me;[1] *let me know you even as I am known.* O Strength of my soul, enter it and make it fit for you, that you may enjoy it *without spot or wrinkle.* This is my hope; therefore I speak, and in this hope I rejoice when I rightly rejoice. The less other things of this life deserve our sorrow, the more we weep for them; and the more they ought to be sorrowed for, the less men weep for them. For behold, you love truth and *he who knows the truth comes to the light.* This I would do in my heart before you in this confession and in my writing before many witnesses.

TWO

What is there in me that could be hidden from you, O Lord, to whose eyes the depths of man's conscience is bare, even though I did not confess it? I might hide you from myself, but not myself from you. But now my groanings bear witness that I am displeased with myself and that you shine brightly and are pleasing, beloved and desired. I am ashamed of myself and renounce myself, and choose you, for I can neither please you nor myself except in you. Therefore I am open to you, Lord, with all that I am, and whatever benefit may come from my confession to you, I have spoken. I do not confess merely with words and fleshly sounds, but with the words of my soul and the cry of my thoughts which your ear knows. For when I am wicked, confession to you is nothing more than to be displeased with myself. But when I am truly devout, it is to ascribe glory to you; because you, Lord, bless the godly, but first you *justify him who is ungodly*.[2] My confession then, O my God, is made both silently and yet not silently, for in sound it is silent, but in affection, it cries aloud. For I neither utter any right thing to others which you have not already heard from me, nor do you hear any such things from me which you have not first said to me.

THREE

But what do I have to do with men that they should hear my confessions, as if they could heal all my infirmities? They are a race, curious to know the lives of others, slow to amend their own. Why do they seek to hear from me what I am, who will not hear from you what they themselves are? And how do they know, when from me they hear of myself, whether I speak the truth, since *no man knows what is in man, but the spirit of man which is in him*? But if they hear from you about themselves, they cannot say, "The Lord lies." For what is it to hear from you of themselves, but to know themselves? And who knows and says, "It is false," unless he lies to himself? But because *charity believes all things*—at least among those whom it knits together with itself as one—I, too, Lord, will confess to you in such a way that men may hear, though I cannot prove to them that my confession is true; yet those whose ears are opened to me by charity will believe me.

But, O my inmost Physician, make plain to me what benefit I may gain by doing it. You have forgiven and covered my past sins that you might make me happy in you, changing my soul by faith and your sacrament. When my confessions of them are read and heard, they stir up the heart. No longer does it sleep in despair and say, "I cannot," but awakes in the love of your mercy and the sweetness of your grace, by which whoever is weak is made strong, when he becomes conscious of his own weakness by it. And the good delight to hear of the past evils of those who are now freed from them—not because they are evils, but because they were and no longer are.

What does it profit me, O Lord my God, what does this book gain me, to confess to men in your presence what I now am? My conscience confesses daily to you, trusting more in the hope of your mercy than in its own innocence. For I have seen and spoken of the fruit of knowing what I have been, but what I now am, at the very time of making these confessions, various people want to know, both those who have known me and those who have not, who have heard from me or of me. But their ear is not at my heart, where I am whatever I am. They wish to hear me confess what I am within, where neither their eye, nor ear, nor understanding can read. They wish it, ready to believe it—but will they know? For charity which makes them good tells them that I do not lie in my confessions, and charity in them believes me.

FOUR

But for what good purpose do they wish to hear this? Do they want to rejoice with me when they hear how near by your grace I approach to you? Do they wish to pray for me when they hear how much I am held back by my own weight? To such I will disclose myself.[3] For it is no little gain, O Lord my God, that thanks should be given to you on our behalf, and that you should be entreated for us. Let the brotherly soul love in me what you teach is to be loved, and lament in me what you teach is to be lamented. Let it be a brotherly, not an alien soul—not one of those strange children, *whose mouth speaks vanity, and whose right hand is the hand of falsehood*. But let it be the soul of my brethren who, when they approve, rejoice for me, and when they disapprove, are sorry for me; because whether they approve or disapprove, they love me. To such I will disclose myself; they will breathe freely at my good deeds, sigh for my ill. My good deeds are your appointments and your gifts. My evil ones are my offenses and your judgments. Let them breathe freely at the one and sigh at the other. Let hymns and weeping go up into your sight from the hearts of my brethren, your censers.[4] And be pleased, O Lord, with the incense of your holy temple; *have mercy on me according to your great mercy* for your own name's sake. And do not on any account leave what you have begun in me, but perfect my imperfections.

This is the fruit, the profit of my confession of what I am, not of what I have been: to confess this, not only before you, in a secret exultation with trembling, and a secret sorrow with hope, but in the ears of the believing sons of men, sharers of my joy, partners in my mortality, my fellow citizens and fellow pilgrims, who have gone before me, and are to follow on—companions of my way. These are your servants, my brethren, who are your sons by your will. They are my masters, whom you command me to serve if I would live with you and in you. But this, your Word, would mean little to me if it only commanded by speaking, without going before in action. This then I do in deed and word. This I do under your wings, for it would be too great a peril if my soul were not subjected to you under your wings and my infirmities known to you. I am but a little one, but my Father ever lives, and my Guardian is sufficient for me. For he is the same who gave me life and defends me, and you yourself are all my good. You, Almighty One, are with me, yes, even before I am with you. To those then whom you command me to serve I will show, not what I have been, but what I now am, and what I continue to be. But I do not judge myself. Thus, therefore would I be heard.

FIVE

You, Lord, are my Judge, because, although *no man knows the things of a man but the spirit of a man which is in him*, yet there is something of man which *the spirit of man that is in him*, itself, does not know. But you, Lord, know him completely, for you made him. And although I despise myself in your sight and account myself *dust and ashes*, I know something of you which I do not know of myself. Truly, *now we see through a glass darkly*, not *face to face* as yet. As long, then, as I am absent from you, I am more present with myself than with you. And I know that you cannot be violated, but I do not know which temptations I can resist and which I cannot. There is hope, because you are faithful, *who will not allow us to be tempted beyond our ability; but will with the temptation also make a way of escape, so that we may be able to bear it.* I will confess then what I know of myself, I will confess also what I do not know of myself. What I know of myself I know by your light shining upon me; and what I do not know of myself, I continue not to know until my *darkness becomes as the noonday* in the light of your countenance.

SIX

I love you, Lord, without any doubt, but with assured certainty. You have stricken my heart with your Word, and I love you. Yes, also, heaven and earth and all that is in them on every side bid me to love you. They will not cease to say so to everyone, so that *they are without excuse*. But more profoundly, *you will have mercy on whom you will have mercy, and compassion on whom you will have compassion.* Otherwise, the heaven and the earth speak your praises to deaf ears.

But what do I love when I love you? Not the beauty of bodies, nor the fair harmony of time, nor the brightness of the light, so gladsome to our eyes; not the sweet melodies of various songs, nor the fragrant smell of flowers and ointments and spices; not manna and honey; not the limbs that physical love likes to embrace. It is none of these that I love when I love my God. Yet I love a kind of light, a kind of melody, a kind of fragrance, a kind of food, and a kind of embrace when I love my God: the light, the melody, the fragrance, the food, and the embrace of the inner man, where there shines into my soul what space cannot contain, and there sounds what time cannot carry away. I breathe a fragrance which no breeze scatters, and I taste there what is not consumed by eating; and there I lie in the embrace that no satiety can ever separate. This is what I love when I love my God.

And what is it? I asked the earth, and it answered me, "I am not he." And whatever is in the earth confessed the same. I asked the sea and its deeps, and the living, creeping things, and they answered, "We are not your God; seek him above us." I asked the moving air; and the whole air with its inhabitants answered, "Anaximenes was deceived; I am not God."[5] I asked the heavens, sun, moon, stars. "No," say they, "we are not the God whom you seek." And I replied to all the things that throng about the senses of my flesh, "You have told me of my God, that you are not he. Tell me something of him." And they cried, "He made us." My questioning of them was my thoughts about them, and their form of beauty gave the answer. And I turned myself to myself, and said to myself, "What are you?" And I answer, "A man." And behold, in me there appear both soul and body, one outside and the other within. By which of these should I seek my God? I had sought him in the body from earth to heaven, as far as I could send my eyesight as messengers. But the better part is the inner, for to it, as to a ruler and judge, all the bodily messengers reported the answers of heaven and earth and all things in them, who said, "We are not God, but he made us." These things my inner man knew by means of the outer. I, the inner man, knew them. I, the mind, knew them through the senses of my body. I asked the whole frame of the world about my God; and it answered me, "I am not he, but he made me."

Is not this outward appearance visible to all who have use of their senses? Why then does it not say the same thing to all? Animals small and great see it, but they cannot ask it anything, because their senses are not endowed with reason, so they cannot judge what they see. But men can ask, *so that the invisible things of God may be clearly seen, being understood by the things that are made.* But in loving them, they are brought into subjection to them, and subjects cannot judge.[6] Nor do these things answer unless the questioners can judge. The creatures do not change their voice, they do not appear one way to this man, another to that; but appearing the same way to both, they are dumb to one and speak to the other. Rather, they speak to all, but only those understand who compare the voice received externally with the internal truth. For truth says to me, "Neither heaven nor earth nor any other body is your God." This, their very nature says to him who sees them, "They are a mass; a mass is less in part than in the whole." Now I speak to you, O my soul; you are my better part, for you quicken the whole mass of my body, giving it life. No body can give life to a body. But your God is the Life of your life.

SEVEN

What do I do, then, when I love my God? Who is he who is so high above my soul? By my very soul I will ascend to him. I will soar beyond that power by which I am united to my body, filling its whole frame with life. But I do not find God by that power, for then, so could *horse and mule that have no understanding* find him, for it is the same power by which their bodies live.[7] But there is another power, not only that by which I am made alive, but that, too, by which I imbue my flesh with sense, which the Lord has made for me, commanding the eye not to hear and the ear not to see; but commanding the eye that I should see through it, and the ear that I should hear through it, and the several other senses, what is to each their own proper places and functions. Through these different senses, I, as a single mind, act. I will go beyond this power of mine, too, for the horse and mule also have this power, for they also perceive through their bodily senses.

EIGHT

I will move on, then, beyond this power of my nature, rising by degrees to him who made me. And I come to the fields and spacious palaces of my memory, where the treasures of innumerable images are stored, brought there from all sorts of things perceived by the senses. Further, there is stored up in memory whatever thoughts we think, either by enlarging or diminishing, or changing in any other way those things which the senses have brought in; and whatever else has been committed and stored up, which forgetfulness has not yet swallowed up and buried. When I enter there, I ask what I want brought forth, and some things appear instantly; others must be sought after longer, and are brought, as it were, out of some inner storage place. Still others rush out in crowds, and while only one thing is desired and asked for, they leap into view as if to say, "Do you perhaps want me?" I drive these away from the face of my remembrance with the hand of my heart until what I wanted is unveiled and appears in sight out of its secret place. Other things come up readily, in unbroken order, as they are called for—those in front giving way to those that follow; and as they make way, they are hidden from sight, ready to come back at my will. All of this takes place when I repeat something by heart.

And all these things are preserved distinctly and under general heads, each having entered my memory by its own particular avenue: light and colors and forms of bodies, by the eyes; all sorts of sounds by the ears; all smells by the avenue of the nostrils; all tastes by the mouth; and by the sensation of the whole body, what is hard or soft, hot or cold, smooth or rugged, heavy or light—either external or internal to the body. All these things the great recesses, the hidden and unknown caverns of memory, receive and store, to be retrieved and brought forth when needed, each entering by its own gate. Yet the things themselves do not enter, but only the images of the things perceived are there, ready to be recalled in thought. But how these images are formed, who can tell? It is plain, however, which sense brought each one in and stored it up. For even while I dwell in darkness and silence, I can produce colors in my memory if I choose, and I can discern between black and white. Sounds do not break in and alter the image brought in by my eyes which I am reviewing, though they also are there, lying dormant and stored, as it were, separately. I can call for these, too, and they immediately appear. And though my voice is still and my throat silent, I can sing as much as I will. Those images of colors do not intrude, even though they are there, when another memory is called for which came in by way of the ears. So it is with other things brought in and stored up by the other senses—I can recall them at my pleasure. Yes, I can tell the fragrance of lilies from violets, though I smell nothing; I prefer honey to sweet wine, smooth surfaces to rough ones—at the time neither tasting nor handling, but only remembering.

These things I do inside myself, in that vast hall of my memory. For present there with me are heaven, earth, sea and whatever I could think on them, in addition to what I have forgotten. There also I meet with myself, and recall myself—what, when and where I did a thing, and what my feelings were when I did it. All that I remember is there, either personal experiences or what I was told by others. Out of the same store I continually combine with the past fresh images of things experienced, or what I have believed from what I have experienced. From these I can project future actions, events and hopes, and I can reflect on all these again in the present. I say to myself, in that great storehouse of my mind, filled with the images of so many and such great things, "I will do this or that, and this or that will follow." "Oh, would that this or that might be!" "May God prevent this or that!" This is the way I talk to myself, and when I speak, the images of all I speak about are present, out of the same treasury of memory. I could not say anything at all about them if their images were not there.

Great is this power of memory, exceedingly great, O my God: a large and boundless chamber! Who has ever sounded the depths of it? Yet this is a power of mine, and belongs to my nature. But I do not myself comprehend all that I am. Therefore the mind is too narrow to contain itself. But where can that part be which it does not itself contain? Is it outside it and not inside? How then does it not comprehend itself? A great wonder arises in me; I am stunned with amazement at this. And men go outside themselves to admire the heights of mountains, the mighty waves of the sea, the broad tides of rivers, the width of the ocean and the circuits of the stars, passing by themselves. They do not wonder at the fact that when I spoke of all these things, I did not see them with my eyes, yet I could not have spoken of them unless I then inwardly saw with my memory the mountains, waves, rivers and stars which I have seen, and that ocean which I believe to exist, and with the same vast spaces between them as if I saw them outside myself. Yet I did not actually draw them into myself by seeing them, when I beheld them with my eyes, but only their images. And I know which sense of the body impressed each of them on me.

NINE

Yet these are not all that the immeasurable capacity of my memory retains. Here also is all that I have learned of the liberal sciences and have not yet forgotten—removed as it were to some inner place, which is yet no place. In this case it is not the images which are retained, but rather, the things themselves. For whatever literature, whatever art of debating, however many kinds of questions I know, they exist in my memory as they are—I have not taken in their image and left out the thing itself. It is not as though it had sounded and passed away like a voice retained in the ear, which can be recalled as if it still sounded when it no longer sounded. Nor is it like an odor that evaporates into the air as it passed, affecting the sense of smell, and from it carries an image of itself into the memory which we renew when we recall it. Nor is it like food, which verily has no taste in the belly, but yet is still tasted in some way in the memory; nor as anything which the body feels by touch and which the memory still conceives when removed from us. For those things themselves are not transmitted into the memory, but their images are caught up and stored, with an admirable swiftness, as it were, in wonderful cabinets, and from there wonderfully brought forth by the act of remembering.

TEN

But now when I hear that there are three kinds of questions—whether a thing is, what it is, of what kind it is—I do indeed hold the images of the sounds which make up these words, and I know that those sounds passed through the air with a noise and then ceased to be. But the questions themselves which are conveyed by these sounds, I never reached with any sense of my body, nor do I ever see them at all except by my mind. Yet I have not laid up their images in my memory, but these very questions themselves.

How they entered into me, let them say if they can; for I have gone over all the avenues of my flesh, and cannot find how they entered. For the eyes say, "If those images were colored, we reported about them." The ears say, "If they made a sound, we gave you knowledge of them." The nostrils say, "If they have any smell, they passed by us." The taste says, "Unless they have a flavor, do not ask me." The touch says, "If it has no size, I did not handle it, and if I did not handle it, I have no account of it."

Whence and how did these things enter my memory? I do not know. For when I learned them, I gave no credit to another man's mind, but recognized them in mine; and approving them as true, I commended them to my mind, laying them up as it were, where I could get at them again whenever I wished. There they were then [in my mind] before I stored them in my memory. Where then, or why, when they were spoken, did I acknowledge them and say, "So it is! It is true," unless they were already in the memory, but so thrown back and buried as it were in deeper recesses, that if the suggestion of another had not drawn them forth, I may have been unable to conceive of them?[8]

ELEVEN

Thus we find that to learn those things whose images do not come to us by way of the senses, but which we know by themselves as they are, without images, is nothing more than taking the things the memory already has—scattered and unarranged. By marking and careful attention we gather them, as it were in that same memory where they lay unknown before scattered and ignored, so that they can readily occur to the mind now familiarized with them. And how many things of this kind does my memory hold which have already been discovered, and, as I said, placed as it were handily, which we are said to have learned and come to know? And if I for some short space should cease to call them back to mind, they would again be so buried, and glide back, as it were, into the deeper recesses, that they would have to be drawn out again as if new from the same place. For there is nowhere else for them to go, but they must be drawn together again that they may be known. That is to say, they must be collected together from their scattering. From this the word *to cogitate* comes. For *cogo* [I collect] and *cogito* [I re-collect] have the same relation to each other as *ago* [I do] and *agito* [I do frequently], *facio* [I make] and *facito* [I make frequently]. But the mind has appropriated to itself this word, *cogito*, so that, not what is collected anywhere, but only what is re-collected, that is, brought together in the mind, is properly said to be cogitated or thought upon.

TWELVE

The memory also contains innumerable principles and laws of numbers and dimensions, none of which have been impressed upon it by any bodily sense, since they have neither color, sound, taste, smell nor touch. I have heard the sound of the words by which they are signified, but the sounds are other than the things themselves. For the sounds are different in Greek than in Latin, but the things are neither Greek nor Latin, nor any other language. I have seen the lines of architects, the very finest, like a spider's thread; but the truths they express are not the images of those lines, which my physical eye saw. The architect knows them without any use whatsoever of a body, by recognizing them within himself. I have perceived, also, with all the senses of my body the numbers of the things which we count, but those numbers themselves by which we count are different. They are not the images of the things we count, and therefore they simply *are*. Let him who does not see these truths laugh at me for saying them. While he derides me, I will pity him.

THIRTEEN

I hold all these things in my memory, and I remember how I learned them. I remember, too, having heard many things erroneously offered against the truth of them, and though they are false, yet it is not false to have remembered them. I perceive that it is one thing to distinguish these things and another to remember that I have often distinguished them when I thought upon them. I remember both that I have often understood these things in the past, and that I am storing up in my memory what I now discern and understand about them, so that later on I can recall what I now understand. Therefore I remember that I have remembered, so that if later on I should call to mind that I was once able to remember these things, it will be by the power of memory that I shall recall it.

FOURTEEN

The same memory contains the feelings of my mind—not in the same way that my mind contains them when it feels them, but in quite a different way, according to a power peculiar to memory. For without rejoicing, I remember that I have rejoiced. Without sorrow, I recollect my past sorrow. And what I once feared, I review without fear; without desire, I call to mind past desire. Sometimes, on the other hand, I remember my past sorrow with joy, and my past joy with sorrow.

This is not to be wondered at as regards the body, for the mind is one thing, the body another. If I therefore remember some past pain of the body with joy, it is not so strange. But this very memory itself is mind—for when we want something remembered, we say, "See that you keep this in mind." And when we forget, we say, "It did not come to my mind," or "It slipped my mind," calling the memory itself the mind.

Since this is so, how is it that, when I remember my past sorrow with joy, the mind has joy while the memory has sorrow? The mind rejoices over the joyfulness which is in it, while the memory is not sad while retaining the sadness in it. Does the memory perchance not belong to the mind? Who will say so? The memory then is, as it were, the belly of the mind, and joy and sadness are like sweet and bitter food. When these are committed to the memory, they are, as it were, passed into the belly, where they may be stowed but not tasted. It is ridiculous to consider this comparison, but yet they are not totally unalike.

But, consider this. It is out of my memory that I say there are four basic emotions of the mind—desire, joy, fear and sorrow. Whatever I may discuss about them, by dividing each into its own particular kind, and by defining what it is, it is from my memory that I find what to say and bring it out from there. Yet I am not disturbed by these emotions when I call them to mind and remember them. Yes, and before I recalled and brought them back, they were there, and so could be brought forth by recollection. Perhaps as meat is brought up out of the stomach by chewing the cud, these things are brought out of the memory by recollection. Why, then, does the man who is thinking of them not taste in his mouth the sweetness of joy or the bitterness of sorrow? Does the comparison fail in this because it is not alike in all respects? For who would ever willingly speak of it, if every time we named grief or fear we should be compelled to feel sad or fearful? And yet we could not speak of them if we did not find in our memory, not only the sounds of their names according to images impressed on it by our bodily senses, but also the notions of the things themselves, which we never received by any avenue of the flesh. But the mind itself recognized them through the experience of its own passions, committed them to the memory; or else the memory itself retained them without having them actually assigned to it [by the conscious mind].

FIFTEEN

But whether this is done by images or not, who can readily say? Thus, I name a stone, I name the sun, and the things themselves are not present to my senses, but their images are present to my memory. I name a bodily pain, yet it is not present with me when nothing aches. Yet, unless its image was present in my memory, I would not know what to say of it, nor how to tell pain from pleasure. I name bodily health. When I am sound in body, the thing itself is present with me; yet unless its image were also present in my memory, I could not recall what the sound of this name signified. Nor would the sick, when health was named, recognize what was being spoken of, unless the same image were retained by the power of memory, although the thing itself was absent from the body. I name numbers by which we count; and it is not their images but the numbers themselves that are present in my memory. I name the image of the sun, and that image is present in my memory. For I do not recall the image of its image, but the image itself is present to me when I call it to mind. I name *memory*, and I recognize what I name. But where do I recognize it but in the memory itself? Is it also present to itself by its image, and not by itself?

SIXTEEN

When I name *forgetfulness* and recognize what I name, how could I recognize it if I did not remember it? I do not speak of the sound of the name, but the thing which it signifies. If I had forgotten, I could not recognize what that sound meant. When I remember memory, memory itself is, by means of itself, present with itself; but when I remember forgetfulness, there are present both memory and forgetfulness: memory by which I remember, and forgetfulness which I remember.

But what is forgetfulness, but the absence of memory? How then can that be present, so that I remember it, which, when it is present keeps me from remembering? But if we hold in memory what we remember, we could never recognize forgetfulness when we hear it named unless we remembered it. So then, forgetfulness is retained by memory. It is present then, so that we do not forget it. This being the case, are we to suppose that forgetfulness, when we remember it, is present to the memory only through its image rather than by itself? Because if it were present by itself, it would not cause us to remember, but to forget. Who can search this out? Who shall understand how it is?

Lord, I truly toil in this; yes, and in myself. I have become a difficult soil, requiring too much sweat of the brow. For I am not now searching out the regions of the heavens, or measuring the distances of the stars, or inquiring about the weight of the earth. It is I myself who remember, I, the mind. It is not so strange if what I am not should be far from me. But what is nearer to me than myself? And lo, I do not understand the power of my own memory, though I cannot even name myself without it. For what shall I say, when it is clear to me that I remember forgetfulness? Shall I say that what I remember is not in my memory? Or shall I say that forgetfulness is in my memory so that I will not forget? Both of these are most absurd. But what third view is there? How can I say that the image of forgetfulness is retained in my memory, not forgetfulness itself, when I remember it? How could I say this either, seeing that when the image of anything itself is imprinted on the memory, the thing itself must first be present from which the image may be imprinted? For this is the way I remember Carthage, and in this way I remember all the places I have been; this is the way it is with men's faces whom I have seen, and things reported by the other senses. Thus it is with health or sickness of the body. For when these things were present, my memory received images from them, which remain present with me, so that I can look on them and bring them back to mind when I remember them in their absence. If then this forgetfulness is retained in the memory through its image, not through itself, then, plainly it was once present itself, so that its image might be taken. But when it was present, how did it write its image in my memory, since forgetfulness by its presence erases even what it finds already recorded? And yet, in whatever way, although it is past conceiving or explaining, I am certain that I remember forgetfulness itself, too, by which is blotted out what we remember.

SEVENTEEN

Great is the power of memory, a fearful thing, O my God, a deep and boundless multiplicity; and this is the mind and this I am myself. What am I then, O my God? What nature am I? A life various and manifold, exceedingly immense. Behold the innumerable plains and caves and caverns of my memory are innumerably full of unnumbered kinds of things—either through images, as in all physical bodies, or by actual presence, as the arts, or by certain notions or impressions, like the emotions of the mind which are retained by the memory even when we no longer feel them, because whatever is in the memory is in the mind. I run over all these, I fly, I dive on this side and on that, as far as I can, and there is no end. The power of memory is as great as the power of life in this mortal life of man.

What shall I do then, O my God, my true life? I will go even beyond this power of mine which is called memory. Yes, I will go beyond it, so that I may approach you, O lovely Light. What do you say to me? See, I am mounting up through my mind toward you who dwell above me. Yes, I now will pass beyond this power of mine which is called memory, desiring to reach you where you may be reached, and to cleave to you where that is possible. For even beasts and birds have memory, otherwise they could not return to their dens and nests, nor do the many other things they do. Nor indeed could they be used in any way except through their memory. I will pass then beyond memory, too, that I may reach him who has separated me from the four-footed beasts and made me wiser than the fowls of the air. So, I will go on beyond memory, but where shall I find you, O truly Good and certain Sweetness? If I find you without my memory, then I cannot retain you in my memory. And how shall I find you, if I do not remember you?

EIGHTEEN

The woman who lost her drachma and searched for it with a light could never have found it unless she had remembered it. And when it was found, how would she know it was the same coin if she did not remember it? I remember having looked for and finding many things, and this I know by it, that when I was searching for any of them, and was asked, "Is this it?" "Is that it?" I said, "No," until the thing I was looking for was offered. But if I had not remembered it—whatever it was—though it had been offered to me, I could not have found it because I failed to recognize it. And so it always is when we look for and find any lost thing. Nevertheless, when anything is lost from sight by chance (not from the memory, as any visible body might be) still its image is retained within us, and we look for it until it is restored to sight; and when it is found, we recognize it by its image within. We do not say that we have found what was lost unless we recognize it, and we cannot recognize it unless we remember it. It was lost to the eye, but it was retained in the memory.

NINETEEN

When the memory itself loses anything, as happens when we forget something and try to recall it, where do we look for it, but in the memory itself? And there, if one thing happens to be offered instead of another, we reject it until we find what we are looking for. And when we find it, we say, "This is it!" We could not say that unless we recognized it, nor recognize it unless we remembered it. Certainly then we had forgotten it. Or, had all of it not been forgotten, and did we look for the part that was missing by the part which we still remembered, as if the memory felt that it could not carry on properly until the missing part was restored to it?

For instance, if we see or think of someone known to us, and having forgotten his name, try to recall it, whatever else occurs does not connect itself with his name, because we are not accustomed to think of that in connection with him. So we go on rejecting these things until something presents itself on which the knowledge we seek rests. And from where does that come, but out of the memory itself? For even when we recognize it as it is brought to mind by someone else, it still comes from memory. For we do not believe it as something new, but upon recollection, agree that what was said was right. But if it had been utterly blotted out of the mind, we would not remember it even when reminded of it. For we have not as yet utterly forgotten what we remember as having forgotten. What we have lost and utterly forgotten, we cannot even search for.

TWENTY

How do I seek you, then, O Lord? For when I seek you, my God, I seek a happy life. I will seek you that my soul may live. For my body lives by my soul, and my soul lives by you. How then do I seek a happy life, seeing that I do not have it until I can rightly say, "It is enough!" How do I seek it? By remembering, as though

I had forgotten it, remembering that I had forgotten it? Or by desiring to learn it as something unknown, either never having known, or having so forgotten as not even to remember that it had been forgotten? Is not a happy life what all seek, and is there anyone who does not desire it? Where have they known it, so that they desire it? Where have they seen it, that they love it so much? Somehow we have it, but how I do not know.

There is indeed a way in which one has it and then is happy, and there are some who are happy in the hope of having it. These have it in a lesser way than those who have it in very fact; yet they are better off than those who are neither happy in fact nor in hope. Yet even these, if they did not have it in some way, would not so greatly desire to be happy—and that they do desire it is most certain. How they have known it then, I do not know. By what sort of knowledge they have it, I do not know, and I am perplexed whether it is in the memory—for in that case, we would have been happy once.

I do not now inquire as to whether everyone was happy separately, or happy in that man who first sinned, in whom also we all died, and from whom we are all born with misery. I only ask whether the happy life is in the memory. For we could not love it if we did not know it. We hear the name, and we all confess that we desire the thing, for we are not delighted with the mere sound. When a Greek hears it in Latin, he is not delighted, not knowing what is being spoken. But we Latins are delighted, as he would be too, if he heard it in Greek; because the thing itself which Greeks and Latins and men of all other tongues long for so earnestly is neither Greek nor Latin. It is therefore known to all, for could they with one voice be asked, "Do you want to be happy?" they would answer, without doubt, "We do." And this could not be unless happiness itself, signified by the name, were retained in their memory.

TWENTY-ONE

But is it the same as when one who has seen Carthage remembers it? No. For a happy life is not seen with the eye, because it is not a body. Is it the same as when we remember numbers? No. For the one who has these in his knowledge does not have to look further to reach them. But a happy life we have in our knowledge and therefore love it, and yet we still desire to attain it, so that we may be happy. Is it the same as when we remember eloquence, then? No. Upon hearing this name, some who are not yet eloquent and desire to be so call eloquence to mind. Through their bodily senses they have observed others to be eloquent, and were delighted by it and wanted to be like them, though actually they would not have been delighted without some inward knowledge of eloquence, nor want to be like them unless they were delighted by it. But in the case of the happy life, we do not experience it in others through any bodily sense.

Do we remember happiness then in the same way we remember joy? Possibly. For I remember my joy even when I am sad, as I remember a happy life even when I am unhappy. Nor did I ever see, hear, smell, taste, or touch my joy with my bodily senses, but I experienced it in my mind when I rejoiced, and the knowledge of it stuck in my memory, so that I can recall it—at times with disgust, at other times with longing, according to the nature of the things which I remember having enjoyed. For I have been immersed in a sort of joy even from foul things which I now abhor and utterly detest when I recall them. At other times I rejoiced in good and honest things which I recall with longing, although they may no longer be present. In that case I recall former joy with sorrow.

Where then, and when, did I experience my happy life that I should remember and love and long for it? Mine is not an isolated case, nor is it that of some few besides me, but all of us desire to be happy. Unless by some certain knowledge we knew what a happy life is, we could not desire it with such certainty. But how is this, that if two men are asked whether they would go to the wars, one might answer that he would and the other that he would not? But if they were asked whether they wanted to be happy, they would instantly, without any hesitation, say they would; and for no other reason would the one choose to go to the wars and the other not, but to be happy. Is it possible that as one looks for his joy in one thing, another in another, all agree in their desire to be happy? In the same way, if they were asked, they would agree that they wished to have joy, and would they call this joy a happy life? Then, although one obtains joy by one means, another by another, both have the same goal they try to reach—joy. Since joy is a thing which all must say they have experienced, it is therefore found in the memory and recognized whenever the name of a happy life is mentioned.

TWENTY-TWO

Far be it, Lord, far be it from the heart of your servant who is confessing here to you, far be it from me to think that I am happy, be the joy what it may. For there is a joy which is not given to the ungodly, but to those who love you for your own sake, whose joy is you yourself. And this is the happy life: to rejoice in you, of you, for you. This is true joy and there is no other. They who think there is another seek some other, and not the true joy. Yet their will is not turned except by some semblance of joy.

TWENTY-THREE

Is it, then, not certain that all wish to be happy, inasmuch as they who do not wish to joy in you (which is the only happy life) do not truly desire the happy life? Or do all men desire this, but *the flesh strives against the Spirit and the Spirit against the flesh*, so that they cannot do what they wish to do? Do they then settle on that which they can do, and are content with that, because they do not desire strongly enough what they cannot do to make them able to do it? For if I ask anyone if he would rather rejoice in truth or in falsehood, he will hesitate as little to say "In the truth," as he would to say that he desires to be happy. But a happy life is joy in the truth, for this is rejoicing in you, who are the Truth, O God, my Light, *the Health of my countenance and my God.* This happy life all desire; all desire this life which is the only happy life, for all desire to rejoice in the truth. I have met with many who would deceive others; none who want to be deceived. And when they love a happy life, which is nothing else than rejoicing in the truth, then they also love the truth—which they could not love if there were not some knowledge of it in their memory. Why then do they not rejoice in it? Why are they not happy? Because they are more strongly occupied with other things which have more power to make them miserable than that which they so dimly remember has to make them happy. For there is yet a little light in men; let them walk, let them walk, *lest the darkness overtake them.*

But why does truth generate hatred, and why does your servant, preaching the truth, become their enemy, since a happy life is loved, which is nothing else but rejoicing in the truth? How is this so unless the truth is loved in such a way that those who love something else want what they love to be the truth? And because they do not want to be deceived, they do not want to be convinced that they are. Therefore they hate the truth, for the sake of the thing they love instead of the truth.

They love the truth when it enlightens, they hate it when it reproves. Since they would not be deceived, yet would deceive, they love it when it reveals itself to them, but hate it when it reveals them to themselves. Thus the truth shall repay them, by exposing those who do not wish to be exposed by it, and yet not revealing itself to them. Thus, thus, yes, thus does the mind of man—blind, sick, foul and ill-behaved—wish to be hidden, but does not want anything hidden from it. But the very opposite happens. The mind is not hidden from the truth, while the truth remains hidden from it. Happy then will it be, when without any other distraction, it shall rejoice in that sole Truth by which all things are true.

TWENTY-FOUR

See what a space I have covered in my memory in seeking you, O Lord! And I have not found you outside it, nor have I found anything concerning you but what I retained in my memory ever since I learned of you. Since I learned of you I have not forgotten you. Where I found truth, there I found my God, the Truth itself. And since I learned this I have not forgotten it. Thus since the time I learned of you, you have resided in my memory. There I find you when I call you to remembrance, and delight in you. These are my holy delights which you have given me in your mercy, being mindful of my poverty.

TWENTY-FIVE

But where do you abide in my memory, O Lord? Where do you abide there? What kind of dwelling place have you made for yourself there? What kind of sanctuary have you built there for yourself? You have given this honor to my memory, to abide in it; but in what part of it you dwell—that I am pondering. For in thinking about you, I passed beyond such parts of it as the animals have, for I did not find you there among corporeal things. And I came to those areas in which I stored the affections of my mind, and did not find you there. Then I entered into the innermost seat of my mind—which the mind has in my memory, since the mind remembers itself—but you were not there. For as you are not a corporeal image, nor the affection of a living being (as when we rejoice, sympathize with, desire, fear, remember, forget, or the like), so neither are you the mind itself. Because you are the Lord God of the mind, and all these things change, but you remain unchangeable over them all—and yet you have vouchsafed to dwell in my memory ever since I learned of you. So why do I now seek to know the part of my memory in which you dwell, as if there were places in the mind? Assuredly, you dwell in it since I have remembered you ever since I learned of you, and since I find you there when I call you to remembrance.

TWENTY-SIX

Where then did I find you that I might learn of you? You were not in my memory before I learned of you. Where did I find you, that I might learn of you, but in yourself, above myself. Place there is none; we go backward and forward, and there is no "place" [location]. Everywhere, O Truth, you hear those who ask counsel of you, and answer all of them at once, though they ask your counsel on many different things. You answer them clearly, though they do not all hear clearly. All consult you on whatever they wish, though they do not always hear back what they wish. He is your best servant who looks not so much to hear what he desires from you, as to desire that which he hears from you.

TWENTY-SEVEN

Too late have I loved you, O Beauty, ancient yet ever new. Too late have I loved you! And behold, you were within, but I was outside, searching for you there—plunging, deformed amid those fair forms which you had made. You were with me, but I was not with you. Things held me far from you, which, unless they were in you, did not exist at all. You called and shouted, and burst my deafness. You gleamed and shone upon me, and chased away my blindness. You breathed fragrant odors on me, and I held back my breath, but now I pant for you. I tasted, and now I hunger and thirst for you. You touched me, and now I yearn for your peace.

TWENTY-EIGHT

When I come to be united with you with my whole self, I shall have no more sorrow or labor, and my life shall be wholly alive, being wholly full of you! You lift up the one you fill, but I am still a burden to myself, because I am not full of you. Lamentable joys strive with joyous sorrows: and on which side the victory will be I do not know. Woe is me! Lord, have mercy on me. My evil sorrows strive with my good joys; and I do not know on which side the victory may be. Woe is me! Lord, have mercy on me! Woe is me! See! I do not hide my wounds; you are the Physician, I the sick. You are the merciful, I the miserable one. Is not the life of man upon earth all trial? Who wishes for troubles and difficulties? You command them to be endured, not to be loved. No man loves what he endures, though he may love to endure. For though he rejoices that he endures, he would rather there were nothing for him to endure. In adversity, I long for prosperity; in prosperity I fear adversity. What middle ground is there between these two—where the life of man is not all trial? Woe to the prosperities of the world, twice woe—woe from fear of adversity and woe from corruption of joy! Woe to the adversities of this world, twice woe, and triple woe: woe from longing for prosperity, woe because adversity itself is a hard thing, and woe for fear that it may make a shipwreck of our endurance! Is not the life of man upon earth all trial without intermission?

TWENTY-NINE

And all my hope is only in your exceeding great mercy. Give what you command, and command what you will. You command self-restraint, and "When I knew," said one, "that no man can be continent unless God gave it, that was a point of wisdom also to know whose gift it is." For by self-restraint, verily, we are bound up and brought back together into wholeness, whereas we had been splintered in many ways. For he loves you too little who loves anything else with you which he does not love for you. O Love, who ever burns and is never quenched! O Charity, my God! Enkindle me. You command continence; give me what you command and command what you will.

THIRTY

Truly you command that I should be continent from the lust of *the flesh, the lust of the eyes, and the pride of life*. You have commanded self-restraint from fornication, and as for wedlock itself, you have counseled something better than what you have permitted. And since you gave it, it was done, even before I became a minister of your Sacrament. But there yet lives in my memory (of which I have spoken at length) the images of such things as my bad habits had fixed there. These rush into my thoughts when I am awake, but in my sleep they not only seem pleasurable, but even to obtain my consent in what very closely resembles reality. Yes, the illusion of the image so far prevails in my soul and in my flesh, that when I am asleep, false visions persuade me to what the true ones cannot when I am awake. Am I not myself at such times, O Lord my God? There is yet so much difference between myself and myself in that instant in which I pass from waking to sleeping, or return from sleeping to waking! Where is reason, then, which resists such suggestions when awake and remains unmoved when such suggestions are urged on it? Is it closed up when my eyes are closed? Is it lulled asleep with the senses of the body? But whence is it that often, even in sleep, we resist and, mindful of our purpose and continuing most chastely in it, give no assent to such enticements? And there is yet so much difference that, when it happens otherwise, upon waking we return to peace of conscience, and by this very difference in the two states, discover that it was not we who did it, while we feel sorry that in some way it was done in us.

Is not your hand able, O Almighty God, to heal all the diseases of my soul and by your more abundant grace able to quench even the lascivious motions of my sleep? You will increase your gifts in me more and more, Lord, that my soul may follow me to you, disengaged from the bird-lime of lust; that it may not be in rebellion against itself, and may not commit in dreams through these sensual images those debasing corruptions, even to pollution of the flesh, nor give consent to them. For it is not too hard for the Almighty to work this—that nothing of this sort should have the very least influence over the pure affections of a sleeper, not even so slight a one as a thought might hold back—not just sometime during this life, but even at my present age, for you are *able to do more than we can ask or think*. But what I still am in this kind of evil, I have confessed to my good Lord, rejoicing with trembling in that which you have given me, and bemoaning that in which I am still imperfect; trusting that you will perfect your mercies in me, even to fullness of peace, which my outward and inward man shall have with you, when *death is swallowed up in victory*.

THIRTY-ONE

There is another *evil of the day*, which I wish were *sufficient* unto it. For by eating and drinking we repair the daily decays of the body, until you *destroy both food and belly*, when you shall slay my emptiness with a wonderful fullness, and clothe this corruptible with an eternal incorruption. But for the present, necessity is sweet to me, and I fight against this sweetness lest I be taken captive by it. I carry on a daily war by fastings, often bringing my body into subjection. And my pains are expelled by pleasure. For hunger and thirst are, in a manner, pains. They burn and kill like a fever unless the medicine of nourishment comes to relieve us. Since they are readily at hand from the comfort we receive through your gifts (with which land, water and air serve our weakness), our calamity is called pleasure.

This much you have taught me, that I should train myself to take food as medicine. But while I am passing from the discomfort of emptiness to the satisfaction of fullness, in that very passage the snare of lust lies in wait for me. For that passage itself is pleasurable; there is no other way to pass to that state of fullness, and necessity forces us to pass. And although health is the reason for eating and drinking, yet a dangerous delight accompanies it, and frequently tries to control it in order that I may do for enjoyment's sake what I say I do, or wish to do, for health's sake. Health and pleasure do not have the same limits. What is enough for health is too little for pleasure. And it is often questionable whether it is the necessary care of the body which still asks nourishment, or whether a sensual snare of desire wants to be served. In this uncertainty, my unhappy soul rejoices and prepares in it an excuse to shield itself, glad that it is not clearly apparent what would suffice for the moderation of health, so that under the cloak of health it may conceal the business of pleasure. These temptations I try to resist daily, and I call your right hand to my aid, and refer my perplexities to you, because as yet I have no clear resolution in this matter.

I hear the voice of my God commanding, *Let not your heart be overcharged with immoderate indulgence and drunkenness.* Drunkenness is far from me; you will have mercy that it may never come near me. But overeating sometimes creeps up on your servant; you will have mercy that it may depart from me. For no man can be continent unless you give it. You give us many things that we pray for, and whatever good we have received before we prayed, we received it from you. Yes, we received it from you that we might afterward know that we received it from you. I was never a drunkard, but I have known drunkards who were made sober by you. It was from you, then, that they who never were drunkards might not be so, and it was your gift that both might know that it was from you.

I heard another voice of yours: "Do not follow your lusts and refrain yourself from your pleasures." And by your grace I have heard that which I have greatly loved: *Neither if we eat are we the better; nor if we do not eat are we the worse.* Which is to say, neither shall the one make me abound, nor the other make me miserable. I heard another also: *For I have learned in whatever state I am, therewith to be content; I know how to abound and how to suffer need. I can do all things through Christ who strengthens me.* See there a soldier of the heavenly camp—the dust as we are. But remember, Lord, *that we are dust,* and that of dust you have made man, and *he was lost and is found.* He [Paul] could not do this by his own strength, because he whom I so love who said these things through the breath of your inspiration, was made of the same dust. He says, *I can do all things through him who strengthens me.* Strengthen me, that I may be able; grant what you command, and command what you will. He confesses to have received, and when he glories, he glories in the Lord. Another person I have heard begging that he might receive: "Take from me," he says, "the greediness of the belly." From this it appears to me, O my holy God, that when that is done which you command, it is by your gift that it is done.

You have taught me, good Father, that *to the pure all things are pure*; but that it is *evil to the man who gives offense in eating.* And that *every creature of yours is good,* and *nothing is to be refused which is received with thanksgiving;* and that *food does not commend us to God,* and that *no man should judge us in food or drink;* that he *who eats should not despise him who does not eat;* and that he *who does not eat should not judge him who eats.* These things have I learned, thanks and praise be to you, my God, my Master, knocking at the door of my ears, enlightening my heart, delivering me out of all temptation. I do not fear the uncleanness of food, but the uncleanness of lust. I know that Noah was permitted to eat all kinds of flesh that was good for food. I know also that Elijah was fed with flesh; that John, endued with a wonderful abstinence, was not polluted by eating locusts alive, which he fed on. I know, too, that Esau was deceived by craving lentils, and that David blamed himself for desiring a drink of water; and that our King was tempted, not by flesh, but bread. Therefore the people in the wilderness deserved to be reproved, too—not so much for desiring flesh, but because, in their desire for food, they murmured against the Lord.

Placed, then, amid these temptations, I strive daily against lust for food and drink. For it is not the kind [of temptation] that I can resolve to cut off once and for all, and never touch it afterward, as I did with fornication. The bridle of the throat, therefore, is to be held moderately between slackness and strictness. And who is he, O Lord, who is not carried in some degree beyond the bounds of necessity in it? Whoever he is, he is a great one! Let him magnify your name. But I am not such a one, for *I am a sinful man.* Yet I, too, magnify your name, and he who has *overcome the world* makes intercession to you for my sins, numbering me among the weak members of his body, because *your eyes have looked on my imperfect being and in your book shall all be written.*

THIRTY-TWO

I am not greatly concerned with all the attractions of sweet scents. When they are absent, I do not miss them; when they are present, I do not refuse them, yet am ready to be without them. So I seem to myself, though possibly I am deceived. For that is also a lamentable darkness which conceals my capabilities from me, so that my mind, inquiring into itself concerning its own powers, does not readily dare to believe itself, because even what is already in it is largely concealed unless it is exposed by experience. And no one ought to be secure in this life, the whole of which is called a temptation, so that he who has been made better from worse may also from better be made worse. Our only hope, our only confidence, our only assured promise, is your mercy.

THIRTY-THREE

The delights of the ear had more firmly entangled and conquered me, but you have unbound and liberated me. Now, I still find some repose in those melodies into which your words breathe soul, when they are sung with a sweet and trained voice. Yet I do not allow myself to be held by them, for I can disengage myself from them when I wish. But with the words which are the life of such melodies and by which they gain admission into me, they seek a place of some honor in my heart, and I can scarcely assign them a fitting one. For at times I seem to myself to give them more honor than is proper, sensing that our minds are more devoutly and fervently inflamed in devotion by the holy words themselves when they are sung this way, than when they are not. I notice that the different emotions of my spirit, by their sweet variety, have their appropriate expressions in the voice and singing, by some hidden relationship which stirs them up. But this gratification of my flesh, which must not be allowed to take control over my mind, often beguiles me.

My feelings do not serve reason, so as to follow it patiently, but after having gained admission for the sake of reason, strive to grab the reins and take the lead. Thus in these things I sin without knowing it, but realize it afterward.

At other times, anxiously shunning this very deception, I err by being too strict, and sometimes to the degree of wishing to have every melody of sweet music to which David's Psalter is often sung banished both from my ears and from the Church itself. That way seems safer which I remember having often heard was followed by Athanasius, bishop of Alexandria. He made the reader of the psalm utter it with such a slight inflection of the voice that it was more like speaking than singing. Yet, again, when I remember the tears I shed at the songs of your Church in the early days of my recovered faith, and how even now I am moved not by the singing, but by what is being sung, when they are sung with a clear voice and skillful modulation, I recognize once more the great usefulness of this practice. Thus I vacillate between the perilous pleasure and proved soundness—inclined rather to approve the custom of singing in the church (though not pronouncing it as an irrevocable opinion), so that the weaker minds may rise to the feeling of devotion by the delight of the ears. Yet when I happen to be more moved by the singing than by what is being sung, I confess that I have sinned gravely, and then would rather not have heard the singing. See my condition now! Weep with me and weep for me, you who can so control your inward feelings that good results follow. For you who do not act this way, these things do not concern you. But O my God, hear me and look upon me, and have mercy on me and heal me, you in whose presence I have become a puzzle to myself; and *this is my infirmity*.

THIRTY-FOUR

There remain the delights of these eyes of my flesh, about which to make my confession in the hearing of the ears of your temple, those brotherly and devout ears, and so to conclude the temptations of *the lust of the flesh* which still assault me, as I groan earnestly, *desiring to be clothed upon with my house from heaven.*

My eyes love beautiful and varied forms, and bright and soft colors. Let these not occupy my soul; let God rather possess it, who made these things *very good* indeed—for he is my Good, not these. Yes, these affect me during the whole waking day. No rest is given me from them, as there sometimes is in silence from music and from all voices. For that queen of colors, the light, flooding all we look upon, wherever I am during the day, gliding past me in various forms, soothes me when I am busied about other things and not noticing it. And it entwines itself so strongly, that, if it is suddenly withdrawn, I look longingly for it, and if it is long absent, my mind is saddened.

O Light that Tobias saw when, with his eyes closed in blindness, he taught his son the way of life, and led the way himself with the feet of charity, never going astray. Or that Light which Isaac saw when, his bodily eyes so dim by reason of old age that he could not see, it was granted him to bless his sons without knowing which was which, but in blessing them to know them. Or which Jacob saw, blind through great age but with an illumined heart, when he shed light upon the different races of people yet to come—foreshown in the persons of his sons—and he laid his hands, mystically crossed, on his grandchildren, the sons of Joseph, not as their father by his outward eye corrected them, but as he himself inwardly discerned them. This is the true Light, the only one, and all who see and love it are one. But that corporeal light of which I spoke seasons the life of this world for those who blindly love it with an enticing and fatal sweetness. They who know how to praise you for this earthly light,

"O God, Creator of All," and sing of it in your hymns, but are not taken up with it in their sleep. Such I desire to be. I resist these seductions of the eyes, lest my feet by which I walk on your path be entangled. And I lift up my inward eyes to you, that you would be pleased to *pluck my feet out of the snare*. You do repeatedly pluck them out, for they are entangled. You do not cease to pluck them out, but I constantly remain fast in the snares set round me on all sides. For you *shall neither slumber nor sleep, who keep Israel.*

What innumerable things, made by various arts and products, in our clothing, shoes, vessels and every kind of work, in pictures, too, and various images—and these far in excess of all necessary and moderate use, and all devotional significance, men have added for the enthrallment of their own eyes! Outwardly they follow what they make themselves, and inwardly forsake him by whom they themselves were made—yes, and destroying that which he made in them!

I also sing a hymn to you, my God and my Joy, for these things, and offer a sacrifice of praise to my Sanctifier for all those beautiful designs which pass through men's minds and are conveyed to artistic hands, coming from that Beauty which is above our souls, which my soul sighs after day and night. But as for the makers and followers of those outward beauties, they derive from that Beauty their power of judging them, but not of using them. And this power, too, is there, though they do not see it, so they might not wander, but keep their strength for you and not dissipate it on delicious lassitudes. And though I speak this way and see this, I, too, get my steps entangled with these outward beauties, but you rescue me. O Lord, you rescue me, *because your lovingkindness is ever before my eyes*. For I am caught miserably, but you rescue me mercifully. Sometimes I am not even aware of this, not having become wholly entangled. At other times, the rescue is painful, because I was held fast in them.

THIRTY-FIVE

To this is added another form of temptation, more complex in its peril. For besides the *lust of the flesh*, which lies in the gratification of all our senses and pleasures, whose slaves wander far from you, are wasted and perish, the soul has, through those same bodily senses, a certain vain and curious desire, cloaked under the name of knowledge and learning—not delighting in the flesh, but in making experiments through the flesh. This longing, since it originates in an appetite for knowledge, and since sight is the sense mainly used to acquire knowledge, is called in divine language *the lust of the eyes*. For seeing properly belongs to the eye, yet we use this word in connection with the other senses, too, when we exercise them in the search for knowledge. For we do not say, "Listen how it glows!" or "Smell how it glistens," or "Taste how it shines," or "Feel how it gleams," for all these are said to be seen. Yet we not only say, "See how it shines," which the eyes alone can perceive; but we also say, "See how it sounds, see how it smells, see how it tastes, and see how hard it is." And so the general experience of the senses, as we said, is called *the lust of the eyes*, because the office of seeing, though properly belonging to the eyes, is applied to the other senses by analogy when they seek after any knowledge.

By this it may be more clearly discerned when the object of the senses is pleasure and when it is curiosity. For pleasure seeks objects that are beautiful, melodious, fragrant, tasty, soft; but curiosity, for the sake of novelty, seeks the very opposite as well, not in order to experience their trouble, but from the passion of experimenting and knowing.

What pleasure is there to see in a mangled corpse that which makes you shudder? And yet, if it is lying near, we flock to it, to be made sad and to turn pale. They fear they will see it in their sleep, as if anyone had forced them to look at it when they were awake, or any report of its beauty had attracted them to it! Thus it is also with the other senses, which would take too long to go through. From this malady of curiosity come all those strange sights exhibited in the theater. From it men go on to search out the secret powers of nature (which do not pertain to us) which to know brings no profit, and which men desire to know simply for the sake of knowing. From this malady, too, with the same goal of gaining perverted knowledge, we consult the magical arts. Even in religion itself God is tempted when signs and wonders are demanded of him—not desired for any saving purpose, but merely to make trial of him.

In such a vast wilderness as this, full of snares and dangers, I have cut many of them off and thrust them out of my heart, as you have given me power to do, O God of my salvation. Yet when do I dare say—since so many things of this kind buzz on all sides about our daily life—when do I dare say that nothing of this sort engages my attention or causes an idle interest in me? True, the theaters no longer carry me away nowadays, nor do I care to know the courses of the stars, nor did my soul ever consult departed spirits. I detest all unhallowed rites. But yet, O Lord my God, to whom I owe humble and single-hearted service, by what subtlety of suggestion does the enemy tempt me to require some sign from you! But I beseech you by our King, and by our pure and holy country Jerusalem, that as any consent on my part to such thoughts is far from me, so may it ever be farther and farther. But when I pray to you for the salvation of anyone, my goal and intention is far different. For you do what you will, and you give me the grace and will give me the grace to follow you willingly.

Nevertheless, in how many petty and contemptible things is our curiosity tempted daily, and who can recount how often we give in to it? How often, when people are telling idle tales, do we begin, as if we were tolerating them to keep from offending the weak, and then gradually begin to take an interest in them! I do not go nowadays to the circus to see a dog chasing a hare, but if by chance I pass such a chase in the field, it may distract me even from some serious thought, and draw me after it—not that I turn aside the body of my horse, but by the inclination of my mind. And unless you, reminding me of my weakness, speedily warn me to lift my thoughts to you above the sight, or to despise it wholly and pass on by, I, vain creature that I am, will stand gazing at it.

When sitting at home, my attention is often distracted by a lizard catching flies, or by a spider entangling flies as they rush into her web. Is the feeling of curiosity different because they are but small creatures? I go on from such distractions to praise you, the wonderful Creator and Disposer of all things; but that is not what first attracts my attention. It is one thing to get up quickly; it is another not to fall. And of such things my life is full, and my only hope is your wonderful, great mercy. For when this heart of ours becomes the receptacle of such things, and bears multitudes of these abounding vanities, then our prayers are often interrupted and disturbed by them, and while in your presence we direct the voice of our heart to your ears, such a great concern as this is interrupted by the influx of I know not what idle thoughts.

THIRTY-SIX

Shall we, then, reckon curiosity among the things to be condemned? Or shall anything restore us to hope but your complete mercy, since you have begun to change us? And you know to what extent you have already changed me, first healing me of the lust of vindicating myself, so that you might forgive all the rest of my *iniquities* and heal all my *infirmities*, and *redeem* my life from corruption, and *crown me with tender mercies and loving-kindness*, and *satisfy* my desire *with good things*; you curbed my pride with fear and tamed my neck to your yoke. And now I bear it and it is *light* to me, because you have so promised and have so made it. And in very truth it was, but I knew it not when I feared to take it up.

But, O Lord, you alone reign without pride, because you are the only true Lord and have no lord. Tell me, has this third kind of temptation left me, or can it ever leave me throughout this lifetime—the desire to be feared and loved by men for no other purpose but that I may enjoy that which is no joy? It is a miserable life and an unseemly ostentation! From this especially it comes that we do not love you nor have a holy fear of you. And therefore you *resist the proud and give grace to the humble*. Yes, you thunder down on the ambitious designs of the world, *and the foundations of the hills tremble*.

Because certain offices of human society make it necessary for the holder to be loved and feared of men, the adversary of our true blessedness presses hard on us, spreading everywhere his snares of "Well done, well done." Greedily reaching for them, we may be caught unawares and separate our joy from your truth and fix it in the deceits of men, and take pleasure in being loved and feared—not for your sake, but in your stead. Having been made like our adversary, then, he may have us for his own, not in the harmony of charity but in the fellowship of punishment. He aspired to *exalt his throne in the north*, so that we men, dark and cold, might serve him who would become a perverse and distorted imitation of you.

But we, O Lord, lo, we are your *little flock*. Possess us as yours. Stretch your wings over us, and let us take refuge under them. Be our glory. Let us be loved for your sake and let your Word be reverenced in us. Those who desire to be praised by the men you condemn will not be defended by men when you judge, nor delivered when you pass sentence. But when—not as when the sinner is praised in the desires of his soul, nor when the unrighteous is blessed in his ungodliness—but when a man is praised for some gift which you have given him, and he is more gratified by the praise for himself than that he possesses the gift for which he is praised, such a one also is praised while you blame. Truly, the man who praised him is better than the one being praised. For the one took pleasure in the gift of God in man, while the other was better pleased with the gift of man than that of God.

THIRTY-SEVEN

We are assaulted by these temptations daily, O Lord; without ceasing we are tried. Our daily furnace is the human tongue. And in this respect, too, you command continence [self-mastery] of us. Give what you command and command what you will. You know the groanings of my heart on this matter, and the rivers that flood my eyes. For I cannot ascertain how far I am clean of this plague, and I stand in great fear of my secret faults which your eyes perceive but mine do not. For in other kinds of temptation I have some way of examining myself; in this, hardly any. For in keeping my mind from the pleasures of the flesh and from idle curiosity, I see how much I have been able to do without them, either voluntarily foregoing them or not having them available. Then I ask myself how much more or less troublesome it is to me not to have them. Riches may be desired that they may serve some one of these lusts, or two, or all three of them. If the soul cannot tell whether it despises riches when it has them, it may cast them aside so that it may prove itself in this way. But to be without praise and to test our abilities in that regard, must we live wickedly, or lead a life so abandoned and atrocious that no one could know us without detesting us? What greater madness could be said or thought? But if praise is usual, and if it ought to accompany a good life and good works, we ought to forego its company as little as we would the good life itself. Yet I cannot tell whether I shall be contented or troubled by being without something unless I am deprived of it.

What, then, do I confess to you, O Lord, in this kind of temptation? What, but that I am delighted with praise, but with truth itself more than with praise? For if it were proposed to me, whether I would rather, being mad or in error on all things, be praised by all men, or being consistent and well assured in the truth, be blamed by all, I see which I would choose. Yet I would rather that the approval of another should not even increase my joy for any good in me. I admit, though, that it does increase it, and more than that, that criticism diminishes it.

When I am troubled at this misery of mine, an excuse presents itself to me—of what value it is, only you know, O God, for it leaves me uncertain. Here it is: It is not self-control [continency] alone which you have commanded of us (that is, that we should hold back our love from certain things), but also righteousness as well (that is, upon what to bestow our love), and have wished us to love not only you but also our neighbor. Often when I am gratified by intelligent praise, I appear to myself to be pleased by the competence or insight I see in my neighbor. In the same way, I seem to be sorry for the defect in him when I hear him criticize either what he does not understand or what is good. For I am sometimes grieved at the praise I get, either when those things are praised in me which I dislike in myself, or when lesser or trifling goods are more valued than they ought to be. But again, how do I know whether I am affected like this because I do not want him who praises me to differ from me about myself—not being influenced by consideration for him, but because those same good things which please me in myself please me more when they please someone else as well? For, in a sense, I am not praised when my judgment of myself is not praised, whenever either those things which displease me are praised, or those which please me less are praised more. It seems then that I am uncertain about myself in this matter.

Behold, O Truth, in you I see that I ought not to be moved at my own praises for my own sake, but for the good of my neighbor. And whether this is so with me, I do not know. For concerning this I know less of myself than you do. I beseech you now, O my God, reveal me to myself, too, that I may confess to my brethren who are to pray for me where I find myself weak. Once again, let me examine myself more diligently. If, in the praise I receive I am moved with consideration for the good of my neighbor, why am I less moved if someone else is unjustly criticized than if it be myself? Why am I more irritated by reproach cast upon me than at that cast upon another in my presence with the same injustice? Do I not know this also? Or is it finally that I deceive myself, and do not the truth before you in my heart and speech? Put such madness far from me, O Lord, lest my own mouth be to me *the sinner's oil to anoint my head.*

THIRTY-EIGHT

I am poor and needy; yet I am better when in secret groanings I am displeased with myself and seek your mercy until what is lacking in my defective condition is renewed and made complete in that peace which the eye of the proud does not know.

The word which comes out of the mouth, and the actions known to men, bring with them a most dangerous temptation from the love of praise, which, to establish a certain glory of our own solicits and collects men's compliments. It tempts, even when I reprove myself for it within myself, on the very ground that it is reproved. Often a man glories even more vainly in his very scorn of praise. And so he is no longer avoiding vainglory when he glories in his scorn of vainglory.

THIRTY-NINE

Within us, also, is another evil, arising out of the same kind of temptation, by which men become vain, pleasing themselves in themselves, though they do not please nor displease nor aim at pleasing others. But by pleasing themselves they greatly displease you. They do not merely take pleasure in things that are not good as if they were good, but take pleasure in your good things as if they were their own; or if, acknowledging the good things to be yours, they think they deserve them, or even if they regard them as from your grace, they do not use them with brotherly rejoicing, but begrudge that same grace to others. In all these and similar perils and labors, you see the trembling of my heart. It is not so much that I never inflict these wounds on myself, as that they are ever anew healed by you.

FORTY

Where have you not walked with me, O Truth, teaching me what to avoid and what to desire when I submitted to you what I could see here below and asked your counsel? With my external senses I surveyed the world as I was able, and observed the life which my body derives from me and from these senses themselves. From this I advanced inwardly into the recesses of memory—those various and spacious chambers, wonderfully filled with unnumbered wealth. I considered and was afraid, and could discern none of these things without you, and found none of them to be you. It was not I, myself, who discovered these things, I, who went over them all and labored to distinguish and evaluate everything according to its worth, taking some things from the report of my senses, asking questions about others which I felt to be mixed up with myself, numbering and distinguishing the reporters themselves. Then, in the vast storehouse of my memory I examined some things carefully, relegating others to the background, taking out others into the light. Yet it was not myself who did these things—that is, the power by which I did them was not my own. Nor was it you, for you are the unfailing light which I consulted concerning all these things, as to whether they were, what they were, and what their real value was. And I heard you teaching and commanding me. And this I often do. It delights me, as far as I can be freed from necessary duties, to have recourse to this pleasure.

But in all these which I go over in consultation with you, I can find no safe place for my soul but in you, in whom all my scattered members may be gathered, so that nothing about me may depart from you. And sometimes you introduce me to a most rare affection in my inmost soul, an inexplicable sweetness that seems to have nothing in it that would not belong to the life to come if it were perfected in me. But by these wretched weights of mine, I relapse again into these lower things, am swept back by my old customs, and am held. I weep greatly, yet I am greatly held. To such an extent does the burden of bad habits weigh us down. I can stay in this condition, but I would not; I would stay there, but I cannot; in both ways, I am miserable.

FORTY-ONE

And thus I have reflected on the weariness of my sins in that threefold lust, and have called your right hand to my help. For with a wounded heart I have seen your brightness, and being beaten back, I said, "Who can attain to it? *I am cut off from before your eyes!*" You are the Truth who presides over all things, but I, through my covetousness, would not indeed forego you, but wished to possess a lie along with you, as no one wishes to speak so falsely as to be ignorant of the truth itself. So then, I lost you, because you do not deign to be enjoyed along with a lie.

FORTY-TWO

Whom could I find to reconcile me to you? Was I to solicit angels? By what prayers? By what sacraments? Many seeking to return to you, and not able of themselves, have, as I hear, tried this, have fallen into a desire for curious visions, and have been deemed worthy to be deluded. For they, being exalted, sought you by the pride of learning, thrusting themselves forward instead of beating their breasts. And so, by a correspondence of heart, they drew to themselves the princes of the air, as conspirators and allies of their pride, by whom through the power of magic they were deceived—seeking a mediator by whom they might be cleansed and *there was none.* For it was the devil himself, *transforming himself into an angel of light.* And he allured proud flesh all the more in that he was without a fleshly body. For they were mortal and sinful; but you, Lord, to whom they proudly sought to be reconciled, are immortal and sinless. But a mediator between God and man must have something in him like God, something in him like men, lest being only like man, he should be far from God, and being only like God, should be too unlike man and so not a mediator. In your secret judgment, then, pride deserved to be deluded by that deceitful mediator who has one thing in common with man: that is sin. Another he would appear to have in common with God: not being clothed with the mortality of flesh, and so would boast himself to be immortal. But since the *wages of sin is death*, this he has in common with mankind, that with them he is condemned to death.

FORTY-THREE

But the true Mediator, whom you have pointed out to the humble in your secret mercy, and sent, that by his example they too might learn that same humility—that *Mediator between God and man, the Man Christ Jesus*, appeared between mortal sinners and the immortal Just One—mortal, as men are mortal; just, as God is just; so that because the wages of righteousness is life and peace, he might cancel the death of justified sinners by a righteousness united with God. He was willing to undergo death in common with them. Hence he was shown forth to holy men of old, so that they, through faith in his Passion to come, even as we through faith in it as already past, might be saved. For as Man, he was Mediator; but as the Word, he was not in the middle between God and man, because he was equal to God, and God with God, and together with the Holy Spirit, one God.

How you have loved us, good Father, who spared not your only Son, but delivered him up for us wicked ones! How you have loved us, for whom he *did not count it robbery to be equal with you, but became obedient unto death, even the death of the cross!* He alone was free among the dead, having power to lay down his life and power to take it up again. For us he was both Victor and Victim, Victor because he was the Victim. He was Priest and Sacrifice for us, and Priest because he was Sacrifice, making us sons to you instead of slaves, by being born himself your Son [in his incarnation], and becoming our slave. Rightly, then, is my hope strongly fixed in him that you will heal all my infirmities by him who *sits at your right hand and makes intercession for us.* Otherwise I should despair. For many and great are my infirmities, many they are and great! But your medicine is greater. We might think that your Word was far from any union with mankind, and despair of ourselves if he had not been made flesh and dwelt among us.

Terrified by my sins and the load of my misery, I had resolved in my heart and had purposed to flee into the wilderness. But you forbade me and strengthened me, saying, *Since Christ died for all, they who live should no longer live unto themselves but unto him who died for them.* See, Lord, I cast all my care upon you, that I may live and *behold wondrous things out of your law*. You know my unskillfulness and my infirmities: teach me and heal me. He, your only Son, *in whom are hid all the treasures of wisdom and knowledge*, has redeemed me with his blood. Let not the proud speak evil of me, because I consider my ransom, and eat and drink and minister it to others. And being poor, I desire to be satisfied with that Food together with those who eat and are satisfied. And *they that seek him shall praise the Lord*.

BOOK XI

Inquiry into Creation and Time

ONE

Lord, since eternity is yours, are you ignorant of what I say to you? Or do you see in time what comes to pass in time? Why, then, do I lay before you so many narrations of such things? Not, surely, that you might learn them through me, but that I might awaken my own love and my readers' devotion toward you, that we may all say, *Great is the Lord, and greatly to be praised.* I have said already, and I will say again, I do this for the love of your love. For we pray also, and yet Truth has said, *your Father knows what things you need before you ask him.* Consequently, it is our love that we lay open to you, confessing to you our own miseries and your mercies upon us, that you may wholly free us, since you have begun, so that we may cease to be wretched in ourselves and be blessed in you—since you have called us to become poor in spirit, meek, mourners, and hungering and athirst for righteousness, merciful, pure in heart and peacemakers. Behold, I have told you as many things as I could and had the will to do, because it was first your will that I should confess to you, my Lord God, for *you are good, and your mercy endures forever.*

TWO

But how shall I be able with the voice of my pen to express all your exhortations, all your terrors, comforts and guidances by which you led me to preach your Word and minister your Sacrament to your people? If I could utter them in order, the drops of time are precious to me. I have long yearned to meditate on your Law and to confess my knowledge and ignorance of it to you, the daybreak of your enlightenment and the remnants of my darkness, *until weakness is swallowed up in strength.* And I would not have anything else take away those hours which I find free from the necessity of refreshing my body and the powers of my mind, and of the service which we owe to men, and which, though we do not owe them, yet we pay.

O Lord my God, hear my prayer and let your mercy regard my desire, because it is not for myself alone, but it desires to serve brotherly charity. You see into my heart, that this is true. I would sacrifice to you the service of my thought and tongue. Give me what I may offer you, *for I am poor and needy. You are rich to all who call upon you*, and while you are free from all care, still you care for us. Circumcise from all rashness and all falsehood, both my inward and outward lips. Let your Scriptures be my chaste delight. Let me not be deceived in them, nor deceive others in them. Hear and pity, O Lord my God, Light of the blind, and Strength of the weak—yes, also Light of those who see, and Strength of the strong. Hearken to my soul and hear it crying *out of the depths*, for if your ears are not open to us in the depths also, where shall we go? To whom shall we call?

The day is yours and the night is yours. At your bidding the moments fly past. Grant, then, space for our meditations in the hidden things of your Law, and do not close it against us who knock. For you would not have the obscure secrets of so many pages written in vain. Nor are those forests without their deer, who retire in them, and range and walk, feed, lie down and ruminate. Perfect me, O Lord, and reveal them to me. Behold your voice is my joy. Your voice exceeds the abundance of pleasures. Give what

I love, for I do love, and this love you have given. Forsake not your own gifts, and do not despise your grass that thirsts for you. Let me confess to you whatever I shall find in your books, and let me *hear the voice of praise*. Let me drink of you and *meditate on the wonderful things out of your Law*, from the beginning when you *made the heaven and the earth*, even to the everlasting reign of your holy city with you.

Lord, have mercy on me and hear my desire, for I believe it is not for the earth, nor for gold and silver, precious stones, nor gorgeous apparel, honors and offices, nor for the pleasures of the flesh, nor necessities of the body, nor for this life of our pilgrimage. All these things *are added to those who seek your kingdom and your righteousness*.

Behold, O Lord, from whence my desire comes. The wicked have told me of delights, but not as your law. See, Father, behold and see and approve, and may it be pleasing in the sight of your mercy, that I may find grace before you, that the secret meanings of your Word be opened to my knock. I beseech you by our Lord Jesus Christ your Son. He is *the Man of your right hand, the Son of Man, whom you made strong for yourself* as your Mediator between you and us, by whom you sought us when we were not seeking you, but sought us that we might seek you. He is your Word, *through whom you made all things*, and among them, me also. He is your only begotten Son, through whom you called your believing people to adoption, and among them me also. I beseech you by him who sits at your right hand and *makes intercession for us, in whom are hidden all the treasures of wisdom and knowledge*. I seek these treasures in your Books. Moses wrote of him; this he says himself. This he says who is Truth.

THREE

Let me hear and understand how *in the beginning you made the heaven and earth*. Moses wrote this, wrote and departed, passed hence from you to you. He is no longer before me. For if he were, I would hold him and ask him, and beseech him by yourself to open these things to me, and lend my physical ears to the sounds coming from his mouth. If he should speak Hebrew, the sounds would fall on my ears in vain; none of it would touch my mind. But if he spoke in Latin, I would know what he said. But how would I know that he spoke the truth? Yes, and if I knew this as well, would I know it from him? No. Verily within me, within the chamber of my thought, Truth—neither Hebrew nor Greek, neither Latin nor barbarian—without the organs of voice or tongue, without the sound of syllables, would say, "He speaks the truth." Then I would say confidently to that man of yours, "You speak truthfully." But, since I cannot inquire of him, I beseech you—you, O Truth, full of whom he spoke truth—you, my God, I beseech to forgive my sins, and as you gave him to speak these things, grant me also to understand them.

FOUR

Behold, the heavens and the earth *are*. They proclaim that they were made, for they change and vary. On the other hand, whatever is, but has not been created, has nothing in it now which was not there before. This is what it is to change and vary, that something is there that was not there before. They also proclaim that they did not make themselves. "We are because we have been made; we did not exist before we existed, and therefore could not have made ourselves." Now the evidence of the thing is the voice of the speakers. Therefore, Lord, you made them. You are beautiful, for they are beautiful. You are good, for they are good. You are, because they exist. Yet they are not beautiful and good in the same way that you their Creator are, nor do they have being as you do. Compared with you, they are not beautiful nor good nor do they have being. This we know, thanks to you, and yet our knowledge, compared with yours, is ignorance.

FIVE

But how did you make the heaven and the earth, and what was your instrument of so mighty a work? For it was not as a human worker, forming one body from another according to the fancy of his mind, who can in some way give it such a form as he sees in his mind by an inward eye. And from where would he be able to do this, if you had not made that mind? And he gives a form to something that already exists and has being—such as clay, stone, wood, gold or the like. And where should these things come from, if you had not supplied them? You made the workman's body for him; his mind able to command his limbs; the material of which he makes anything; the capacity to understand his art and to see inwardly what he does outwardly; the senses of his body, by which as by an interpreter, he may convey what he does from mind to the material, and report it back, so that his mind may consult the truth which presides within it, whether it is done well or not.

All these things praise you, the Creator of all. But how did you make them? How, O God, did you make heaven and earth? Truly, neither in the heaven nor in the earth did you make heaven and earth, nor in the air, nor waters, since these also belong to the heaven and the earth; nor did you make the whole world in the whole world, because there was no place where it could be made before it was made. Nor did you have anything in your hand out of which to make heaven and earth. For where could you obtain what you had not made, of which to make anything? Does anything exist, except by the fact that you are? Therefore you spoke and they were made, and in your Word you made them.

SIX

But how did you speak? Was it in the manner of the voice that came out of the cloud, saying, *This is my beloved Son*? For that voice was uttered and passed away, began and ended. The syllables sounded and vanished, the second after the first, the third after the second, and so on, in order, until the last followed all the rest, and then silence. From this it is clear and plain that the action of a creature spoke it, the creature itself temporal, obeying your eternal will. And these your words, formed at the time, the outward ear reported to the intelligent mind whose inward ear lay attentive to your eternal Word. But the mind compared these words sounding in time with your eternal Word in silence, and said, "It is different, far different. These words are far beneath me, nor are they real, because they flee and vanish; but *the Word of the Lord abides* above me *for ever*." If, then, in sounding and passing words you said that the heaven and earth should be made, and made heaven and earth in this way, there was already a corporeal creature before heaven and earth, by whose temporal motions that voice might take its course in time. But there was nothing corporeal before heaven and earth—or if there were, surely without such a passing voice you had created something through which to make this passing voice, by which to say that the heaven and earth should be made. For whatever such a voice was made of, unless it was made by you, it could not exist at all. By what Word of yours was it decreed that a bodily thing be made by which those passing words could be uttered?

SEVEN

You call us, then, to understand the Word, the God who is God with you, which is spoken eternally, and by which all things are spoken eternally. For what was spoken was not finished and another spoken until all was spoken; but all things at the same time and forever. Otherwise, we have time and change, and not a true eternity nor true immortality. This I know, O my God, and give thanks. I know, I confess to you, O Lord, and whoever is thankful for assured truth knows and blesses you with me. We know, Lord, we know this much: that to the same degree that anything is not what it was, and is what it was not, it dies and comes into existence. But there is nothing of your Word that becomes something or passes away, because it is truly immortal and eternal. Therefore to the Word co-eternal with you, you say at once and forever all that you say; and whatever you say shall be made, is made; nor do you create in any way other than by speaking. Yet all things which you make by speaking are not made at once or forever.

EIGHT

Why is this, I ask you, O Lord my God? In a way I see it, but I do not know how to express it, unless it is that whatever begins to be, and then ceases to be, begins when it does and ceases when your eternal Reason knows that it ought to begin or cease. In your Reason nothing begins or ceases. This your Word, *the Beginning*, also speaks to us. Thus in the Gospel he [the Word] speaks through the flesh, and this is heard outwardly in the ears of men that he might be believed and sought inwardly, and that he might be found in the eternal Truth where the one good Teacher teaches all his disciples. There, Lord, I hear the voice of One speaking to me, since he who teaches us so that we understand really speaks to us. But one who does not teach us, although he speaks, does not truly speak to us. Moreover, who teaches us now, but the unchangeable Truth? For when we are admonished through a changeable creature, we are only led to the unchangeable Truth. There we truly learn while we stand and hear him, and *we rejoice greatly because of the Bridegroom's voice*, restoring us to the Source from which we came. Therefore unless *the Beginning* remained unchangeable, there would be nothing to return to when we had strayed. But when we return from error, it is by knowing that we return. But that we may know, he teaches us, because he is *the Beginning* and is speaking to us.

NINE

In this Beginning, O God, you have made heaven and earth, in your Word, in your Son, in your Power, in your Wisdom, in your Truth: wondrously speaking and wondrously creating. Who shall comprehend it? Who can declare it? What is that which gleams through me and strikes my heart without injury, making me shudder and burn? I shudder inasmuch as I am unlike it, and I burn inasmuch as I am like it. It is Wisdom itself that shines through me, clearing my cloudiness which so readily overwhelms me, causing me to shrink from it through the darkness which my punishment brings upon me. For my strength is brought down in need, so that I cannot endure my blessings until you, O Lord, who have been gracious to all my iniquities, heal all my infirmities. For you shall also *redeem* my life *from corruption, and crown* me *with loving kindness and tender mercies*, and *shall satisfy my desire with good things, so that my youth shall be renewed like the eagle's. For we are saved in hope*; and *through patience we wait for your promises*. Let him who is able, hear you inwardly speaking. I will boldly cry out from your Word, *How wonderful are your works, O Lord. In wisdom you have made them all.* And this wisdom is the Beginning, and in that *Beginning* you *made heaven and earth.*

TEN

Lo, are they not full of their old way who say to us, "What was God doing before he made heaven and earth?" "For if," they say, "he were unemployed and did nothing, why does he not also cease from working forever, as he did in times past? For if any new motion or a new will has arisen in God, to make a creation which he had never made before, how then would that be a true eternity, where a will emerges which was not there before? For the will of God is not a creature, but is prior to the creation—since nothing could be created unless the will of the Creator had preceded it. The will of God then, belongs to his very substance. But if anything has emerged in God's substance which was not there before, then his substance cannot be truly called eternal. But if it was the will of God from eternity that the creation should exist, why was not the creation also from eternity?"

ELEVEN

Those who speak in this way do not yet understand you, O Wisdom of God, Light of the soul. They do not yet understand how the things are made which are made by you and in you; yet they strive to comprehend eternal things, but their heart flits between the movements of things past and things to come, and is still wavering. Who shall hold it, and fix it, that it may rest awhile and then by degrees catch the glory of that eternity that stands for ever, and compare it with the times which are never stable, and see that it is incomparable; and that a long time cannot become long except by the many motions that pass by, which cannot all pass at the same time; but that in the Eternal, nothing passes away, but all is present? On the other hand, no time is all present at once, and the past is forced on by the future, and all the future follows upon the past; and all past and future time is created and flows out of that which is always present. Who will hold the heart of man, that it may stand still and see how eternity, always standing still, utters past and future times, but is itself neither past nor future? Can my hand accomplish this, or can the instrument of my mouth by persuasive speech bring about a thing so great?

TWELVE

Behold, I answer him who asks, "What did God do before he made heaven and earth?" I do not answer as one is reported to have done facetiously (avoiding the pressure of the question), "He was preparing hell for those who pry into his mysteries!" It is one thing to answer questions, another to make fun of the questioner. So I have no answer. For I had rather say, "I do not know what I do not know," than to answer in a way that raises a laugh at him who asks deep things, and gain praise for a false answer. But I say that you, our God, are the Creator of every creature. And if by the name *heaven and earth* every creature is included, I boldly say that before God made heaven and earth, he did not make anything. For if he created, what did he make but a creature? And would that I knew all that I desire to know for my profit as well as I know that no creature was made before any creature was made!

THIRTEEN

But if the roving thought of anyone should wander over the images of bygone times, and wonder that you, the omnipotent

God, the All-creating, All-supporting Architect of heaven and earth, refrained for innumerable ages from so great a work before you would create it, let him wake up and consider that he wonders at a faulty concept. From where could innumerable ages come, which you have not made, since you are the Author and Creator of all ages? Or what times should there be which were not created by you? Or how should they pass by if they had never been? Since you are the Creator of all times, if any time was before you made heaven and earth, why do they say that you refrained from working? For you made that very time, nor could times pass by before you had made those times. But if there was no time before heaven and earth, why is it asked what you did *then*? For there was no *then* when time was not.

Nor do you precede time by time—else you would not precede all times. But you precede all times past by the excellency of an ever-present eternity, and you outlast all future times, because they are future, and when they have come, they shall be past. But you are the same, and your years fail not. Your years neither come nor go; but ours both come and go, that all of them may come. All your years stand at once, since they abide. The departing ones are not excluded by the coming years, because they do not pass away. But these years of ours shall all be until they are no more. Your years are as one day; and your day is not daily, but today, because your today does not give way to tomorrow, not does it follow yesterday. Your today is eternity. Therefore you begat the Co-eternal, to whom you said, *This day have I begotten you.* You have made all time, and you are before all time, and there was never a time when time was not.

FOURTEEN

At no time, then, had you not made anything, because you made time itself. And no times are co-eternal with you, because you remain for ever; but if times remained they would not be times.

For what is time? Who can readily and briefly explain this? Who can, even in thought, comprehend it sufficiently to express himself clearly concerning it? But what do we mention in conversation more familiarly and knowingly than time? And we certainly understand it when we speak of it. We understand it, too, when someone else speaks of it. What, then, is time? If no one asks me, I know. If I wish to explain it to one who asks, I do not know. Yet I say boldly that I know that if nothing passed away there would be no time past. And if nothing were coming, there would be no future time. And if there were nothing, there would be no present time. Those two times, then, past and future—how are they, when the past is no longer and the future is not yet? But should the present always be present and never pass into time past, truly it would not be time, but eternity. If, then, the very condition of the present's being "time" is that it passes away into the past, how can we assert the existence of that whose only cause of *being* is that it shall *not be*—so that in truth we assert the present to be time only because it tends toward *not-being*?

FIFTEEN

And yet we speak of a long time and a short time—but only of time past or future. For example we call a hundred years ago a long time past, and a hundred years hence a long time to come. A short time past we call, say, ten days ago, and a short time to come, ten days hence. But in what sense is something long or short which does not exist? For the past is not now, and the future is not yet. Let us not say of the past then, "It is long," but rather, "It has been long"; and of the future, "It will be long." And yet, O Lord, my Light, will your truth not mock at man even here also? For that past time which was long, was it long when it was already past, or when it was still present? For then it might have been long when there was something that could be long, but when it is past, it no longer was—so what did not exist could not be long. Let us not say therefore that a past time was long; for we shall not find in past time anything capable of being long, since once it was past it was no more. Let us say instead that that present time was long, because when it was present, it *was* long. For it had not yet passed away so as not to be, and therefore there was something that could be called long. But after it passed into what *was not*, it also ceased to be long.

Let us see then, O human soul, whether present time can be long. For it is given to you to feel and measure periods of time. How will you answer me? Are a hundred years when present a long time? See, first, whether a hundred years can be present. For if the first of these years is now current, that is present, but the other ninety-nine are future, and therefore are not as yet. But if the second year is current, the first is already past, another present, the rest future. And so if we assume any middle year of this hundred as present, those prior to it are past, and those after it are future. Therefore a hundred years cannot be present all at once.

But see at least whether the current year itself can be present. For if the current month is its first, the rest are future; if the second, the first is already past, and the others are future. Therefore neither is the current year present as a whole. For a year has twelve months, and whatever month is now current is itself present, and the rest are either past or future. But even that current month is not present as a whole, but only one day—the rest being future if it is the first day, or past, if it is the last; any other day of the month stands between the past and future.

See how the present time, which alone we found could be called long, is shortened to the length scarcely of one day. But let us look at that, too, because even one day is not present as a whole. For it is made up of twenty-four hours of night and day. Of these, the first has the rest future, the last has them past, and any of the middle has those before it past and the rest future. And that one hour passes away in fleeting moments. Whatever of it has flown away is past; whatever remains, is future. If any portion of time is conceived, which cannot now be divided into even the minutest particles of moments, that alone is what may be called present. And that flies by with such speed from future to past that it cannot be lengthened out in the least, for if it is extended, it is divided between past and future. The present has no extension or length.

Where, then, is the time which we can call long? Is it future? Concerning it we do not say, "It is long," because it does not yet exist, so as to be long, but we say, "It will be long." When, then, will it be? For since it is future, it will not be long, because what could be long does not yet exist. It will be long when, from the future (which is not yet), it has begun to exist and to be present, so that there would then exist what *could* be long. But then present time cries out in the words above that it *cannot* be long.

SIXTEEN

And yet, Lord, we perceive intervals of time, and we compare them, and say that some are shorter and others are longer. We even measure how much longer or shorter this time is than that; and we answer, "This is double, or treble, while this other is but once, or only just as long as that." But we measure times as they are passing, by perceiving them. But past times, which no longer are, or future times, which are not yet, who can measure? Unless, perhaps, anyone would dare to say that what *is not* can be measured. When, therefore, time is passing, it can be perceived and measured; but when it is past, it cannot, because it is not.

SEVENTEEN

I ask, Father, I do not affirm. O my God, rule and guide me. Who will tell me that there are not three times, as we learned when we were boys, and as we taught boys, the past, present and future, but only present, because past and future do not exist? Or do they also exist, and when from the future it becomes present, does it come out of some secret place, and the same when from the present it becomes past, does it retire to something secret? For where have they, who foretold things to come, seen them if they do not yet exist? For what is not cannot be seen. And they who relate things past could not relate them if they did not perceive them in their mind, and if they were not, they could not be discerned in any way. Therefore, future and past times *are*.

EIGHTEEN

Allow me, Lord, to seek further. O my Hope, do not let my purpose be confounded. For if times past and future do exist, I want to know where they are. I realize that if I cannot know this, that wherever they are, they are not there as future or past, but as present. For if there, also, they are future, they are not as yet there. If there, also, they are past, they are no longer there. Wherever they are, whatever they may be, they are only there as present.

Although past facts are related as true, the things themselves are not drawn out of the memory (the things that have passed), but rather, words which are conceived from the images of things which they have left as traces in the mind in their passage through the senses. My childhood, for instance, which no longer exists, is in time past, which is not now. But when I recall its image and tell of it, I see it in the present, because it is still in my memory. Whether there is a similar cause in foretelling future things, so that the images of things which are not as yet can be perceived as already existing, I confess, O my God, I do not know. This indeed I do know, that we generally think ahead of time on our future actions, and that such premeditation is present, but the action which we premeditate does not yet exist, because it is in the future. When we have determined on such action and begun to do what we premeditated, then that action has being, because then it is no longer future but present.

However, then, this secret foreseeing the future may come to be, only that can be seen which actually is. But what is present is not future, but present. When, then, future things are said to be seen, it is not themselves (which do not yet exist, that is, which are yet to be) but their causes, possibly, or signs are seen—which already are. Therefore, to those who now see them they are not future but present, from which future things, conceived in the mind, are foretold. Again, these conceptions exist in the present and those who foretell these things behold these conceptions before them as present.

Let me find some example from the abundance of such circumstances as I am thinking of. I see the daybreak. I foretell that the sun is about to rise. What I see is present. What I predict is future—not the sun, which already exists, but the sunrise, which is not yet. And yet, if I did not imagine the sunrise itself in my mind (as I do now while I speak of it), I could not foretell it. But that dawn which I see in the sky is not the sunrise, although it precedes it. Nor is that imagination in my mind the sunrise. Both of these I see as present so that the other which is future may be foretold. Future things, then, are not as yet, and if they are not as yet, they simply are not. And if they do not exist, they cannot be seen at all. Yet they can be foretold from things present which already are and are seen.

NINETEEN

And so, O Ruler of your creation, how can you teach souls things to come? Certainly you did teach your prophets. How do you, to whom nothing is future, teach things to come? Or rather, of future things teach in the present? For what does not exist certainly cannot be taught. This way of yours is too far from my view: it is too mighty for me, I cannot reach it, but I will be enabled by you, when you have granted it, O sweet Light of my hidden eyes.

TWENTY

What is now clear and plain is that neither past things nor future things have any existence. Nor is it properly said, "There are three times: past, present and future." Yet possibly it might be properly said, "There are three times: a present of things past, a present of things present, and a present of future things." For these three do somehow exist in the mind, for otherwise I do not see them; there is present of things past, memory; present of things present, sight; present of things future, expectation. If we were permitted to speak in this way, I see three times, and I acknowledge that there are three. Let it be said, too, that there are three times, past, present and future, in our incorrect way. See, I do not object or contradict, or find fault, provided it is said in such a way as to be understood that neither future or past exists in the present. For we only speak properly of a few things; of most things we speak improperly—yet the things we intend are understood.

TWENTY-ONE

I have just said then, that we measure time as it passes in order to be able to say that this time is twice as much as that one; or this one is just the same as that one; and so of any other parts of time which are measurable. So, as I said, we measure times as they pass. And if anyone should ask me, "How do you know this?" I can answer, "I know because we measure it, and we cannot measure what is not; and things past and things to come are nonexistent." But present time—how do we measure it, since it has no length? It is measured while it passes, but when it has passed it is not measured, because there is nothing to be measured.

But where does it come from, how does it pass, and where does it go while it is being measured? From where, but from the future? Which way, but through the present? To where, but into the past? Therefore it is from that which is not as yet, through that which has no extension, into that which no longer is. But what do we measure if not time in some extent of length? For we do not say a single time, and twice as long, and three times as long, and as long as—or any other way we speak of time—unless we talk in terms of lengths of time. In what extent of time, then, do we measure passing time? Is it in the future, from which it is passing through? But we do not measure what does not yet exist. Or is it in the present, by which it passes? But there is no length to measure. Or in the past, into which it is passing? But neither do we measure that which no longer is.

TWENTY-TWO

My soul yearns to know the answer to this most entangled enigma. Do not shut away these familiar yet hidden things from my desire, O Lord my God, good Father; through Christ I beseech you, that my mind not be hindered from penetrating into them, but let them dawn through your enlightening mercy, O Lord. Whom shall I question concerning these things? To whom shall I more profitably confess my ignorance than to you, to whom these my studies, so ardently seeking the light of your Scriptures, are not troublesome? Give what I love: for I do love, and this [love] you have given me. Give, Father, for you truly know *how to give good gifts to your children*. Give, since I have undertaken to know, and a wearisome task confronts me until you open it up. Through Christ I beseech you in his name, Holy of Holies: let no man disturb me. For *I believed, and therefore I speak*. This is my hope, for this I live, that *I may see the joys of the Lord*. *Behold, you have made my days grow old*, and they pass away—and how, I do not know.

And we talk of time and a time, of times and times: "How long a time is it since he did this?" "How long a time since I saw that?" And "This syllable has twice as much time as that single short syllable." We speak words like these and we hear them, and we are understood and we understand. They are most clear and most ordinary; yet again, the meanings of these same things lie hidden too deeply, and their discovery would be a new thing.

TWENTY-THREE

I once heard a learned man say that the motions of the sun, moon and stars constituted time, and I did not assent to it. For why should not the motions of all bodies rather be time? Or, if the lights of heaven should cease, and a potter's wheel still turned, should there be no time by which we might measure those turnings, and say either that it moved with equal pauses, or if it turned sometimes slower, other times faster, that some revolutions were longer, some shorter? Or while we were saying this, should we not also be speaking in time? Or, how could there be some short syllables in our words, others long, unless those short ones sounded in a shorter time, these in a longer? God grant to men to see in a small thing the conceptions that are common to things both small and great. Both the stars and lights of heaven are *for signs, and for seasons, and for years and for days*. They are, without a doubt. But I would not say that the revolution of that wooden wheel was a day, nor should that learned man say that then there would be no time.

I long to know the power and the nature of time, by which we measure the motions of bodies and say, for instance, this motion is twice as long as that. For I ask, since "day" denotes not only the period of the sunlight upon the earth (according to which, day is one thing, night another), but also its whole circuit from east to east again. According to this we say, "So many days have passed," including the night when we say, "So many days." The nights are not counted apart.

Seeing, then, that a day is completed by the motions of the sun and by its circuit from east to east again, I ask, does the motion alone make the day, or the period in which that motion is completed, or both? For if the sun's passage is the day, then we should have a day even if the sun should finish that course in as small a space of time as an hour. If the period of time is what is counted to make a day, it would not make a day if, between one sunrise and another there were only as short a period as an hour. The sun would have to go round twenty-four times to complete one day. If both [the period of time and the circuit of the sun from east to east comprise one day], then that could not be called a day if the sun should run its whole circuit in one hour, nor if the sun stood still as long as it usually takes to run its whole course, from morning to morning. So I will not ask now what is called day, but what time is, for it is that by which we measure the circuit of the sun and would say that it was finished in half the usual time, if it happened to be finished in as small a period as twelve hours. Comparing both times, we would call this a single time, that a double time, as if supposing that the sun might run its round from east to east, sometimes in that single, sometimes in that double time.

Let no man tell me, then, that the motions of the heavenly bodies constitute time, because when at the prayer of one man, the sun had stood still till he could achieve victory in his battle, the sun stood still, but time went on. For that battle was waged and ended in such a space of time as was sufficient. I see, then, that time is a certain extension. But do I really see it, or only seem to see it? O Light and Truth, you will show me.

TWENTY-FOUR

Do you bid me to agree if anyone defines time to be a motion of a body? You do not so command me. For I hear that no body moves except in time. This you say. But I do not hear that the motion of the body is time. You do not say it. For when a body is moved, I measure by time how long it moves, from the time it begins to move until it ceases. And if I did not see where it began and it continued to move so that I did not see when it ended, I could not measure, save possibly from the time I began to look until I ceased to see. But if I look long, I can only say that it was a long time, but not how long; because when we say how long, we do it by comparison; as "This is as long as that," or "This is twice as long as that," or the like. But if we were able to mark the distances of the places, where it started and where it stopped, or its parts, if it moved as in a wheel, then we can say precisely how much time it took to move that body or its part from this place to that. Since the motion of the body is one thing and that by which we measure the length of the movement another, who does not see which of the two is rather to be called time? If a body is sometimes moved, and sometimes stands still, we measure not only its motion, but also its standing still by time, and we say, "It stood still as long as it moved," or "It stood still twice or three times as long as it moved," or any other period which our measuring has determined, or, roughly estimated, as we say, plus or minus. Time, then, is not the motion of a body.

TWENTY-FIVE

And I confess to you, Lord, that I do not yet know what time is, and I confess to you, O Lord, that I know that I speak this in time, and that I have already spoken a long time of time, and that very "long" is not long, but by its continuance in time. How, then, do I know this, since I do not know what time is? Or is it possibly that I do not know how to express what I know? Alas for me, that I do not even know what I do not know! Behold, O my God, before you I do not lie. As my heart is, so I speak. *You will light my candle; you, O Lord my God, will enlighten my darkness.*

TWENTY-SIX

Does not my soul most truly confess to you that I do measure time? But do I then measure, O my God, and not know what I measure? I measure the motion of a body by time. Do I not measure time itself? Could I indeed measure the motion of a body, how long it is and how long a period it took to come from this place to that, without measuring the time in which it is moved? This time itself, then—how do I measure it? Do we measure a longer time by a shorter one, measure a longer one, as by the length of a cubit measure the length of a crossbeam? Indeed we seem to measure the space of a long syllable by a short one, saying it is double the other. Thus we measure the length of stanzas by the length of verses, and the length of verses by the length of the feet, and the length of the feet by the length of the syllable, and the length of the long syllables by the length of the short ones—not measuring by pages, for then we measure space rather than time. But when we speak words, and they pass by, and we say, "It is a long stanza, because it is composed of so many verses; long verses, because they consist of so many feet; long feet, because they are lengthened by so many syllables; a long syllable because it is double a short one."

But we do not obtain any certain measure of time in this way, because it may be that a shorter verse, pronounced more fully, may take up more time than a longer one, pronounced hurriedly. And the same would be true of a verse, a foot, or a syllable. From this it appears to me that time is nothing else than protraction—but of what, I do not know. And I wonder if it could be of the mind itself. For what, I beseech you, O my God, do I measure when I say, either indefinitely, "This is a longer time than that," or definitely, "This is double that"? I know that I measure time, and yet I do not measure future time, for it is not yet, nor the present, because it is not extended by any space; nor do I measure past time, because it no longer is. What then do I measure? Is it time as it passes but not past? This is what I have said.

TWENTY-SEVEN

Persevere, O my mind, and pay earnest attention. *God is our helper. He made us, and not we ourselves.* Press on where truth begins to dawn.

Suppose, now, the voice of a body begins to sound, and does sound, continues to sound, and then stops. It is now silence and that sound is gone. It is no longer a sound. Before it sounded, it was future, and could not be measured, because it did not yet exist. It cannot be measured now, because it no longer is. But while it was sounding it could have been measured, because there was something there to measure. But even then, it was not stationary, for it was in process and passing away. Could it then be measured better on that account? For while it was passing, it was being extended into some space of time so that it could be measured, since the present has no space. If, then, it might have been measured, suppose that another voice had begun to sound and is still sounding in one continuous course without any interruption.

We can measure it while it sounds, for when it stops sounding it will be gone and nothing will be left to be measured. Let us measure it accurately and say how long it is. But it is still sounding and cannot be measured except from the instant it began to the point that it ends. For the very interval between is the thing we measure, from some beginning to some end. On that account a sound that is not yet ended cannot be measured, so that we may say how long or short it is, nor can it be called equal to another, twice as long, or the like. But when it is ended, it no longer is. How may it then be measured? And yet we measure times, but not those which are future nor those which are past, nor those which are not lengthened out by some delay, nor those which have no limits. Therefore, we measure neither future time nor time past, nor time present, nor time passing. Yet we do measure time!

Deus, Creator omnium. This verse of eight syllables alternates between short and long syllables. The four short then, the first, third, fifth and seventh, are but single, in respect of the four long, the second, fourth, sixth and eighth. Each of the long ones is twice as long as the short ones. I pronounce them, report on them, and find it so, as one's common sense perceives. By common sense, then, I measure a long syllable by a short one, and I find that it has twice as much. But when one sounds after the other, if the former is short and the latter long, how shall I detain the short one, and how, measuring, shall I apply it to the long one, so that I may find this has twice as much, since the long one does not begin to sound unless the short one stops sounding? And how do I measure that very long one as present, since I do not measure it until it has ended? But its end is its passing away. What, then, is it I measure? Where is the short syllable by which I measure? And where is the long one I measure? Both have sounded, have flown, have passed away and are no more. And yet I measure, and confidently answer (so far as the exercise of my sense is trustworthy), that as to length of time this syllable is single, that one double. And yet I could not do this unless they were already past and ended. It is not then themselves, which no longer exist, that I measure, but something in my memory, which remains fixed there.

It is in you, O my mind, that I measure time. Do not interrupt me by clamoring that time has objective existence! I measure time in you. The impression which things cause in you as they pass by remains even when they are gone. This, which is still present, is what I measure, not those things which have passed by to make this impression. This is what I measure when I measure time. Either, then, this is time, or I do not measure time.

How, then, do we measure silence and say that this silence lasted as long as that sound? Do we not extend our thought to the length of the voice, as if it sounded, so that we can report something of the intervals of silence in a given space of time? For where both voice and tongue are still, yet we go over poems and verses in thought, and any other discourse, or measures of motions, and we report as to the spaces of times—how much this is in comparison with that—just as if we were uttering them aloud. If anyone uttered a lengthened sound, and had already determined how long it should be, that person has already gone through a space of time in silence, and committing it to memory, begins to utter that speech which goes on until it reaches its proposed end. Yes, it has sounded and will sound, for what is already finished has sounded, and the rest of it will sound. And thus it passes on, until the present intent carries the future over into the past. The past increases by the reduction of the future, until by the consumption of the future, all is past.

TWENTY-EIGHT

But how is that future diminished or consumed, which does not yet exist? Or how is that past increased, which no longer is, except that the mind which does this, does three things? It expects, it considers, it remembers, so that what it expects, through what it considers, passes into what it remembers. Who, then, denies that things to come as yet are not? But there is already in the mind an expectation of things to come. And who denies that past things no longer are? And yet there is still a memory in the mind of things past. And who denies that the present moment has no space, because it passes away in an instant? And yet our consideration continues, and it is through this that what is present may proceed to become past. It is not, then, future time that is long, for it is not at all, but a long future period is a long expectation of the future. In the same way, it is not time past which does not exist at all that is long, but a long past is a long memory of the past.

I am about to repeat a Psalm I know. Before I begin, my attention is extended over the whole; but when I have begun, however, much of it becomes past by my saying and it is extended along my memory; and the life of this action of mine is divided between my memory as to what I have repeated, and the expectation of what I am about to repeat. But my attention is in the present with me, that through it what was future may be carried over so as to become past. The more of it I repeat the more my expectation is shortened and the memory is enlarged, till the whole expectation at length is exhausted, and when the action is ended, it shall have passed into the memory. And what takes place in relation to the whole Psalm, takes place in each individual part of it and in each separate syllable. The same holds in the larger action of which this Psalm may be a part. The same holds in the whole life of a person, of which all the actions of that person are parts. The same holds in the whole of humanity, of which all the lives of men are parts.

TWENTY-NINE

But, *because your loving kindness is better than life*, behold, my life is but a distraction, and *your right hand upheld me* in my Lord, the Son of Man, the Mediator between you, the One, and us the many. (We are many also through our many distractions amid many things.) By him I may lay hold on the One by whom I have been apprehended, and may be recollected from my old way of life, to follow the One, *forgetting what is behind*, not distended, but drawn on not to those things which shall be and shall pass away, but *reaching out to those things which are before*, not drawn this way and that with distracted attention but with concentration of mind. I follow on *for the prize of my heavenly calling*, where I may hear the voice of your praise and contemplate your delights, which are neither coming to be, nor passing away. But now my years are spent in mourning. And you, O Lord, are my comfort, my Father everlasting. But I have been divided amid times, the order of which I do not know, and my thoughts, even the inmost depths of my soul, are torn and mangled with tumultuous confusions, until I flow together to you, purified and molten in the fire of your love.

THIRTY

And I will stand and become firm in you, in my mold, your truth. I will not endure the questions of men, who by a punishing disease thirst for more than they can contain, and say, "What did God do before he made heaven and earth?" Or, "How did it come into his mind to make anything, having never made anything before?" Grant them, O Lord, to think carefully what they say, and to see that where there is no time, they cannot say "never." Then speaking of what he is said "never to have made"—what is it saying but that in no time was it made? Let them therefore see, that time cannot be without a creation, and let them stop speaking such foolishness. May they also look *toward those things which are before*, and understand that you are before all time, the eternal Creator of all times, and that no time is co-eternal with you, nor is any creature, even if there should be any creature beyond all time.

THIRTY-ONE

O Lord my God, what a deep is that secret place of your mysteries, and how far from it have my transgressions cast me! Heal my eyes that I may enjoy your light. Surely, if there is a Mind abounding with such vast knowledge and foreknowledge as to know all things past and future as well as I know a single well-known Psalm, truly that Mind is surpassingly wonderful and fearfully awesome. Nothing past and nothing to come in later ages is any more hidden from him than the past and future of that Psalm was unknown to me when I was singing it, how much of it had already been said, and how much there remained to the end.

But far be it that you, the Creator of the universe, the Creator of souls and bodies—far be it that you should know all things past and to come, in the same way I know that Psalm. You know them far, far more wonderfully and far more mysteriously. For it is not as the varied feelings of one who sings what he knows, or hears some well-known song, by expecting the words to come and remembering those that are past, with his senses divided. Not so does anything happen to you, unchangeably eternal, that is, the truly eternal Creator of minds. As in the beginning you knew both the heaven and the earth, with no change of your knowledge, in the beginning you made heaven and earth without any division of your action. Whoever understands this, let him confess to you; and whoever understands it not, let him confess it to you. Oh how exalted you are! And yet the humble in heart are your dwelling place, for you raise up those who are bowed down, and they do not fall, for you are their exaltation.

BOOK XII

Further Inquiry into the Mystery of Creation

ONE

In this poverty-stricken life of mine, O Lord, my heart, smitten by the words of your sacred Scriptures, is greatly exercised by them. For the most part, this poverty of human understanding is plentiful in words, because inquiry says more than discovery, demanding is longer than obtaining, and our hand that knocks is more active than the hand that receives. We hold the promise; who shall break it? *If God be for us, who can be against us? Ask and you shall receive; seek and you shall find; knock and it shall be opened to you. For everyone who asks receives, and he who seeks finds; and to him who knocks, it shall be opened.* These are your own promises. Who need fear to be deceived, when it is the Truth who promises?

TWO

The weakness of my tongue confesses to your majesty, that you *made heaven and earth.* This heaven which I see and this earth which I walk upon (from which came this earth that I carry about me), you have made. But where is that heaven of heavens, O Lord, of which we hear in the words of the Psalm: *The heaven of heavens are the Lord's; but the earth he has given to the children of men?* Where is that heaven which we do not see? In relation to it all this we see [the visible universe] is "earth." For since this physical universe is not wholly everywhere, it has received its portion of beauty in such a way that this, our earth, is the lowest part. Still, compared to that heaven of heavens, even the heaven of our earth is but earth. Yes, it is not absurd to call both these great bodies "earth" as compared to that unknown "heaven" which is the Lord's, not the sons' of men.

THREE

And truly this earth was invisible and without form, and there was an abyss beyond measure, upon which there was no light, because it had no form. Therefore, you commanded that it should be written that there was *darkness upon the face of the deep*. What else was this than the absence of light? For if there had been light, where would it have been but by being above all, showing itself aloft and enlightening? Where as yet there was no light, why was darkness present except that light was absent? Darkness then, was upon it, because light was not upon it—just as there is silence where there is no sound. And what is it to have silence there, but to have no sound there? Have you not, O Lord, taught this soul who confesses to you? Have you not taught me, O Lord, that before you formed and separated this formless matter there was nothing—neither color, nor figure, nor body, nor spirit? And yet, it was not absolutely nothing, for there was a certain formlessness without any shape.

FOUR

What then should it be called, that even in some way it might be conveyed to those of slower minds, but by some common word? And what, among all the parts of the world, can there be found anything nearer to absolute formlessness than the earth and the deep? Because they occupy the lowest place, they are less beautiful than the other higher parts are, all transparent and shining. Why, therefore, may I not consider the formlessness of matter (which you had created without shape, out of which to make this shapely world) to be suitably expressed to men by the name of *earth invisible and formless*?

FIVE

When our thought seeks what the senses may arrive at, it says to itself, "It is no intelligible form, such as life or justice; because it is bodily material, yet it is not an object of the senses, because it is invisible and formless and there is nothing to be seen or felt." While man's thought talks this way to itself, it may try either to know it by being ignorant of it; or to be ignorant by knowing it.

SIX

But, Lord, if I were to confess to you by my tongue and pen the whole of whatever you have taught me about that formless matter, I would say this: when I heard the word before, I did not understand it, and neither did they who were telling me of it. I then conceived of it as having innumerable and different forms. Therefore, I did not grasp it properly—my mind tossed up and down all sorts of weird and horrible forms, out of all order, but yet forms—and I called it formless, not that these forms lacked all shape, but because they were such shapes as my mind would recoil from, if they should appear, as unwanted and disturbing to my human frailty. And still what I conceived to be formless was not as being deprived of all shape, but shapeless in comparison with more beautiful forms. True reason persuaded me that I must utterly remove from it all form whatsoever if I were to conceive matter absolutely formless. But I could not, for I could more easily have imagined that which was formless to be nothing, than to imagine a thing between form and nothingness, neither formed nor nothing, a formless "almost nothing."

And my mind stopped questioning my spirit—filled (as it was) with the images of formed bodies, changing and varying them as it would. And I devoted myself to the bodies themselves, and looked more deeply into their changeable character, by which they ceased to be what they had been, and began to be what they were not. This same shifting from form to form I suspected to be through some formless condition, not through a mere nothing. Yet I longed to know, not only to guess it. But if my voice and pen confessed to you the whole, whatever knots you untied for me concerning this question, what reader would endure to take in the whole? Still, my heart shall not cease to give you honor, and a song of praise for those things which it is not able to express. The changeableness of changeable things is itself capable of all those forms into which these changeable things are changed. But what is this changeableness? Is it soul? Is it body? Is it the outward appearance of soul or body? If one could say "A nothing something," and "That which is, is not," I would say that this was it, and yet in some manner it was already capable of taking the visible, complex forms we know.

SEVEN

But from where did it get this degree of being, unless from you, from whom are all things insofar as they exist. But the farther from you they are, the more unlike you they are, for it is not distance of space. For you, Lord, are not one thing in one place and another in another, but the Same, and the Selfsame, and the very Selfsame, *Holy, Holy, Holy, Lord God Almighty. In the Beginning*, which is of you, in your wisdom, which was born of your own Substance, you created something, and that out of nothing. You created heaven and earth—not out of yourself, for they would then have been equal to your Only Begotten and thereby equal even to you. And in no way would it be right that anything should be equal to you which was not of you. And there was nothing else except you out of which you might create them, O God, one Trinity, and threefold Unity. Therefore, out of nothing *you created the heaven and the earth*, a great thing and a small—for you are almighty and good, and made all things good, both the great heaven and the small earth. You were, and there was nothing else. Out of nothing you created heaven and earth. You created two kinds of things, one close to you, the other close to nothingness—one to which you alone should be superior, the other to which only nothing should be inferior.

EIGHT

But that heaven of heavens was for yourself, O Lord. But the earth which you gave to the sons of men, to be felt and seen, was not such as we now see and feel. For it was then *invisible and without form*, and there was a deep upon which there was no light; or, darkness was over the deep; that is, more than just in the deep. Because this deep of earthly waters now visible has even in its depths a light suitable to its nature, perceptible in some degree to the fish and creeping things on the bottom of it. But that other deep was almost nothing, because up to that time it was completely formless. Yet there was already something that could be formed. For you, Lord, made the world out of formless matter, which, out of nothing, you made "almost nothing." Out of that "almost nothing" you made those great things which we sons of men wonder at. For this corporeal heaven is very wonderful. The firmament located between water above and water below was made the second day after the creation of light. You said, "Let it be made," and it was made. You called that firmament *heaven*; that is, the heaven of this earth and sea, which you made the third day by giving a visible shape to the formless matter you had made before all the days. For you had already made a heaven before all days, but that was the heaven of this heaven, because *In the beginning* you had *made heaven and earth*. But this earth itself which you had made was formless matter, because it was invisible and without form, and darkness was upon the deep. Out of this invisible and formless earth, out of this formlessness, out of this "almost nothing" you made all these things which make up this changeable world, a world without stability. For its very changeableness shows itself in the fact that time can be observed and measured in it. For periods of time are measured by the changes of things, while the shapes, made of this invisible matter mentioned earlier, vary and change.

NINE

And therefore the Spirit, the Teacher of your servant, when he tells that you *in the Beginning created heaven and earth*, says nothing of time, nothing about days. For doubtless that heaven of heavens which you created in the Beginning is some intelligent creation which, although in no way co-eternal with you, the Trinity, yet partakes of your eternity, and through the sweetness of that most happy contemplation of yourself, strongly diminishes its own changeableness. Without any failure from its first creation, by clinging so close to you, it is placed beyond the rolling changes of time. But this formlessness—this earth *invisible and without form*—was not numbered among the days [mentioned in Genesis 1]. For where there is no form nor order, nothing comes or goes; and where nothing comes or goes, plainly there are no days, nor any succession of periods of time.

TEN

Oh let the Truth, the Light of my heart, not my own darkness, speak to me! I had fallen to that and was darkened by it. But even from there, even from there I loved you. I went astray, yet I remembered you. I heard your voice behind me, bidding me to return, though I scarcely heard it through the uproar of the enemies of peace. And now, behold, I return yearning and panting for your fountain. Let no one forbid me! Of this I will drink and so live. Let me not be my own life, for of myself I have lived badly—I was death to myself. In you I revive. Speak to me. Preach to me. I have believed your Books, and their words are very deep.

ELEVEN

You have already told me with a strong voice, in my inner ear, O Lord, that you are eternal and alone have immortality. You cannot be changed by any shape or motion. Your will is not altered by time, since no will which changes is immortal. This is very clear to me in your presence. Let it become clearer and clearer, I beseech you; and in that clarity let me abide more soberly under your wings.

You have also told me with a strong voice in my inner ear, O Lord, that you have made all natures and substances which are not what you yourself are, and yet are. And only that which is not from you has no being at all. Further, you have told me that the movement of the will away from you who are, toward that which to a lesser degree is, is an offense and a sin. Yet no one's sin can either hurt you nor disturb the order of your rule in the greatest thing or the least. All this in your presence is very clear to me. Let it become clearer and clearer, I beseech you; and in that clarity, let me abide more soberly under your wings.

You have also told me with a strong voice in my inner ear that that creature [the heaven of heavens] is not co-eternal with yourself. Though its only happiness is you alone, though by drawing its nourishment from you with a most persevering purity, it should never show its natural changeableness; even though, having you present with it, it keeps its whole affection toward you, expecting nothing from the future and having nothing from the past to remember unaltered by any change nor stretched out into time periods, it still is not co-eternal with you. O blessed creation—if any such there be, clinging to your blessedness—blest in you, its eternal Inhabitant and its Enlightener! I find no better name for the heaven of heavens which is the Lord's than to call it your house, which contemplates your delight ceaselessly with one pure mind, most peacefully one, by that settled peace of holy spirits, the citizens of your city *in the heavenly places*—far above those heavenly places that we can see.

By this let the soul whose wanderings have been long and far away understand, if it now thirsts for you; if its tears have now become its bread, while they daily say to it, *"Where is your God?"*; if it now seeks of you one thing and desires it, that it *may dwell in your house all the days of its life.* And what is its life but you? And what are your days but your eternity? For *your years fail not,* because you are ever the same. By this, then, may the soul that is able understand how far you are above all time, eternal. And so your house, which has never wandered into a far country, although it is not co-eternal with you, by continually and steadfastly holding to you, experiences no ravages of time. This is very clear to me in your presence. Let it become clearer and clearer, I beseech you, and in that clarity let me abide more soberly under your wings.

Behold, I do not know what formlessness there is in the changes of the last and lowest creatures. Who shall tell me, unless it be someone who, through the emptiness of his own heart wanders and tosses himself up and down among his own fancies? Who but such a one would tell me that if all forms dwindled and disappeared and only formlessness remained, in which the creation changed and turned through that formlessness, from one shape to another, that such formlessness would be able to exhibit any succession of periods of time? Surely this could not be, because without the change of motions there is no time, and where there is no shape, there can be no change.

TWELVE

When I consider these things as you, O my God, give them, as you stirred me up to knock, as you open to me when I knock, I find that you have made two things outside the compass of time, neither of which is co-eternal with you. One is so formed that without any failure of purpose or intention, without any interval of change, although it is capable of change, yet not changed, it may thoroughly enjoy your eternity and unchangeableness. The other was so formless that it did not have anything that could be changed from one form to another, either by moving or by being still, by which it could become subject to time. But you did not leave this formless, because before all days, you *in the beginning created heaven and earth*, these two things I am speaking of. But the earth was invisible and formless, and darkness was upon the deep. By these words this formlessness is expressed to us, so that the idea might gradually lay hold upon the minds which cannot conceive of the absence of all form without them coming to nothing. And out of this formlessness another heaven was created and another earth, visible and well-formed, and the water beautifully ordered with all the rest that is recorded in the formation of this world as having been created in days, because such things are of such natures that the successive changes of time may take place in them, since they are subject to appointed changes of motions and forms.

THIRTEEN

This is what I envisage, O my God, when I hear your Scripture saying, *In the beginning God created heaven and earth; and the earth was invisible and without form, and darkness was upon the deep*—not mentioning what day you created them. This is what I understand, that it is on account of that heaven of heavens, that intellectual heaven where to understand means to know all at once—not in part, not darkly, not *through a glass*, but as a whole, in full view, *face to face*. It is to know not this thing now and that thing then, but all at once, without any succession of time. And I understand the Scripture this way on account of the invisible and formless earth, without any succession of time, which presents one thing now, another thing then, because where there is no form there can be no distinction between "this" and "that." It is, then, on account of these two, one originally formed, the other originally formless, the one, *heaven* (but actually the heaven of heavens), the other, *earth* (but the earth invisible and formless). It was because there were these two that your Scriptures say, without mentioning days, *In the beginning God created heaven and earth*. For it added immediately what earth it spoke of, and furthermore, when the *firmament* is recorded to have been created on the second day, and called *heaven*, it suggests to us which other heaven he spoke of before, without mention of days.

FOURTEEN

Wonderful depth of your Words! Their surface meaning is before us, plain to children; and yet wonderful is their depth, O my God—a wonderful depth! It is awesome to look in them, an awesome honor and a trembling of love. I hate their enemies vehemently. Oh that you would slay them with your two-edged sword, that they might no longer be the enemies of your Words! For

I would love to have them slain to themselves that they might live to you. But behold others—not faultfinders, but those who extol the book of Genesis: "The Spirit of God," they say, "who wrote these things by his servant, Moses, did not mean to have those words understood this way. Moses would not have understood it the way you say it, but as we do." O God of us all, yourself our Judge, I answer them in this way.

FIFTEEN

Will you call that false which Truth tells me with a strong voice in my inner ear, concerning the very eternity of the Creator, that his essence is in no way changed by time, and that his will is not separate from his very substance? So, he does not will one thing at one time, another at another, but once, at the same time and forever he wills everything that he wills—not again and again, now this, now that; nor does he will afterward what he did not will before; nor does he cease to will what he willed before, because such a will is changeable, and nothing changeable is eternal; *but our God is eternal.*

These things I sum up and put together, and I find that my God, the eternal God, has not made any creature on the basis of any new will, nor does his knowledge receive anything in a transitory way.

What will you say, then, all you objectors? Are these things false?

"No," they say.

What, then? Is it false to say that every nature already formed, or any matter capable of form, is only from him who is supremely good because he *is* supremely?

"Neither do we deny this," they say.

What, then? Do you deny that there is a certain sublime creature, clinging with such a chaste love to the true and truly eternal God that, although it is not co-eternal with him, yet it is not separated from him, nor does it turn away into any variation or into successive periods of time, but reposes in the truest contemplation of him alone? Because you, O God, show yourself to him who loves you as much as you command, and you are sufficient for him, and therefore this creature does not turn away from you nor toward itself. This is *the house of God*, not an earthly house nor of any heavenly material—but a spiritual house, and a partaker of your eternity because it remains without blemish forever. *For you have established it for ever and ever. You have given it a law which it shall not pass.* Yet it is not co-eternal with you, O God, because it was not without a beginning. It was created.

Although we can find no time before it, for *wisdom was created before all things*, this certainly is not that Wisdom altogether equal and co-eternal with you, our God, his Father, and by whom all things were created, and in whom, as in the Beginning, you created heaven and earth. Rather, this wisdom which has been created, namely, the intellectual nature, in its contemplation of light, is light. For this, though it was created, is also called wisdom. But there is as much difference between the Light which enlightens and that which is enlightened as there is between the Wisdom that creates and the wisdom that is created; as between the Righteousness that justifies and the righteousness which has been made by justification. Are we not called your righteousness, as your servant Paul says, *That we might be made the righteousness of God in him*? Therefore, since a certain created wisdom was created before all things, the rational and intellectual mind of that chaste city of yours, *our mother which is above, is free and eternal in the heavens.* And in what heavens, unless in those that praise you, *the heaven of heavens*? Because this is *the heaven of heavens which is the Lord's.* And though we find no time before it, because that which has been created before all things also precedes the creation of time, yet the eternity of the Creator himself is before it, from whom it took its beginning, since it was created. It was not created in time, since time was not as yet—but of the nature that belonged to it.

Hence created wisdom comes into being altogether other than yourself, and it is not the Selfsame, because though we do not find time before it nor in it (since it is ever fit to behold your face and never is drawn away from it, and therefore is not varied by any change) yet it has in it the possibility of change, so that it might become dark and cold if it was not clinging to you by a strong love so that it shines and glows from your radiance like a perpetual noontime. O house, full of light and splendor! *I have loved your beauty and the place of the habitation of the glory of my Lord, your Builder and Owner.* In my wandering let me sigh after you. I ask him who made you that he may possess me also in you, since he also made me. *I have gone astray like a lost sheep.* But I hope to be brought back to you on the shoulders of my Shepherd, your Builder.

What do you say to me now, you objectors that I was speaking to, who yet believe Moses to have been the holy servant of God and his books to be the utterance of the Holy Spirit? Is not this the *house of God*, not co-eternal indeed with God, yet in its own way, *eternal in the heavens*, where you look in vain for changes of time, because you will not find them? For that creature surpasses all those that exist in time-extensions and revolving periods of time, whose good is to *hold fast to God*.

"It is," they say.

What, then, of all those things which my heart cried out to my God when it inwardly heard the voice of his praise? Which of them do you claim to be false? Is it not because matter was formless, in which, because there was no form, there was no order? And where there was no order, there could be no changing periods of time; and yet this "almost nothing," inasmuch as it was not altogether nothing, was certainly from him from whom comes whatever is, in whatever degree it is.

"This, too," they say, "we do not deny."

SIXTEEN

I would like to talk a little further in your presence, O my God, with those who admit all these things are true which your Truth indicates to my mind. Let those who deny these things bark and deafen themselves as much as they pleased. I will try to persuade them to be quiet and to allow your Word to reach them. But if they refuse and reject me, I ask you, my God, "Be not silent to me." Speak truly in my heart. For only you speak thus. And I will let them alone to stir up the dust and blow it up into their own eyes. As for myself, I will enter my chamber and sing songs of love there to you, groaning with groanings unutterable in my pilgrimage and remembering Jerusalem with my heart uplifted toward it, Jerusalem my homeland, Jerusalem my mother, and yourself, its Ruler, Light, Father, Guardian, Spouse, its pure and strong delight, its solid joy, and all good things ineffable, even all at the same time, because you are the one supreme and true Good. And I will not be turned away until you gather all that I am from my scattered and deformed state into the peace of that very dear mother where the first-fruits of my spirit already dwell, from which these things are assured to me. Conform and confirm it for ever, O my God, my Mercy. But as for those who do not deny all these truths, who honor your Holy Scripture set forth by holy Moses, placing it, as we do, on the summit of authority to be followed, and yet who contradict me in some things, I have given this answer. Be yourself the Judge, O our God, between my confessions and their contradictions.

SEVENTEEN

For they say, "Although these things are true, yet Moses did not intend those two things [the spiritual and material heavens] when, by revelation of the Spirit, he said, *In the beginning God created heaven and earth.* By the word *heaven* he did not mean that spiritual or intellectual creature which always beholds the face of God; nor under the name *earth* did he mean that formless matter."

"What then?" I ask.

"That man of God," they say, "meant what we mean. This is what he declared by those words."

"What is that?"

"By the words *heaven and earth*," they say, "he meant first to express, universally and briefly, all this visible world; and afterward, by specifying the different days, to arrange in detail, and as it were, piece by piece, all those things which it pleased the Holy Spirit thus to reveal. For the people to whom he spoke were so uncouth and carnally minded, that he judged it prudent that only those works of God which were visible should be entrusted to them."

They agree, however, that the words, *earth invisible and without form*, and the darksome deep (out of which it is subsequently shown that all these visible things which we all know, were made and arranged during those *days*), may quite properly be understood to refer to this formless, primal matter.

If anyone wish, he may say that the term *heaven and earth* was used for this formless matter because the whole visible universe and everything in it was made from it.[1]

Another might say that everything visible and invisible is included in the term *heaven and earth*, the whole creation which God made in his Wisdom, in the Beginning. But nothing was made out of God's substance, because they are not divine and they are all capable of change and destruction. Even if they remain unchanged (as does the eternal dwelling place of God), or are constantly changing (like the human soul and body), they are still capable of change. And the same formless matter was used to make both heaven and earth. So it is right to think of *everything* visible and invisible as referred to by the phrase *earth invisible and formless and darkness was upon the face of the deep*, provided that *the earth invisible and formless* refers to physical matter before it had any form, while *darkness upon the deep* refers to spiritual matter before it underwent limitations of its gaseous or fluid nature, and before it received any light from Wisdom.

EIGHTEEN

Having heard and considered all these things well, I will not argue about words, *for that is profitable for nothing but the subverting of the hearer*. But *the law is good for edification if a man use it lawfully*, because *its end is charity out of a pure heart and good conscience and out of genuine faith*. And our Master knew well upon which *two Commandments all the Law and the Prophets hung*. And what harm does it do to me, O my God, Light of my eyes in secret, if while I ardently confess these things—since many things may be understood by these words, all of which are true—what harm, I say, is done if I think something other than the original writer thought? All of us who read endeavor to trace out and understand his meaning; and since we believe that he speaks truly, we dare not suppose that he has said anything which we either know or think to be false. Since every person endeavors to understand in the Holy Scriptures what the writer understood, what hurt is it, if a man understand what you, the Light of all true minds, show him to be true—even if the author, though he understood a Truth, did not understand it in the same way?

NINETEEN

For it is true, O Lord, that you *made heaven and earth*; and it is true, too, that the Beginning is your Wisdom, in which you created all. It is true again, that this visible world has for its major divisions the heaven and the earth, including all natures that have been made and created. And it is true, too, that everything changeable suggests to our minds a certain formless substance which then receives form. It is true that what so clings to the unchangeable Form as never to be changed is not subject to time. It is also true that the formlessness which is almost nothing cannot have changes of times. It is true that that of which a thing is made may, by a certain manner of speaking, be called by the name of the things made of it. So that formlessness, out of which heaven and earth were made, might be called *heaven and earth*. It is true that of all things having form, nothing is nearer to formlessness than the earth and the deep. It is true that you created and formed, not only every created and formed thing, but whatever is capable of being created and formed, for all things are from you. It is true that whatever is formed out of that which had no form was formless before it was formed.

TWENTY

From all these truths, which they whose inner eye you have enabled to see such things do not doubt, who unshakenly believe your servant Moses to have spoken in the Spirit of truth—from all these, then, one chooses the words, *In the Beginning God made the heaven and the earth* to mean "In his Word, co-eternal with himself, God made the intelligible and the sensible, or the spiritual and the physical creation."

Another takes *In the beginning God created heaven and earth* to mean "In his Word, co-eternal with himself, God made the whole mass of this corporeal world, together with all those apparent and known creatures which it contains."

Another says, *In the beginning God created the heaven and earth* means "In his Word, co-eternal with himself, God created the formless matter of the physical creation, in which heaven and earth were as yet mixed, which are now distinguished and formed, and which at this day we see in the mass of this world."

Yet another says, *In the beginning God made heaven and earth* means that "In the very beginning of creating and working, God made formless matter, containing in itself both heaven and earth mixed indistinguishably together; out of which, being given form, they now stand out and are apparent with all they contain in them."

TWENTY-ONE

And with regard to the understanding of the words that follow, out of all those truths he selected one truth for himself, who says, "*And the earth was invisible and formless and darkness was upon the deep* means that that physical thing which God made was as yet the formless matter of physical things, without order, without light."

Another truth is chosen by one who says, "*The earth was invisible and unformed, and darkness was upon the deep* means that all this which is called heaven and earth was still a formless, darkish matter. Out of this was to be made the physical [or corporeal] heavens and the corporeal [physical] earth, with everything in them which are known to our physical senses."

Yet another says, "But *the earth invisible and formless* means this whole universe which is called heaven and earth was as yet a formless, darkened matter out of which were to be made both that heaven which is called elsewhere the *heaven of heavens* and the earth—that is the whole physical nature, including this physical heaven also; that is, from which *every* visible and invisible creature would be created."

Still another truth is chosen by one who says, "*The earth was invisible and without form and darkness was upon the deep* means that there was already a certain formless matter which Scripture had spoken of, saying, *God made heaven and earth, namely, the spiritual and corporeal creation.*"

Yet another is chosen by one who says that these words, *the earth invisible and formless,* refer to the whole corporeal mass of the world divided into two great parts, upper and lower, with all those familiar and known creatures that are in them.

TWENTY-TWO

If anyone should attempt to argue against these last two opinions, saying, "If you will not allow that this formlessness of matter seems to be called by the name of heaven and earth, then it follows that there was already something which God had not made, out of which he could make heaven and earth. For Scripture has not told us that God made this matter, unless we understand it to be implied by the term *heaven and earth,* or of earth only when it says, *In the beginning God made the heaven and earth* as that which follows—*and the earth was invisible and formless.* Although it pleased him to speak of formless matter like this, we are to understand it to refer to no other matter than that which God had made in that text which has already stated, *God made heaven and earth.*"

The maintainers of either of these last two opinions [mentioned above] will, when they have heard this, answer that they do not deny that this formless matter was indeed created by God, the God who made all things very good; for just as we say that that is a greater good which is created and formed, so we acknowledge that to be a lesser good which is only capable of being created and formed—yet it is still good. We say, however, that Scripture has not stated that God made this formlessness any more than it has many other things—Cherubim, Seraphim, and those which the apostle distinctly speaks of—Thrones, Dominions, Principalities and Powers, for example. That God made all of them is most apparent.

Or if all things are included in the phrase, *he made heaven and earth*, what shall we say of the waters upon which the Spirit of God moved? For if they are included in this word earth, how then can formless matter be meant in that word, *earth*, when we see the waters so beautiful? Or if it is to be taken in this way, why then is it said that out of the same formlessness the firmament was made, and called *heaven*, and yet it is not written that the waters were made? For the waters do not stay formless and invisible, since we see them flowing in so beautiful a manner. But if they then received that beauty when God said, *Let the waters under the firmament be gathered together*, so that the gathering together is itself the forming of them, what will be answered as to those waters that are above the firmament? If they were formless they would not have been worthy of so honorable a seat, nor is it written by what word they were formed.

If, then, Genesis is silent as to anything that God has made, and neither sound faith nor well-grounded understanding doubts that he made it, let no serious teaching dare to say that these waters were co-eternal with God on the ground that we find them mentioned in Genesis, but do not find when they were created. Since Truth teaches us, why may we not understand that the formless matter which this Scripture calls the *earth invisible and formless and the dark abyss* was created by God out of nothing, and therefore not co-eternal with him, although the narrative has failed to show when it was created?

TWENTY-THREE

I have heard and understood these things according to the weakness of my apprehension, which I confess to you, O Lord. You know that I see that two sorts of differences may arise when a thing is related in words, even by true reporters—one concerning the truth of the things related, the other concerning the meaning of the one who relates them. For in one way we inquire about the truth concerning the forming of the creation. But in another way, we ask what Moses, that faithful servant of your faith, would have wished his reader and hearer to understand by those words. As for the first—away with all those who imagine themselves to know as a truth what is false! And for the other—let all those depart from me who imagine Moses to have spoken false things! But let me be united in you, O Lord, and let me delight myself in you with those who feed on your truth, in the breadth of charity. Let us approach the words of your Book together and search in them for your meaning through the meaning of your servant by whose pen you have dispensed them.

TWENTY-FOUR

But among so many truths which occur to inquirers in those words, understood as they are in different ways, which of us shall so discover that one meaning as to state, "This is what Moses thought," and, "That is what he wanted understood in that narrative," as confidently as he would say, "This is true, whether Moses thought this or that"? For behold! O my God, I, your servant, who have in this book vowed a sacrifice of confession to you, and pray that by your mercy I may pay my vows to you, can I, with the same confidence I have when I say that in your immutable Word you created all things visible and invisible, also affirm that Moses meant nothing else than this when he wrote *In the beginning God made heaven and earth*? No. Because I do not see his mind, that he thought of this when he wrote these things as I see it to be certain in your truth. For he might have had his thoughts on the very beginning of the creation when he said *In the beginning*, and when he said *heaven and earth*, he may have wanted it to be understood that they were of no formed nor perfected nature, either spiritual or physical—but that both of them, newly begun, were inchoate and as yet formless. For I perceive that whichever of the two had been said, it might have been said truly; but which of them he may have thought of in these words, I do not clearly see. Whether it was one of these, or some other meaning altogether which I have not mentioned here, which this great man saw in his mind when he uttered these words, I do not doubt that he saw it truly and expressed it suitably.

TWENTY-FIVE

Let no one trouble me, then, by saying, "Moses did not think what you say, but what I say." For if he should ask me, "How do you know that Moses thought what you infer out of his words?" I ought to take it calmly and reply as I have already done, or even more fully if he is stubborn. But when he says, "Moses did not mean what you say, but what I say," and does not deny that what both of us are saying may be true—O my God, life of the poor, in whose bosom is no contradiction, pour down a softening dew into my heart, that I may patiently bear with such a one! It is not because they are divine and have seen into the heart of your servant [Moses] what they say, but because they are proud; not because they know Moses' opinion, but love their own; not because it is truth, but because it is theirs. Otherwise they would equally love another true opinion, as I love what they say when they speak what is true, not because it is theirs but because it is true, and therefore it is not theirs, because it is truth. But if they love it because it is true, then it is both theirs and mine, as belonging to all lovers of truth. But when they contend that Moses did not mean what I say, but what they say, I do not like it; I do not love it. For though it were so, their rashness is not of knowledge, but of audacity. Not insight but vanity brought it forth. O Lord, your judgments are to be dreaded, since your truth is neither mine, nor theirs, nor another's, but it belongs to us all whom you call publicly to have it in common, warning us terribly not to hold it specially to ourselves, lest we be deprived of it. For whoever claims as a private thing that which you appointed for all to enjoy, and wants as his own what belongs to all, is driven from what is common to all to what really is his own—that is, from truth to falsehood. For *he who speaks a lie speaks it out of himself.*

Hear, O God, best Judge, Truth itself; hear what I say to this objector. Hear, because I speak before you and my brethren who employ your Law lawfully, to the end of charity; hear and see if what I shall say to him pleases you. I return this brotherly and peaceful word: if we both see what you say is true, and if we both see that what I say is true, where, I ask, do we see it? I do not see it in you and you do not see it in me, but both in the unchangeable truth itself, which is above our minds. Since, therefore, we do not contend about the very light of the Lord our God, why do we strive about the thoughts of our neighbor, which we cannot see as we see the unchangeable truth? If Moses himself had appeared to us and said, "This is what I meant," even in that case we would not see his thought, but simply believe it. Let us, then, not be puffed up one against another, going beyond what is written. *Let us love the Lord our God with all our heart, with all our soul, and with all our mind; and our neighbor as ourselves.* Unless we believe that whatever Moses meant in those books, he meant according to these two precepts of charity, we would make God a liar, for we would ascribe something to our fellow servant's mind other than what he has taught us. See now, how foolish it is, with such an abundance of true meanings as can be extracted from those words, rashly to affirm which of them Moses particularly meant, and to offend charity itself with pernicious arguments. For it is for the sake of charity that he spoke all the things whose words we try to explain.

TWENTY-SIX

O my God, Exaltation of my humility, Rest of my labor, you hear my confessions and forgive my sins. Yet you command me to love my neighbor as myself. I cannot believe that you gave Moses, your faithful servant, a smaller gift than I would wish or desire you to have given me if I had been born in his time. This is what I would want if you had placed me in that position, that by the service of my heart and tongue those books might be published, which for so long afterward were to profit all nations, and through the whole world from such a high pinnacle of authority were to surmount the words of all false and proud teachings. Suppose I had been Moses (for we all come from the same lump, and *what is man, but that you are mindful of him?*). If I had been what he was and you had commanded me to write the book of Genesis, I would have desired such a power of expression and such a style of arrangement to be given me that they who cannot as yet understand how God creates might not reject the words as surpassing their powers. And I would wish that they who had reached that understanding might find that whatever true opinion they had arrived at by thought was not omitted in those few words of your servant. And if another man by the light of truth should have discovered something else, that too should not fail to be found in those same words of mine.

TWENTY-SEVEN

A fountain in a little space is more plentiful and affords the supply of water for many streams, and waters a wider area than any one of the streams which take their rise from it, though their course may spread over wide regions. In just the same way, the narrative of the dispenser of your Word [Moses], destined to supply material for many preachers from a limited amount of language, pours forth streams of clear truth from which each interpreter draws out the longer and more winding channels of discourse on whatever of truth he is able to attain concerning these subjects, one taking one truth and one another.

For some people, when they read or hear these words, think that God, like a man or some large body gifted with immense power, by some new and sudden decision, had, outside himself, as it were at a certain distance, created heaven and earth, the two great bodies above and below, in which all things were to be contained. And when they hear *God said, Let it be made, and it was made*, they think of words begun and ended, sounding in time, and passing away, after whose departure that which had been commanded came into being, including whatever else of the same kind their familiarity with the world would suggest. In these, since they are yet babes, while their weakness is being borne up by this humble kind of speech as if in a mother's bosom, their faith is wholesomely built up, by which they hold most assuredly that God made all elements which their eyes see in a wonderful variety. If any one despises these words as too simple, and with proud weakness shall stretch himself beyond the protective nest, he will, alas, fall miserably. Have pity, O Lord, lest they who pass by trample on the unfledged bird; send your angel to put it back in its nest, that it may live until it can fly.

TWENTY-EIGHT

But others, to whom these words are no longer a nest, but deep shady bowers of fruit, see the fruits hidden in them and fly joyously around, and with cheerful notes seek out and pluck them. When they read or hear these words, they see that all times past and to come are surpassed by your eternal and stable abiding, and yet that there is no creature formed in time that is not made by your will, and because your will is one with yourself, it underwent no change nor did anything emerge in it which was not there before. Yet by it you made all things, not from your own Being in your own image which gives form to all things, but from nothing you made a formless matter wholly unlike you but destined to be formed through your image (by a recourse to you, the One, according to the measure of the capacity allotted to each thing in its kind). And all was made very good, whether they remain close to you, or whether, removed in time and space, they make or undergo the beautiful variations of the universe. They see these things and rejoice in the light of your truth, to the degree that they can.

Another directs his attention to the words, *In the beginning God made heaven and earth*, and sees in them Wisdom, the Beginning, because it also speaks to us. In the same way, another directs his attention to the same words, and by *beginning*, understands the commencement of things created. He reads *In the beginning he made*, as if it were said *At first he made*. And among those who understand *In the beginning* to mean *In your Wisdom you created heaven and earth*, one believes that matter out of which the heaven and earth were to be created is called there *heaven and earth*. Another believes that it means natures already formed and distinct. Another sees it to mean one formed element, a spiritual one, under the name *heaven*, and the other formless, of physical material, under the name *earth*. But those who understand the names *heaven and earth* to refer to the formless matter out of which both heaven and earth were to be formed do not all interpret that in the same way. Some think matter is that out of which both the intelligible and conscious creation were to be completed. Others think that it refers only to the matter out of which that which can be perceived by the senses was to be made, containing in its vast bosom these clear and visible elements. Nor do they all agree who believe that *heaven and earth* refer to creation already ordered. Some of them include both the visible and invisible world, while others, the visible only, in which we admire the luminous heaven and the dark earth, with the things that are contained in them.

TWENTY-NINE

Those, however, who understand *in the beginning* as meaning "at first," must understand *heaven and earth* as the primal matter of the universe; that is, the spiritual and material creation. For if they understand *heaven and earth* as the organized universe, they will be hard put to it to answer the question, "If God made this first, what did he make afterward?" And after the universe they will find nothing. Thereupon they must, however unwilling, hear, "How can this be first if there is nothing afterward?"

But if they say that God made matter first formless, then formed, it is not absurd to understand that this does not mean a precedence in time. They need only discern the difference between what precedes by eternity, what precedes by time, what by choice and what by origin, as follows: by eternity, as God is before all things, by time, as the flower before the fruit, by choice, as the fruit before the flower, by origin, as the sound is before the tune.

Of these four mentioned, the first and last are hard to understand, while the two middle ones are easy. For it is a rare and lofty vision, O Lord, to behold your eternity, unchangeably making things changeable, and thereby always before them. And who, again, is of such an acute mind that he can without great pains discern how the sound is before the tune? For a tune is formed of sound, and a thing not formed may exist, but what does not exist cannot be formed. So is the material prior to the things made of it, not because it makes it, since it is made itself, nor is its priority a matter of time. For we do not chronologically first utter sounds without singing, and then adapt or fashion them into the form of a song as when we form wood or silver into a chest or vessel. For such materials do precede the forms into which they are made in time. But in singing it is not so. For when it is sung, its sound is heard at the same time—not first a formless sound, which is afterward formed into a song. Each sound, as soon as it is made, passes away, and you cannot find anything of it to recall and compose by art. So, then, the song is absorbed in its sound, which is its material. And this indeed is formed so that it may be a tune. Therefore, as I said, the material of the sound precedes the form of the tune, not preceding it as if it had any power of its own to make it a tune, for the sound is not the composer of the tune in any way, but it is sent forth from the body and is subjected to the soul of the singer, that from it he may make a tune. Nor is the sound prior in time, for it is given forth together with the tune. Nor is it first in choice, for a sound is not better than a tune, since a tune is not only a sound, but a beautiful sound. But it is first in origin, because the tune does not receive form to become a sound, but a sound receives a form to become a tune. By this example, let those who are able understand how the matter of things was first made, and called *heaven and earth*, because *heaven and earth* were made out of it. Yet that matter was not made first in time, because the form of things give rise to time, but that was *formless*. But now in time, it is perceived by the senses, together with its form. Yet nothing can be told about that formless material without making it apparently first in time, although it is last in value, because things formed are assuredly superior to formless things; and it is preceded by the eternity of the Creator, so that the substance from which things were to be made should itself be made out of nothing.

THIRTY

In this diversity of true opinions, let Truth itself produce concord; and may our God have mercy upon us that we may *use the Law lawfully, to the purpose of the commandment, which is pure charity.*[2]

By this, if anyone asks of me, "Which of these was the meaning of your servant, Moses?" these would not be my confessions if I did not confess to you, "I do not know." And yet I know that those senses are true—with the exception of those carnal ones—of which I have spoken what seemed necessary. And the words of your Book, treating lofty things in a lowly manner, and abundant meanings with few words, do not frighten your little ones of good hope. But let all whom I acknowledge to see and speak the truth in these words love one another and likewise love you, our God, Fountain of truth, if we thirst for it and not for vain things. Yes, let us so honor your servant, the dispenser of the Scripture, full of your Spirit, as to believe that when he wrote these things by your revelation, he intended that which will chiefly excel both for light of truth and the increase of our fruitfulness.

THIRTY-ONE

So when one says, "Moses meant what I mean," and another says, "No, but as I mean," I suppose that I speak more reverently when I say, "Why not as you both mean, if both are true?" And if there is a third, or a fourth—yes, if any other sees any other truth in those words, why may he not be believed to have seen all these things, through whom one God has tempered the Holy Scriptures to the understanding of many, who see in them things that are true but different? Certainly (and I speak it fearlessly from my heart) if I were to write anything that would have supreme authority, I should prefer to write it in such a way that whatever truth anyone might apprehend on those matters might be re-echoed in my words, rather than to set down my own meaning so clearly as to exclude the rest, which could not offend me, since they were not false. I am unwilling, therefore, O my God, to be so headstrong as not to believe that this great man has received as much from you. Without doubt, when he wrote those words, he perceived and thought whatever truth we have been able to find, and also what we have not been able to find, and are still unable, but which may yet be found in them.

THIRTY-TWO

Finally, O Lord, you are God and not flesh and blood. Even if a man sees less, can anything lie hidden from your *good Spirit, who shall lead me into the land of uprightness*, which you yourself, through those words, were revealing to future readers, even if Moses through whom they were spoken may have thought of only one meaning among many possible true ones? And if this is so, let that which he thought be the highest of all indeed be the highest! But Lord, do reveal that same truth to us or any other truth which you please, so that whether you make known the same truth to us that you did to Moses, or some other truth, using those same words, yet you may feed us and we shall not be deceived by error.

See, O Lord my God, how much I have written on a few words— how much, I beseech you! What strength of ours, yes, what ages would suffice for all your books in this manner. Permit me then, to summarize more briefly before you, and to choose one true, certain and good meaning that you shall inspire, although many meanings offer themselves, where indeed many may be possible. Let this be the understanding upon which I undertake this confession, namely, that if I should say that which your servant, Moses, intended, that is right and best. For this I should strive. If

I do not attain this, yet may I say that which your Truth willed to say to me by his words—the same Truth which also said to him what he willed to say.

ONE

I call upon you, O my God, my Mercy, who made me and who did not forget me, though I forgot you. I call you into my soul, which you prepare for your reception by the longing you inspire in it. Do not forsake me now as I call on you who anticipated me before I called, and urged me with many kinds of repeated calls, that I should hear you from afar, be converted, and call upon you, who called me.

Lord, you blotted out all my evil desserts, not recompensing the work of my hands, by which I have acted rebelliously against you. And you have anticipated all my good desserts, so as to repay the work of your hands by which you made me, because before I came to be, you were, and I was not anything to which you might grant being. And yet, behold, I am—out of your goodness, anticipating all that you made me to be, and all out of which you made me. For you had no need of me, nor am I such a good one as to be helpful to you, my Lord and God; not in serving you, as though you were fatigued in working, or lest your power might be less if it lacked my assistance. Nor is my service to you like the cultivation of land, that you should go uncultivated if I did not cultivate you. But it is that I may serve and worship you to the end that I may have well-being from you, from whom I am one capable of well-being.

TWO

For the fullness of your goodness your creation exists so that a good which could not benefit you in any way might be. That creation is not out of you nor equal to you, but it was given existence by you. For what did *heaven and earth*, which you made *in the beginning*, deserve from you? Let those spiritual and material elements which you made in your Wisdom declare what they deserve of you to make a claim—even in their inchoate and formless state, whether spiritual or physical—ready to fall away into disorder and complete unlikeness to you. The spiritual, though without form, was superior to the physical, though formed, and the physical, though without form, was better than if it were altogether nothing. Thus they would hang upon your word in formlessness unless they were brought back to your Unity by the same Word, endued with form and all made very good by you, the one Sovereign Good. How did they deserve you to be even *without form*, since they could not even have been this except from you?

How did corporeal matter deserve you to be even invisible and without form? It would not even have been this if you had not made it, and therefore it was not and could not deserve to be made by you. Or how could the inchoate spiritual creation deserve you even to ebb and flow in darkness like the abyss and unlike you?—unless it had been turned to that by the same Word who made it and unless it had been so enlightened by that Word that it became light. Even so, it was not equal to you, yet conformed to that Image which is equal to you. For to be a body is not the same as being beautiful—else it could not be deformed. So, likewise, to a created spirit, to live is not the same as living wisely—for then it would be wise unchangeably. But *it is good for it always to hold fast to you*, lest it should lose by turning away from you the light it has obtained by turning to you, and thus relapse into a life resembling the dark abyss.

For even we ourselves, who in respect of the soul are spiritual creatures, having turned away from you, found that our light in that life was *sometimes darkness*. And still we work amidst the relics of our darkness until in your only Son we *are made your righteousness, like the mountains of God, for we have seen your judgments, which are like the great deep.*

THREE

That you said in the beginning of the creation, *Let there be light, and there was light,* I understand to be the spiritual creation, because there was already a sort of life which you might illuminate. But just as it had no claim on you for a life that could be illuminated, so neither, when it already existed, had it any claim to be enlightened. For its formless condition could not be pleasing to you until it became light. And it became light not merely by existing, but by beholding the illuminating light and cleaving to it. It follows that it owes its living, and its living happily, to nothing but your grace, being turned by a change for the better toward that which cannot be changed for better or worse. That, you alone are, because you alone simply *are*. To you it is not one thing to live, another to live happily, because you, yourself, are your own blessedness.

FOUR

What would be lacking to your goodness which you yourself are, even if these things had never existed or had remained without form? You made them, not out of any need of them but out of the plentitude of your goodness, shaping them and turning them to form as though your joy were not perfected in them. For since you are perfect, their imperfections were displeasing, and so they were perfected by you, and were pleasing to you. But it was not that you were imperfect, and were to be perfected by their perfection yourself. For indeed your good Spirit *moved over the surface of the waters*, not borne up by them as if he rested upon them. For he causes to rest in himself those on whom your good Spirit is said to rest. But your incorruptible and unchangeable will which in itself is all-sufficient for itself was borne upon that life which you had created. To that created life, living is not the same as living blessedly, since it lives ebbing and flowing in its own darkness. There it remains, waiting to be converted to him by whom it was made, and to live more and more by the *fountain of life*, and in his *light to see light*, to be perfected, given light and made happy.

FIVE

Behold, now the Trinity appears to me *in a glass darkly*, which you, my God, are: because you, O Father, created heaven and earth in him who is the Beginning of our wisdom, who is your Wisdom, born of yourself, equal and co-eternal with you, that is, in your Son. We have said much about the *Heaven of heavens*, and about the earth *invisible and without form*, and about *the dark abyss* in reference to the wandering defects of its spiritual deformity. When the *heaven of heavens* turned to him from whom it had its first degree of life and was illuminated by him, it became a beauteous life, the heaven of that heaven which afterward was set between water and water.

Under the name of God, I now understand the Father, who made these things; and under the name of the Beginning, I understand the Son, in whom he made these things; and believing, as I did, my God as the Trinity, I searched further in his holy words, and lo! your *Spirit moved above the waters*. Behold the Trinity: my God, Father, Son and Holy Spirit, Creator of all creation!

SIX

But why was it, O true-speaking Light—I lift up my heart to you: do not let it teach me vanities; dispel its darkness and tell me, I beseech you, by your mighty charity, tell me the reasons, I beseech you—why was it that your Scripture should then at long last refer to your Spirit after the mention of heaven and of the earth invisible and formless, and darkness upon the abyss? Was it because it was appropriate that he should be spoken of as "moving above," and this could not be said unless that were first mentioned upon which your Spirit could be understood to have moved? For he did not move over the Father nor the Son, and he could not have been described as moving above [or upon] if he were moving upon nothing. First, then, that over which he might move was described, and then he was mentioned, whom it is not proper to describe otherwise than as *moving upon*. But why was it not fitting that our knowledge of him should be conveyed otherwise, than as *moving upon*?

SEVEN

Let him who is able now follow with his understanding the words of your apostle, where he says, *Because your love is shed abroad in our hearts by the Holy Spirit who is given to us*, and where, *concerning spiritual gifts*, he teaches and shows us *a more excellent way* of charity; and where he bows his knee to you for us, that we *may know the love of Christ that surpasses knowledge*. Thus from the beginning he who is above all *moved upon the waters*.

To whom shall I tell this? How can I speak of the weight of evil desires, pressing downward to the steep abyss? And how charity rises up again through your Spirit who *moved upon the waters*? For we are not immersed in space nor emerge from it. What can be more similar, and yet more dissimilar? They are the feelings, the loves, the uncleanness of our spirit flowing downward with the love of cares. And your holiness raising us up by love of freedom from cares, that we may lift our hearts to you, is your Spirit *moving upon the waters*, that we may come at last to that surpassing rest, when our soul shall have passed through the waters which are without substance.[1]

EIGHT

Angels fell, the soul of man fell, and by this they have pointed out the abyss in that dark depth. That abyss was ready for the whole spiritual creation, if you had not said from the beginning, *Let there be light, and there was light,* and if every obedient intelligence of your heavenly City had not clung to you and rested in your Spirit—moving unchangeably over everything changeable. Otherwise, even the heaven of heavens would have been in itself a dark abyss; but now it is light in the Lord. For even in that miserable restlessness of the spirits who fell away, and when stripped of the garments of your light, discovered their own darkness, you sufficiently reveal how noble you made the rational creation, to which nothing less than you will suffice to produce a happy rest. It is not a rest even to itself. For you, O God, *shall lighten our darkness.* From you shall come our garments of light; and then *our darkness shall be as the noonday.*

Give yourself to me, O my God. Restore yourself to me. Behold I love you, and if it be too little, let me love you more strongly. I cannot measure my love, so that I may know how much love there is yet lacking in me before my life can run to your embrace and not be turned away, until it is hidden in the secret place of your Presence. This only I know: that woe is me except in you—not only outwardly, but also within myself. And all plenty that is not my God is poverty to me.

NINE

But were neither the Father nor the Son *moving upon the waters?* If this means in space, like a body, then neither was the Holy Spirit. But if it means the unchangeable supremacy of Divinity above all changeable things, then both the Father and Son *and* the Holy Spirit *moved upon the waters.* Why, then, is this said of your Spirit only? Why is it said only of him, as though he had been in space, who is not spatial, of whom only it is written that he is your gift? In your gift we rest. There we enjoy you. Our rest is our place. Love lifts us up to it, and your good Spirit lifts up our lowliness from the gates of death. In your good pleasure lies our peace. The body by its own weight gravitates toward its own place. Weight does not bring it necessarily to the lowest place, but to its own place; fire tends upward, a stone downward. They are propelled by their own weights; they seek their own places. Oil poured under water rises above the water. Water poured on oil sinks under the oil. They are propelled by their own weights; they seek their own places. Out of order, they are restless; restored to order, they are at rest.

My weight is my love. By it I am carried wherever I am carried. By your Gift we are inflamed and carried upward. We glow inwardly and go forward. *We ascend the upward way in our hearts and sing a song of degrees.* We glow inwardly with your fire, with your good fire as we go, because we go upward to the peace of Jerusalem; for *I was glad when they said to me, "We will go up to the house of the Lord."* There your good pleasure has placed us, that we may desire nothing else but to dwell there forever.

TEN

Blessed creation! [The spiritual heaven of heavens.] Although it was not what you are, it never had the experience of being anything else. It would have been something else if it had not, as soon as it was made, without any interval of time, been exalted by your Gift, the Spirit, which is borne aloft above all changeable things. In virtue of that call you said to it, "*Let there be light*," and so it was made light.

On the other hand, this process took place in us at different times—in that we were once darkness, and now have been made light But of that heaven of heavens the only thing said is what *would* have been if it had not been illuminated. And this is so spoken as if it had been unsettled and dark before, so that the cause by which it was made to be otherwise might be clear, namely, that being turned to the unfailing Light, it became light.

Whoever is able, let him understand this. Let him ask of you. Why should he trouble me, as though I could enlighten any one who comes into this world?

ELEVEN

Which of us understands the almighty Trinity? And yet who does not speak of It, if it really is It he speaks of? It is a rare soul who knows what he is speaking of when he speaks. Men contend and strive; yet no one sees that vision without peace. I would wish that men would consider the trinity they have in themselves. These three are indeed far different from the Trinity, but I merely tell them so that they may exercise and test themselves, and see how far they are from that Trinity.

Now the three things I speak of are, To *be*, to *know*, and to *will*. For I am, and I know and I will; I *am* knowing and willing; I *know* myself to be and to will; and I *will* to be and to know. In these three, then, let him see how inseparable a life there is—yes, one life, one mind, and one essence; yes, finally, how inseparable a distinction there is—and yet a distinction. Surely a man has this distinction in front of him. Let him look into himself and see, and tell me. But when he discovers and can say anything about these, let him not think then that he has found that Trinity which is above these, the Unchangeable who *is* unchangeably, and *knows* unchangeably and *wills* unchangeably; and whether on account of these three (being, knowing and willing) there is also a Trinity, or whether these three are in each Person (so that the three belong to Each), or whether both things are true at once, wondrously, simply and yet diversely, in Itself a limit unto Itself, yet illimitable (so that the Trinity is, and is known to Itself, and suffices in Itself, unchangeable, the Selfsame in the abundant greatness of Its Unity)—who can readily conceive? Who could in any way express it? And who would in any rash way make a pronouncement on it?

TWELVE

Proceed in your confession, my faith. Say to the Lord your God, "Holy, Holy, Holy, O Lord my God; we have been baptized in your name, Father, Son and Holy Spirit; in your name we baptize, Father, Son and Holy Spirit, because among us also God in his Christ made heaven and earth, namely, the spiritual and carnal people of his Church. Yes, and our earth, before it received the "form of doctrine," was *invisible and without form*, and we were covered with the darkness of ignorance For *you chastened man for iniquity and your judgments were a great abyss.* But because your Spirit *moved upon the waters*, your mercy did not forsake our misery, and you said, *"Let there be light, repent for the kingdom of heaven is at hand; repent, let there be light!"* And because our soul was troubled within us, from the land of Jordan we remembered you and that mountain[2]—high and holy but lowly for our sakes—and displeased with our darkness we turned to you, *and there was light*. And behold, *we were sometimes darkness, but now we are light in the Lord.*

THIRTEEN

But as yet *we walk by faith and not by sight, for we are saved by hope; but hope that is seen is not hope.* As yet *deep calls unto deep, but now in the noise of your waterfalls.* As yet Paul, who says *I could not speak to you as to spiritual ones, but only as unto carnal,* even he *does not think himself to have apprehended, but forgetting those things which are behind, and reaching forth to those things which are before, groans, being burdened.* And his soul *thirsts after the living God, as the hart after the water brooks,* and says, *"When shall I come?"* desiring *to be clothed upon with his house which is from heaven.* And he calls upon this lower deep, saying, *Be not conformed to this world, but be transformed by the renewing of your mind,* and *be not children in understanding, but in malice be children that in understanding you may become perfect,* and *O foolish Galatians, who has bewitched you?* But now it is no longer in his own voice, but in your voice, who sent your Spirit from above through him who *ascended upon high,* and set open the floodgates of his gifts, that the force of his streams might *make glad the city of God.* For it is for him this *friend of the Bridegroom* longs, *having now the first fruits of the Spirit* laid up with him, yet still groaning *within himself and waiting for the adoption, namely, the redemption of the body.* To him he sighs, as a member of the Bride; he is jealous for him, as being a *friend of the Bridegroom;* for him he is jealous, not for himself; because in *the voice of your waterfalls,* not in his own voice, he calls to that other deep, for whom, being jealous, he fears lest as the serpent beguiled Eve through his subtlety, so their minds should be corrupted from the purity that is in our Bridegroom, your only Son. Oh what a light of beauty that will be when we shall see him as he is! *and when those tears have passed away which have been my food day and night, while they continually say to me, "Where is your God?"*

FOURTEEN

Behold, I, too, say, "O my God, where are you? Behold, where are you?" In you I breathe a little while I pour out my soul by myself *in the voice of joy and praise, in the voice of him who keeps holy day.* And yet again it is cast down because it relapses and becomes a deep, or rather feels that it is still a deep. My faith which you have kindled to brighten my path in the night speaks to it, "*Why are you cast down, O my soul, and why are you troubled within me? Hope in God. His word is a lantern for your feet.* Hope and endure until the night passes, that mother of the wicked, until the wrath of the Lord is past, for we *were once children of wrath,* who were *sometimes darkness,* whose relics we still carry about as in our bodies, dead because of sin, *until the day break and the shadows flee away.* Hope in the Lord." *In the morning I shall stand in your presence* and contemplate you. *I shall ever offer praise to you. In the morning I shall stand in your presence* and shall see *the health of my countenance, my God,* who *shall also quicken our mortal bodies* by the Spirit that dwells in us, because in his mercy he has *moved over* our inner dark and restless deep. From him we have received an earnest in this pilgrimage of what is to come, that we should now be light even while we are being *saved by hope,* and are *children of the light and children of the day,* not the children of the night nor of the darkness which at one time we were.

Between him and us, in this as yet uncertain state of human knowledge, only you can rightly divide [light from darkness in us]—you who test our hearts and call the light day, and the darkness night. For who truly knows us but you? And *what do we have that we have not received* from you? *Out of the same clay some vessels are made to honor, while others are made to dishonor.*

FIFTEEN

Or who, but you, our God, made for us that firmament of authority over us in your divine Scripture? As it is said, *For heaven shall be rolled up like a scroll*, and now it is stretched over us like a skin. Your divine Scripture is of more sublime authority since those mortals through whom you conveyed it to us have died. And you know, Lord, you know, how you clothed men with skins when they became mortal through sin. And so, like a skin you stretched out the firmament of your Book; that is, you have spread your harmonious words over us by the ministry of mortal men. For by their very death that solid firmament of the authority that was in your sayings set forth by them was more sublimely stretched over all that are under it. That authority was not so eminently extended while they were living here. You had not as yet spread abroad the heaven like a skin. You had not yet spread the glory of their deaths in all directions.

Let us look, O Lord, *at the heavens, the work of your fingers*. Clear from our eyes that cloud which has covered them. There is your testimony, which *gives wisdom to the little ones. Perfect, O my God, your praise out of the mouth of babes and sucklings.* For we know no other book so destructive to pride, so destructive to the enemy and the defender who resists your reconciliation in defense of his own sins. I do not know, Lord, I do not know any other such pure words, which so persuade me to confess, and make my neck submissive to your yoke, and invite me to serve you for nothing. Let me understand them, good Father. Grant this to me, placed under them as I am, because you have established them for those placed under them.

There are other "waters" above this "firmament," I believe—immortal and removed from earthly corruption. Let them praise your name; let them praise you, those super-celestial beings, your angels, who have no need to gaze up at this firmament, or to know your Word by reading it. For they always behold your face, and there they read without any time-bound syllables what your eternal will wills. They read, they choose, they love. They are always reading, and what they read never passes away; for by choosing and by loving, they read the very unchangeableness of your counsel. Their book is never closed, nor is their scroll rolled up, because you yourself are this to them, and you are this eternally to them, because you have appointed them to be above this firmament. These Holy Scriptures you have firmly established over the weakness of the lower people, so they might look up and learn your mercy, which always proclaims you in time who made all times. For *your mercy, O Lord, is in the heavens, and your truth reaches to the clouds.* The clouds pass away, but the heavens abide. The preachers of your Word pass away from this life into another, but your Scripture is spread abroad over the people, even to the end of the world. *Heaven and earth also shall pass away, but your words shall not pass away.* Because the scroll shall be rolled together, and the grass over which it was spread *shall pass away with the goodliness of it.* But *your Word endures for ever,* which now appears to us under the dark image of the clouds, and through the glass of heaven, and not as it truly is; because we also, even though we are now well-beloved through your Son, yet it *does not yet appear what we shall be.* He looks through the lattice of our flesh, and he speaks tenderly to us, and enkindles us, and *we follow his sweet perfume.* But *when he shall appear, then we shall be like him, for we shall see him as he is.* As he is, O Lord, we shall see him—but the time is not yet.

SIXTEEN

For only you know altogether what you are. You *are* unchangeably, and *know* unchangeably and *will* unchangeably.

And your essence *knows* and *wills* unchangeably; and your knowledge *is* and *wills* unchangeably; and your will *is* and *knows* unchangeably. It does not seem right in your eyes that as the Unchangeable Light knows Itself, It should be so known by the thing that is enlightened and changeable. Therefore *my soul is like a land where no water is*, because, as it cannot of itself enlighten itself, so it cannot of itself satisfy itself. Thus *the fountain of life is with you* and *in your light we shall see light.*

SEVENTEEN

Who gathered the embittered ones together in one society? For they all have the same end, that of a temporal and earthly happiness, and to attain it they do everything, although they toss up and down with an innumerable variety of cares. Who, Lord, but you, said, *"Let the waters be gathered together into one place,"* and *"Let the dry land appear,"* and *thirst after you*? For *the sea also is yours and you made it, and your hands formed the dry land*. The gathering together of the waters called sea is the bitterness of men's wills, for you restrain the wicked desires of men's souls, and set their bounds for them—how far they may be allowed to pass, that their waves may break against one another; and thus you make it a sea by the order of your dominion over all things.

But as for the souls that thirst after you and appear before you (being divided by other boundaries from the society of the sea), you water them by a sweet spring, so that *the earth may bring forth its fruit*, and you so commanding it, O Lord God, our souls may bud forth in works of mercy according to their kind—loving our neighbor in the relief of his bodily necessities, having seed in itself after its kind, so that the feeling of our own infirmity moves us with compassion to relieve the needy, helping them as we would wish to be helped if we were in like need—not only in easy things, as in *the herb-yielding seed*, but also in the protecting aid of our very strength, like the tree yielding fruit. By this I mean our well-doing in seeking to rescue him who suffers injury from the hands of the powerful, and giving him the shelter of protection by the mighty strength of just judgment.

EIGHTEEN

So, Lord, I beseech you, let it spring up just as you have made it, just as you give cheerfulness and ability—let *truth spring out of the earth and righteousness look down from heaven*, and *let there be lights in the firmament. Let us break our bread with the hungry, and bring the homeless poor into our house. Let us clothe the naked, and not despise those of our own flesh.*

These fruits springing out of the earth show that it is good. And let our light break forth as the morning, and let us from this inferior fruit of action possess the delights of contemplation and of the Word of Life above. And let us appear as lights in the world, holding fast to the firmament of your Scripture. For there you instruct us to distinguish between things intellectual and things of the senses, as between the day and the night. In the same way you distinguish between souls, some given to intellectual things, others to things of sense. Before the firmament was made you distinguished between the light and the darkness in the secret of your judgment. But now, your spiritual children, also set and ranked in the same firmament (now that your grace is manifest throughout the world), may give light on the earth, and distinguish between the day and the night. They are, as it were, *signs of the times*, that *old things have passed away, and, behold, all things have become new*; and that *our salvation is nearer now than when we first believed*; and that *the night is far spent, and the day is at hand*; and that you will *crown your year with blessing*, sending *the laborers* of your goodness *into your harvest*, where *others have labored to sow*. You send them also into other fields, whose harvest shall not be until the end. Thus you grant the prayers of him who asks, and bless the years of the just. But you *are the same*, and in *your years that fail not*, you prepare a harvest for our passing years. For by an eternal decree you bestow heavenly blessings on the earth in their proper seasons.

For indeed *to one is given by the Spirit the word of wisdom*, as it were, the greater light, for the sake of those who are delighted with the light of clear truth (as given for the ruling of the day). *To another is given the word of knowledge by the same Spirit*, as it were, the lesser light. *To another is given faith; to another, the gift of healing; to another, the working of miracles; to another, prophecy; to another, discerning of spirits; to another, various kinds of tongues.* And all these are like stars. For *in all these the one and same Spirit is at work, dividing to every man his own as he wills,* causing these stars to shine clearly to the profit of the whole. But the word of knowledge contains all the sacraments, varied in their seasons like the moon. And it includes those other kinds of gifts, which one after another are considered like stars, since they come short of the brightness of wisdom which gladdens the day. They are only for ruling the night, but they are necessary to those to whom your most prudent servant, Paul, *could not speak as to those who were spiritually mature, but as to carnal men*—even he who *speaks wisdom among those who are mature*. But the natural man—like a babe in Christ, must be fed on milk until he is strengthened for solid meat and his eye is able to look at the sun. Let him not dwell in a night void of all light, but let him be content with the light of the moon and the stars. So you speak to us, our all-wise God, in your Book, your firmament, that we may discern all things in wondering contemplation—though as yet *in signs and seasons, in days and years*.

NINETEEN

But, first, *Wash yourselves; make yourselves clean; remove the evil of your doings from your souls and from before my eyes*, that the dry land may appear. *Learn to do good; judge the fatherless, plead for the widow*, that the earth may bring forth the green herb for food and the tree bearing fruit. And *come, let us reason together, says the Lord*, that there may be lights in the firmament of heaven, and that they may shine upon the earth.

That rich man asked of the good Master what he should do to gain eternal life. Let the good Master tell him, whom he thought no more than a man (but he is *good* because he is God), and let him tell him that if he would enter life, he must *keep the commandments*; let him put away from him the *bitterness of malice and wickedness*; let him *not kill, not commit adultery, not steal, not bear false witness*, that the dry land may appear and bring forth the honoring of father and mother and the love of our neighbor.

"All these," he says, "I have kept from my youth."

Why, then, so many thorns, if the earth is fruitful? Go, root up the woody thicket of covetousness. *Sell what you have*, and be filled with fruit by giving to the poor, *and you will have treasure in heaven*. And follow the Lord *if you would be perfect*, in association with those among whom he speaks wisdom—he who knows what to distribute to the day and to the night, that you may also know it, and so that there may be lights in the firmament of heaven for you, too, which will not be, unless your heart is there. And your heart will not be there unless your treasure is there, as you have heard from the good Master. But that "barren earth" was grieved at this, and the thorns choked the word.

But you, *chosen generation, weak things of the world*, who have forsaken all that you may follow the Lord: go after him and *confound the mighty*. Go after him, O beautiful feet, and shine in the firmament, that *the heavens* may *declare his glory*, discerning between the light of the perfect (though not as the angels) and the darkness of the little ones (though they are not to be despised). Shine over the earth, and let the day, lightened by the Sun, *utter day to day the speech* of wisdom; and let the night, shining with the moon, *show night to night* the word of knowledge. The moon and stars shine for the night; yet the night does not obscure them, since they give it light to a degree. For behold, it is as if God says, *Let there be lights in the firmament of heaven*, and *there came suddenly a sound from heaven, as of the rushing of a mighty wind, and there appeared cloven tongues of fire and sat upon each of them*. And they were made lights in the firmament of heaven, having the Word of Life.

Run to and fro, everywhere, you holy fires, you beautiful fires: for *you are the light of the world*, and you are not to be hid under a bushel. He to whom you cling is exalted and he has exalted you. Run to and fro, and be known to all the nations.

TWENTY

Let the sea also conceive and bring forth your works; and let the waters bring forth the moving creatures that have life. For by *separating the precious from the vile* you have been made *as the mouth of God*, by whom he says, *Let the waters bring forth*, not the living creatures which the earth brings forth, but the creeping creatures that have life, and the fowls that fly above the earth. For your sacraments, O God, by the ministry of your holy ones, have made their way amid the billows of the temptations of the world, to instruct the nations in your name in your baptism. And among these things, many great wonders have been wrought, as it were great whales. And the voices of your messengers fly above the earth near the open firmament of your Book which has been set over them as their authority, under which they are to fly wherever they go. For *there is no speech nor language where their voice is not heard*, since *their sound has gone through all the earth*, and *their words to the end of the world*; because you, Lord, have multiplied them by your blessing.

Do I speak falsely, or do I mingle and confuse, and fail to distinguish between the lucid knowledge of these things in the *firmament of heaven*, and the corporeal works in the wave-tossed sea, and *under the firmament of heaven*? For there are those things, the knowledge of which is solid and defined, without any increase generation by generation, like the lights of wisdom and knowledge. But even of these, the physical manifestations are many and varied. And one thing grows out of another, and as they multiply by your blessing, O God, you have refreshed the weakness of our mortal senses that in the understanding of our mind one thing may be expressed in many ways by the motions of the body.

These sacraments [or signs] the waters have produced through your Word. The necessities of the people estranged from the eternity of your truth have brought them forth through your Gospel, because the waters themselves cast them out—the waters whose diseased bitterness was the reason they came forth through your Word.

Now all things that you made are fair, but lo, you are inexpressibly fairer who made them all. If Adam had not fallen from you, the saltiness of the sea would never have flowed out of him—that is, the human race so profoundly curious, so furiously raging, so restlessly moving up and down. And then there would have been no need of your dispensers to work in these many waters to show forth in a corporeal and sensible way mysterious deeds and sayings. For this is what those creeping and flying creatures now seem to me to mean. By them people are instructed and consecrated by material sacraments, but without further profit to themselves unless these souls had a higher spiritual life, and unless, after the sacrament of admission, they look forward to maturity.

TWENTY-ONE

And thus through your Word, it is not the depth of the sea but "the earth,"[3] separated from the bitterness of the waters, that brings forth, not the creeping and flying creatures that have life, but the living soul itself. For now it has no more need of baptism as the heathen have, and as it had itself when it was covered with the [bitter] waters, for there is no other entrance into the kingdom of heaven, since you have appointed that this should be the entrance. Nor does this soul seek after great, miraculous works any longer in order to produce belief. For it is not such that *unless it sees signs and wonders, it will not believe*, now that the faithful earth is separated from the waters made bitter by infidelity. *And tongues are for a sign, not to them that believe, but to them that do not believe.* That earth which you have founded upon the waters has no need of those flying kinds of creatures which the waters brought forth at your word. Rather, send forth your Word into it by your messengers. For we tell of their works, but it is you who work in them that they may bring forth a living soul. The earth brings forth the soul, because the earth is the cause that they work these things in it, just as the sea was the cause that produced the creeping creatures that have life and the fowls that fly under the firmament of heaven, of whom the earth now has no need.

Yet the earth feeds upon that FISH that was taken out of the deep upon that Table which you have prepared in the presence of those who believe. For this reason he was raised from the deep, that he might feed the dry land. And the birds, though bred in the sea, are yet multiplied on the earth.

For man's infidelity was the cause of the first preachings of the Evangelists, but the faithful are also exhorted and greatly blessed by them in many ways from day to day. But the living soul takes its origin from the earth, for it profits only the faithful to keep themselves from the love of this world so that their soul may live unto you, their soul which was dead while it lived in pleasures, in death-bringing pleasures, Lord. For you, Lord, are the life-giving delight of the pure heart.

Now, therefore, let your ministers work on the earth—not as in the waters of infidelity, by preaching and speaking, by miracles and signs and mysterious words, in which ignorance, the mother of marvels, may be intent upon them out of a fear of occult signs. For such is the entrance to the faith for the sons of Adam, forgetful of you while they hide themselves from your face and become a dark deep. But let your ministers work now as on the dry land, separated from the swirling eddies of the great deep. Let them be an example to the faithful by living before them and stirring them up to imitation. People listen to them not only to hear, but also to act. *Seek the Lord and your soul shall live*, that the earth may bring forth the living soul. *Be not conformed to the world*. Keep yourselves from it. The soul lives by avoiding what dies by loving. Keep yourselves from the unbridled savagery of pride, the lazy, sensual pleasures of luxury, and from what is falsely called knowledge. Thus the wild beasts may be tamed, the cattle subdued to the yoke, the serpents rendered harmless. For these are the movements of our mind allegorically figured; that is to say, the haughtiness of pride, the delight of lust and the poison of curiosity are the movements of a dead soul—not so dead as to lose all motion, however. It dies by forsaking the fountain of life, and so is received by this transitory world and conformed to it.

But your Word, O God, is the fountain of eternal life and does not pass away. Therefore, this departure of the soul is kept in check by your Word when it says to us *Be not conformed to this world*, so that the earth may bring forth a living soul in the fountain of life—that is, a soul restrained in your Word through your Evangelists by imitating the followers of your Christ. For this is what *after its kind* means, because a man is likely to follow his friend. *Become as I am*, Paul says, *because I have become as you are*. Thus in this living soul there shall be good beasts in gentleness of action. For you have commanded, *Do your work in meekness and you will be loved by all.* And there will be good cattle, which neither if they eat shall overabound, nor starve if they eat too little; and good serpents, not destructive to do harm, but *wise*, to take heed; and only exploring as much into this temporal creation as is sufficient that eternity may be clearly seen, *being understood through the things that have been made.* For these creatures are obedient to reason when, kept in check from their deadly propensities, they live and are good.

TWENTY-TWO

Thus, O Lord our God, our Creator, when our affections have been turned from the love of the world, by which we were dying by evil living, and when we have begun to be a living soul by good living, and when your Word *Be not conformed to this world* which you spoke by your apostle is made good in us, you immediately add another word to it, *But be transformed by the renewing of your mind.* Now it does not say *after your kind*, as if following your neighbor who went before you, nor as living after the example of some better man, for you did not say, "Let man be made after his kind," but *Let us make man after our own image and likeness*, so that we might prove what your will is.

This is why that dispenser of yours who fathered children by the Gospel said, *Be transformed by the renewing of your mind that you may prove what is that good and acceptable and perfect will of God*, in order that they might not forever remain as babes who needed to be fed with milk, nor have to be cared for by a nursemaid.

Therefore you did not say, "Let man be made," but *Let us make man.* Nor did you say, "according to his kind," but *after our image and likeness.* For when man is renewed in his mind, and sees and understands your truth, he does not need another person as his director, that he may imitate his kind. But by your direction he proves *what is that good, that acceptable and perfect will of yours.* Yes, you teach him, now made capable, to perceive the Trinity of the Unity and the Unity of the Trinity. And so it is said in the plural, *Let us make man.* Then this is added in the singular: *And God made man.* To the plural, *After our likeness,* is added the singular, *After the image of God.* Thus mankind is renewed in the knowledge of God after the image of him that created him, and being made spiritual, he *judges all things* (all things, that is, which are to be judged), yet *he himself is judged of no man.*

TWENTY-THREE

The words, *he judges all things,* mean that mankind has *dominion over the fish of the sea, and over the birds of the air, and over all cattle and wild beasts, and over all the earth, and over every creeping thing that creeps on the earth.* For he does this by the discernment of his mind, by which he *perceives the things of the Spirit of God.* Without this, *man being placed in honor, had no understanding, and is compared to the brute beasts and became like one of them.*

In your Church, therefore, O our God, according to your grace which you have bestowed on it (*for we are your workmanship, created for good works*), you made not only those who are in spiritual authority, but those who are spiritually subject to them (*male and female you made mankind*). But in your grace spiritually, *there is neither male nor female* according to the sex of the body, *neither Jew nor Greek, neither bond nor free.* Therefore spiritual persons, whether they are those in authority or those who obey, judge spiritually. They do not judge by that spiritual knowledge which shines in the firmament, for they ought not to presume to judge by so sublime an authority; nor does it become them to judge your Book itself, even though some things there do not seem clear, because we submit our understanding to it and hold it certain that even what is hidden from our understanding is still rightly and truly spoken. In this way man, though now spiritual and *renewed in the knowledge of God after the image of him who created him*, ought to be *a doer of the Law, not a judge*. Neither does he judge concerning the division between spiritual and carnal men, who are known to your eyes, O God, and who have not as yet revealed themselves to us by works, that *by their fruits we may know them*. But you, O Lord, already know them, and you have divided and called them in secret before the firmament was made. Nor does this person, though spiritual, judge the storm-tossed people of the world. *For what has he to do to judge those who are outside*, knowing not which of them shall hereafter come into the sweetness of your grace, and which of them will continue in the perpetual bitterness of their ungodliness?

Humanity, therefore, whom you have made after your own image, did not receive dominion over the lights of heaven, nor over that hidden heaven itself, nor over the day and night, which you called into being before the creation of heaven, nor over the gathering together of the waters which is called the sea. But he received *dominion over the fishes of the sea, and the fowls of the air, and over all cattle, and over all the earth, and over all creeping things which crawl on the earth.*

He judges and approves what he finds right, and disapproves what he finds amiss, whether in the celebration of those sacraments by which those are initiated whom your mercy searches out in many waters; or in that, in which that FISH is set forth, which, raised from the deep, the devout "earth" feeds upon; or in the expressions and signs of words, subjected to the authority of your Book, which burst forth sound out of the mouth, as it were, under the firmament, by interpreting, explaining, discoursing, disputing, blessing, or praying to you, so that the people may answer *Amen*.

The reason all these words must be vocally pronounced is the deep of this world, the blindness of the flesh which cannot see thoughts, so that it is necessary to speak aloud in the ears. Thus, although winged birds are multiplied on "the earth," yet they derive their beginning from "the waters."

The spiritual man also judges by approving what is right and disapproving what he finds wrong in the works and morals of the faithful, in their alms, which is signified by the earth bringing forth fruit; and he judges concerning the living soul, living by the taming of its passions by chastity, by fasting, by holy meditations. And he judges concerning those things which are perceived by the bodily senses, for it is now said that he should judge concerning everything in which he also had the power of correction.

TWENTY-FOUR

But what is this? What kind of mystery, that you bless mankind, Lord, that they may *increase and multiply and replenish the earth*? Do you not give us a hint to understand something in this? Why did you not also bless the light, which you called day, nor the firmament of heaven, nor the [greater and lesser] lights, nor the stars, nor the earth, nor the sea? I might say, O God, who created us after your image, that it was your good pleasure to bestow this blessing exclusively on mankind if you had not in the same way blessed the fishes and the whales, that they should increase and multiply and replenish the waters of the sea, and that the birds should be multiplied on the earth. In the same way, I might say that this blessing pertained properly to such creatures as are bred of their own kind if I had found it given to the fruit trees and herbs, and beasts of the earth. But it is not said *Increase and multiply* either to the herbs, nor the trees, nor the beasts nor the reptiles. Yet all of these increase by propagation and preserve their kind.

What shall I say then, O Truth, my Light? Shall I say that it was said idly and vainly? Not so, Father of goodness! Far be it from a minister of your Word to say so. And if I do not understand what you mean by that phrase, let my betters—those who have more understanding than I have—make better use of it, in proportion as you, my God, have given to each one to understand. But let my confession also be pleasing in your eyes, which I confess to you, that I believe, Lord, that you have not spoken this way in vain; and I will not suppress what this lesson suggests to me. For it is true, and I do not see what should hinder me from understanding the figurative sayings of your Bible in this way. For I know a thing may be conveyed many ways by bodily expressions, which is understood in only one way by the mind, and that the mind may understand in many different ways what is signified by one bodily expression. Behold the single love of God and of our neighbor is expressed by how many sacraments and innumerable languages and how many different ways of speaking there are in each language. Thus do the offsprings of the waters increase and multiply.[4] Observe again, whoever reads this; see what Scripture declares and the voice pronounces only one way: *In the Beginning God created heaven and earth.* Is it not understood in many different ways, not by any deceit of error, but by different kinds of true meanings? Thus do man's "offspring" *increase and multiply.*

If, then, we conceive of the different natures of the things themselves (not allegorically, but properly), then the phrase *increase and multiply* corresponds to all things that come from seed. But if we treat the words as spoken figuratively, which I rather suppose to be the purpose of the Scripture (which surely does not superfluously ascribe this blessing only to the offspring of marine animals and man), then we find that *multitude* applies to spiritual creatures as well as physical ones, as *heaven* and *earth*, and to souls both righteous and unrighteous, as *light* and *darkness*; and the word refers to holy writers through whom the Law was ministered to us as the *firmament* which is placed between the *waters* [above] and the *waters* [below]; and to the society of bitter people as *the sea*; and to the zeal of holy souls as *the dry land*; and to the works of mercy belonging to this present life as *green herbs, bearing seed*, and *trees bringing forth fruit*; and to spiritual gifts which are manifest for our edification as *the lights of heaven*; and to passions shaped to temperance as *the living soul*. In all these instances we meet with multitudes, abundance, and increase. But it will increase and multiply in such a way that one thing may be expressed many ways, and one expression may be understood many ways. We do not find this true except in ideas mentally conceived and expressed through bodily signs. I interpret the phrase, *the generation of the waters*, to refer to the bodily signs [words and sacraments] made necessary by our involvement in the flesh. By things mentally conceived— human generations—I take to refer to that in which reason brings forth its fruit. And therefore I believe, Lord, that you have said to both these kinds, *Increase and multiply*. For in this blessing I see that you have granted us a power and a faculty to express in several ways what we understand in only one, and to understand in several ways what we read expressed obscurely in only one way. Thus the *waters* of the sea are replenished which can be moved only by a variety of signs. Thus the *earth* is also replenished with human offspring, its dryness appearing in its thirst for truth and by the fact that reason rules over it.

TWENTY-FIVE

I would also say, O Lord my God, what the following Scripture reminds me of. I will say it without fear. For I will say the truth, you inspiring me with what you will that I say out of these words. For I believe myself to speak truth by no other inspiration than yours since you are the Truth and every man a liar. He, therefore, who *speaks a lie speaks of his own.* So I will speak of you that I may speak truth.

You have given us for food *every seed-bearing herb on all the earth, and every tree that has seed-bearing fruit,* and not to us alone, but also *to the birds of the air and to the beasts of the earth,* and to all creeping things. But you have not given them to the fish and to the great whales. Now we were saying that these *fruits of the earth* signified and allegorically expressed the works of mercy which are provided for the necessities of this life out of the fruitful earth. Such an *earth* was the devout Onesiphorus, to whose house you gave mercy because he often refreshed your Paul and was not ashamed of his chains. This also the Macedonian brethren did, and they bore the same fruit, supplying what he [Paul] needed. But how he grieved over some "*trees*" who did not afford him the fruit due to him, where he says, *At my first answer no man stood by me; but all forsook me! I pray God that it may not be laid to their charge.* For these *fruits* are due to such as minister spiritual doctrine to us through their understanding of the divine mysteries, and they are due to them as men. Yes, and they are due to them also as *the living souls* who give themselves as examples in their own self-denial. And they are due to them as *flying creatures,* because of their blessings which *are multiplied on the earth, for their sound has gone forth into all the earth.*

TWENTY-SIX

Those who are delighted by these truths are fed by them. Those *whose god is their belly* find no delight in them. For it is not what is given that bears the fruit, but the spirit in which it is given. Therefore, I see clearly why he [Paul] rejoiced over one who served God and not his own belly. I see it and I rejoice with him. For he had received from the Philippians what they had sent by Epaphroditus to him. I understand why he rejoiced. He rejoiced at what he fed on. For, speaking in truth, he says, *I rejoiced greatly in the Lord that now at last your care of me has flourished again, in which you were once so careful,* but it had become *a weariness to you.* These Philippians, then, had dried up with a long weariness and withered, as it were, as to bearing this fruit of a good work; and he rejoices for them because they flourished again, not for himself, that they ministered to his needs. So he adds, *Not that I speak in respect of my lack, for I have learned in whatever state I am, to be content with it. I know how to be abased and how to abound; in any and all circumstances I have learned the secret of facing plenty and hunger, abundance and want. I can do all things through Christ who strengthens me.*

At what, then, do you rejoice in all things, O great Paul? At what do you rejoice? On what do you feed, O man *renewed in the knowledge of God after the image of him who created you,* O *living soul* of so much self-denial, O tongue, speaking mysteries like *flying birds*? (For to such creatures, this food is due.) What is it that feeds you? Joy! Hear what follows: *Nevertheless, you have done well in that you have shared my trouble.* This is what causes him to rejoice; this is what he feeds on, because they had done well, not because his need was relieved. For he said to you, *you have enlarged me when I was in distress,* because he knew *how to abound and how to suffer want* in you, who strengthened him. And he goes on to say, *For you Philippians yourselves know that in the beginning of the gospel, when I left Macedonia, no church entered into partnership with me in giving and receiving except you only. For even in Thessalonica you sent me help for my needs once and again.* He now rejoices that they have returned to these good works, and he is gladdened that they flourished again, as when a fruitful field becomes green again.

Was it for his own necessities that he said, *You sent help for my needs?* Is he rejoicing for that? Surely not for that. But how do we know this? Because he himself continues, *not because I desire a gift, but I desire fruit.*

I have learned of you, my God, to distinguish between a *gift* and a *fruit.* A gift is the thing itself which he gives who bestows those necessities on us: money, food, drink, clothing, shelter, help. But the fruit is the good and right will of the giver. For the good Master says not only, *He who receives a prophet,* but adds, *in the name of a prophet.* And he does not say only, *He who receives a righteous man,* but adds, *in the name of a righteous man.* So verily shall the one receive the reward of a prophet, and the other the reward of a righteous man. He does not say only, *He who shall give one of my little ones a cup of cold water to drink,* but adds, *in the name of a disciple,* and so he concludes, *Verily I say to you, he shall not lose his reward.* The *gift* is to receive a prophet, to receive a righteous man, to give a cup of cold water to his disciple. But the *fruit* is to do this in the name of a prophet, in the name of a righteous man, in the name of a disciple.

With *fruit* Elijah was fed by the widow who knew he was a man of God and therefore fed him. But he was fed by the raven with a gift. The inner man of Elijah was not fed by the raven's gift, but the outer man only, which might have perished from the lack of that food.

TWENTY-SEVEN

Therefore I will speak in your presence, O Lord, what is true, that when carnal men and unbelievers (for gaining and preparing of whom the sacraments and the mighty workings of miracles are necessary—people we suppose to be signified by the terms *fishes* and *whales*), when such people undertake the bodily refreshment or otherwise give your servant aid with something useful for this present life, since they are ignorant as to why this is done, and to what purpose, they neither feed these servants nor are these [spiritually] fed by them, because they do not do it out of a holy and righteous intent, nor do the receivers rejoice at their *gifts*, since they yet see no *fruit*. For it is *fruit* that the soul feeds on, for which it is glad. And therefore the *fishes* and *whales* do not feed on such food as the *earth* alone brings forth until after they have been separated and divided from the bitterness of the waters of the sea.

TWENTY-EIGHT

And you, O God, *saw everything that you had made, and behold, it was very good.* Yes, we also see the same, and behold, all things are very good. Of the several kinds of your works, when you said, *Let them be*, and they came to be, you saw each one that it was good. I have counted it written seven times that you saw that what you made was good, and this is the eighth time, that you saw everything that you had made, and behold it was not only *good*, but *very good*. Apart, they were only *good*, but then being all together, they are both *good* and *very good*. All beautiful bodies also express this, for a body consisting of members, all of them beautiful, is far more beautiful than the same members by themselves. By a well-ordered union, the whole is completed even though the members separately are also beautiful.

TWENTY-NINE

And I looked closely to see whether it was seven or eight times you saw that your works were good when they pleased you. But I found no periods of time in your seeing, by which I might understand that you saw so often what you made. And I said, "Lord, is not this your Scripture true, since you are true, and being Truth have set it forth? Why, then, does it say to me that in your sight there are no times, while this Scripture tells me that what you made each day you *saw that it was good* ?" And when I counted them, I found how often. To this you reply to me, for you are my God, and with a strong voice you tell your servant in his inner ear, bursting through my deafness and crying, "O man, I say what my Scripture says. And yet they speak in terms of time, but time has no relation to my Word, because my Word exists in equal eternity with myself. So the things which you see through my Spirit, I see; just as what you speak by my Spirit, I speak. And so when you see those things in time, I do not see them in time, just as when you speak in time, I do not speak them in time."

THIRTY

And I heard, O Lord my God, and drank up a drop of sweetness from your truth, and understood that there are some men who dislike your works, and say that you made many of them compelled by necessity—such as the fabric of the heavens and the courses of the stars; and that you made them, not of what was yours, but that they were from elsewhere and were created from other sources, that you might collect them, compact them and combine them when you raised up the walls of the universe from your conquered enemies, so that they, bound down by this structure, might not be able to rebel against you again. For other things, they say that you neither made them nor even fashioned them—such as all flesh and all the very minute creatures, and whatever has its roots in the earth; but that a mind hostile to you, and another nature not created by you and in every way contrary to you, gave birth to and framed these things in the lowest depths of the world. They who speak this way are mad, because they do not see your works by your Spirit nor recognize you in them.

THIRTY-ONE

But as for those who see these things by your Spirit, it is you who see in them. Therefore, when they see that these things are good, you see that they are good. And whatever things are pleasing for your sake, you are pleased in them. And what pleases us through your Spirit, pleases you in us. *For what person knows a man's thoughts except the spirit of the man which is in him? Even so no one comprehends the thoughts of God except the Spirit of God. Now we*, he says, *have received not the spirit of the world, but the Spirit which is from God, that we might understand the gifts bestowed on us by God.* And I am reminded that truly *no one comprehends the things of God, but the Spirit of God*; but how, then, do we know what things are given to us by God? The answer comes to me: "Because the things which we know by his Spirit, even these no one knows but the Spirit of God." For as it is rightly said to those that were to speak by the Spirit of God, *It is not you who speak*, so it is rightly said to them that know by the Spirit of God, "It is not you who know." And no less then is it rightly said to those who see by the Spirit of God, "It is not you who see"; therefore, whatever they see by the Spirit of God to be good, it is not they, but God who sees that it is good.

It is one thing for a man to suppose that which is good to be bad, as those mentioned above think. It is another thing that a man should see as good what is good (as your creatures are pleasing to man because they are good, yet you are not pleased in them when they choose to enjoy them rather than to enjoy you). It is still another thing that when a man sees a thing to be good, God in him sees that it is good—that in truth he may be loved in what he has made, who cannot be loved but by the Holy Spirit which he has given. *Because the love of God is shed abroad in our hearts by the Holy Spirit which is given to us*, by whom we see that whatever in any degree *is*, is good. For it is from him, who himself *is*—not in any partial degree, but *is* what he *is*.

THIRTY-TWO

Thanks be to you, O Lord. We see *heaven and earth*, whether a corporeal part, upper and lower, or a spiritual and physical creation. And we see the light made and divided from the darkness for the embellishment of these parts, consisting of the universal mass of the world or the whole created universe. We see the firmament of heaven, either that primal body of the world between the spiritual "upper" waters and the material "lower" waters, or since this is also called heaven, that expanse of air through which the birds of heaven fly, between those waters which are carried in clouds above, and on clear nights distill down in dew and those heavier waters which flow along the earth. We see waters gathered together in the plains of the sea; and the dry land rising clear of the water so as to be visible and settled, and the material of herbs and trees. We see the lights shining from above—the sun to serve the day, the moon and the stars to cheer the night; and that by all these, periods of time can be marked and noted. We see on every side a humid element, replete with fishes, beasts and birds, because the density of the air which bears up the flight of birds is increased by the evaporation of the waters. We see the face of the earth decked out with terrestrial creatures, and man, created after your image and likeness, in that very image and likeness of you (that is, having the power of reason and understanding), set over all irrational creatures. And as in his soul there is one power which rules by directing, another is made subject that it might obey; so, woman was made (as regards the body) for man. In the mind of her rational understanding she was created equal in nature, but pertaining to the sex of her body, she was made subject to the sex of her husband in the same way that the appetite for action is subjected by the reason of the mind to conceive the skill of acting rightly. These things we behold, and they are severally good, and all together they are *very good*.

THIRTY-THREE

Let your works praise you, that we may love you; and let us love you, that your works may praise you, which have their beginning and ending in time, their rising and setting, their growth and decay, perfection and imperfection. They have, then, their succession of morning and evening, in part secretly, in part apparent; for they were made from nothing by you, not of you, and not of any matter which was not yours, nor which was created before, but of matter "concreated"—that is, matter that was created by you at the same time, because you gave form to its formless state without any interval of time. For since the material of heaven and earth is one thing, the form another, you made the matter of absolutely nothing, but the form of the world, you made out of the formless matter. Yet you made both together at the same time, so that form followed matter with no interval of delay.

THIRTY-FOUR

We have also examined what you willed to be figuratively expressed, either by their creation or the description of things in their particular order. And we have seen that things separately are good and together, very good, in your Word, in your only begotten Son, heaven and earth, the Head and body of the Church, in your predestination before all time, without morning and evening. But when you began to execute in time the things predestined beyond time, to the end that you might reveal hidden things and adjust our disorders (for our sins hung over us and we had sunk into profound darkness), your good Spirit moved upon us to help us in due season. And you justified the ungodly, and divided them from the wicked; and you made your Book the firmament of authority between those placed above, who would be obedient to you, and those placed under, who were to be obedient to them. And you gathered together the society of unbelievers into one conspiracy, so that the zeal of the faithful might appear, and that they might bring forth works of mercy to you, even distributing to the poor their earthly riches to obtain heavenly ones. And after this, you kindled certain *lights in the firmament*, your saints, having the Word of life, and shining with a sublime authority given them by their spiritual gifts. After that, again, for the instruction of unbelieving nations, you produced the sacraments from corporeal matter, and visible miracles, and the preached word according to the firmament of your Book, by which the faithful should be blessed and multiplied. Next, you formed the living soul of the faithful through the taming of their passions by vigorous self-denial; and then, the mind, subjected to you alone and needing no human authority, you renewed after your image and likeness, and subjected its rational actions to the higher excellence of the understanding, as the woman to the man. And to all offices of your ministry, necessary for the perfecting of the faithful in this life, you willed that these same faithful ones should themselves bring forth good things for their temporal uses, good things, fruitful in the time to come.

All these we see, and they are very good, because you see them in us—you, Lord, who have given us your Spirit by which we may see them and so love you in them.

THIRTY-FIVE

O Lord God, grant us peace, for you have given us all things. Grant us the peace of quietness, the peace of the Sabbath which has no evening. For all this most goodly order of things, all very good, having finished their courses, will pass away, for in them there is morning and evening.

THIRTY-SIX

But the seventh day has no evening, nor has it any setting, because you have sanctified it to an everlasting continuance; so that what you yourself did after your works, which were very good, resting on the seventh day (even though you made them in unbroken rest), the voice of your Book may announce beforehand to us that we also, after our works (which are also very good because you have given them to us), may rest in you in the Sabbath of eternal life.

THIRTY-SEVEN

For you shall rest in us then, as you work in us now. And your rest shall be through us, just as your works are now done through us. But you, Lord, ever work and are ever at rest. You do not see in time, nor do you move in time, nor rest in time. And yet you make the scenes of time, and indeed time itself, and the rest which results from time.

THIRTY-EIGHT

Therefore, we see those things which you made because they are. But they are, because you see them. And we see them outwardly, what they are, and inwardly, that they are good. But you saw them as made when you saw that they were to be made. And we were at a later time moved to do well, after our hearts had so conceived by your Spirit. But in the former time we were moved to do evil, forsaking you. But you, the One, the good God, have never ceased to do good. And we also have some good works by your good gift, but they are not eternal. After them, we hope to rest in your great hallowing. But you, the Good, needing no other good, are ever at rest, because you yourself are your rest. And what man can teach man to understand this? Or what angel can teach the angels? Or what angel, a man? We must ask it of you, seek for it in you, knock for it at your gate. Only so, even so shall we receive; so shall we find; so it shall be opened to us. Amen.

THE END
Deo gratias!

NOTES

Introduction

1 Pilkington, Rev. J. C., Translator. *The Confessions of St. Augustine*, 1876.
2 Gibb, John and William Montgomery, Editors. *The Confessions of Augustine* [Latin Version], Introduction. Cambridge University Press, 1927.
3 *Ibid.*
4 Augustine. *Epistle ccxxi.*

BOOK I
Infancy to age fifteen

1 Note that the book begins with an ascription of praise. The word *Confessio* in St. Augustine's use has a wider meaning than the English *confession*, and includes ascriptions of praise as well as acknowledgment of sin.

Throughout the *Confessions* Augustine uses an Old Latin version of the Old Testament, which he preferred even after he became acquainted with St. Jerome's new translation from the Hebrew (the Vulgate). He disapproved of the new translation, believing that the Greek Septuagint version of the Old Testament had been inspired, and that it was presumptuous for a single scholar to undertake such a revision.

2 Mortality is the evidence that God resists the proud—the penalty of that self-exaltation in which Augustine finds the ultimate motive of man's primary disobedience—aimed as setting self in the place of God.

3 Referring to St. Ambrose, who was then bishop of Milan.

4 He combines the thought of Exodus 33:20, "For man shall not see me and live," with that of Deuteronomy 31:17, "And I will forsake them and hide my face from them, and they will be devoured."

5 Augustine's memories of his early childhood were far from happy. His reference to physical punishment at school indicates that he still felt that some of it was unjust and unwarranted.

6 Augustine was a catechumen. Infant baptism had not yet come into general use. The sign of the cross and reception of salt were part of the ceremony of preparation, and in Africa, salt was used throughout the period of training.

7 Because baptism was considered indispensable to salvation and was held to remove all sin committed up to that time, it was common in the fourth century for people to postpone it until the hour of death, fearing the possibility of sin afterward more than the risk of failing to receive it. By the fifth century, the practice of infant baptism was firmly established as the norm.

BOOK II
Object of these confessions

1 Throughout this book the words *soul* and *mind* are often translations of the Latin word *animus*. Various translators choose one or the other, to try best to convey Augustine's thought.

2 It is not surprising that, in revulsion from this unworthy idea of marriage, Augustine should have felt that the genuineness of his conversion demanded celibacy. It is good to note, however, that his ascetic sympathies did not prevent his adopting a considerably higher view of marriage exhibited in *De Bono Conjugali* in his later life.

3 Madaura was about 20 miles south of Tagaste. Its schools attained some distinctions, and its ruins indicate that it was a place of importance. Augustine later wrote to its people urging them to abandon their idols, and addresses them as "My fathers and brothers."

4 In the *Confessions* we see a growth in Monica's spiritual life. His expression here means that she still entertained some of the old ambitions for worldly success for her son, and still retained some of the superstitious practices learned in Africa.

5 This whole discussion illuminates Augustine's doctrine of sin. He holds that in sinning men do not seek evil *per se* but some supposed good in the evil. This theft is discussed with special care because at first sight it seems to have no good in view, but to have been done for the sheer delight of sinning. The final solution is that the good was the pleasure in companionship—in itself a good thing.

6 Lucius Sergius Catilina, c. 108–62 BC. Cicero's four speeches against him and Sallust's essay on his plot to overthrow Rome were well known to rhetoricians in Augustine's day.

7 Augustine classifies the different kinds of beauty to correspond to the various degrees of life—moral, intellectual, sensuous [meaning feeling], and organic. All are "good" but in different degrees.

BOOK III
From age sixteen to eighteen

1 "There was something peculiarly enthralling to an ardent mind like Augustine's in the Manichean system. That system was kindred in many ways to modern Rationalism. Reason was exalted at the expense of faith. Nothing was received on mere authority, and the disciple's inner consciousness was the touchstone of truth. The result of this is well pointed out by Augustine (Contr. Faust xxxii. sec. 19): 'Your design, clearly, is to deprive Scripture

of all authority, and to make every man's mind the judge of what passage of Scripture he is to approve or disapprove. This is not to be subject to Scripture in matters of faith, but to make Scripture subject to you. Instead of making the high authority of Scripture the reason for approval, every man makes his approval the reason for thinking a passage correct.'

"It was Augustine's desire for knowledge concerning the origin of evil that united him to Manicheism and which also led him to forsake it when he found in it nothing but empty fables. Manicheus taught that evil and good were primeval, and had independent existences. Augustine on the other hand, maintains that it was not possible for evil to exist by itself." Quoted from Pilkington, *op. cit.*

BOOK IV
From age eighteen to twenty-seven

1 Manicheism was placed under an Imperial Edict in Rome in 372, the year before Augustine became a "hearer" in Africa. It was a religious system developed by Mani, a Persian leader, sometime in the third century. From the fourth to the twelfth centuries it spread as far as France in the west and all the way to China in the east. Marco Polo found Manichean communities at the end of the thirteenth century. Much material on the movement has been discovered in the twentieth century, throwing new light on its origin and development. A Manichean community consisted of (l) "the elect," who lived ascetic lives, laboring at the separation of the good from the evil (light from darkness); (2) the "hearers," who followed the teaching, but with less strictness; and (3) the "adherents" who were interested but undertook no obligations.

2 According to the Manichean belief [to which Augustine then subscribed], there were two substances—in effect, two gods—

one good, the other evil. The human soul they believed to be of the same substance or nature as God, though not created by him. The soul originated in the intermingling of God's substance with evil matter. "Not a temple, but a part and member of God," is the way Augustine describes their view of the soul. They also denied original sin, and attributed their sin to "the race of darkness," which was in process of being overcome by their religious acts.

3 Manicheans held that the soul was "a spark of divinity" [not unlike some modern systems].

BOOK V
At age twenty-eight

1 Augustine frequently restates that in God's overruling providence, mankind's foulness, failure and sin do not disturb the essential order or beauty of the universe.

2 Since the "good soul" in humankind was, according to Manichean teaching, a part of God's substance, when one sinned, God himself suffered defeat from the dark powers—the material creation.

3 A deliberate and ironic contradiction on Augustine's part. Infinite cannot be greater or smaller!

4 The reference here is to II Corinthians 3:6: "The letter kills, but the spirit gives life."

BOOK VI
At age twenty-nine

1 Dr. Pusey interprets this as referring to the privilege of purchasing at special prices enjoyed by officials connected with the court.

2 Marriageable age was twelve years old!

3 This first attempt at community life proved abortive. Later on, with some modifications, it was begun again at Cassiciacum. (See Book Nine, Chapter 6.)

4 "This incident, with the sequel, is the most painful in the life of Augustine, and for it he expresses no adequate regret. Others

appear to have influenced him, probably his mother and his friends, but it is impossible to acquit him of blame. He was probably deterred by his social ambition from making her his wife." Gibb and Montgomery, *op. cit.*

BOOK VII
At age thirty

1 *Adolescentia* extended from ages 15 to 30. *Iuventutem* (here translated "early manhood") when used alone covered the ages from 20 to 40, but was often limited to the period which followed *adolescentia*.

2 Augustine held that man lost this light when Adam, after his disobedience, fled from God.

3 The philosophers now known as Neoplatonists. Plotinus (c. 205–270) was the earliest and most famous. They drew their inspiration from Plato, but their beliefs were more closely knit and more directly religious. Their aim was to provide a sound intellectual basis for a religious and moral life.

4 A good example of Augustine's allegorical use of Scripture. In this one sentence the "gold" of Egypt becomes the spiritual truth of the philosophers, who were Gentiles. But they worshiped "the idols of Egypt"—their own pride—and they perverted the "gold" from its proper use.

5 "Augustine has at length found standing ground in regard to the problem of evil. Evil is negative, therefore he need no longer think of God as its creator. It requires as its presupposition a good thing which suffers loss or corruption. It is a negation because it tends to destroy the material on which it feeds." Gibb and Montgomery, *op. cit.*

6 He refers here to Genesis 1:31: "God saw all things that he had made and they were very good." Harmony, Augustine means, is better than uniformity, but harmony implies variety and variety

involves gradation. Even different degrees of goodness fit into
the divine scheme of things.

7 Photinus was an Arian bishop of Sirmium about 344. He taught
that Christ was a man, born of the Virgin and illuminated by
a special divine influence. He was deposed by a Council held
at Sirmium in 351. Photinus' followers were condemned at
the Council of Constantinople in 381. Arians denied the true
divinity of Jesus Christ. It was one of the most widespread
and dangerous of the early heresies, and had the support of
several emperors.

8 When Augustine took up the letters of Paul, a new era opened
for the thought and life of the Church. The historian Harnack
says, "Marcion after the Apostolic Fathers; Irenaeus, Clement
and Origen after the Apologists; Augustine after the Greek
Fathers; the great reformers of the Middle Ages from Agobard
to Wessel in the bosom of the medieval Church; Luther after
the Scholastics; Jansenism after the Council of Trent: everywhere
it has been Paul in these men who produced the reformation."
Gibb and Montgomery, *op. cit.*

9 Augustine uses the word *creasti* (formed or made) to refer to
Christ's human nature, not his divinity. His Biblical reference
here is Proverbs 8:22, "The Lord created me at the beginning of
his way, the first of his acts of old." This is a famous battleground
of the Arian controversy, who denied the eternal coexistence of
Christ with the Father.

BOOK VIII
At age thirty-one

1 This belief that St. Paul's change of name was related to his
conversion of Sergius Paulus (Acts 13:4–12) was apparently
widely held among some of the Church Fathers. It is now
recognized that it was usual for the Jews of the Dispersion to

adopt a second name for use among the Gentiles, and that the choice of the name was frequently suggested by assonance with the Jewish name (e.g. Saul–Paul).

BOOK IX
At age thirty-two

1 The language implies that the celebration of the Eucharist at the grave was customary in Rome, but not in Africa.

2 This is the only time Augustine mentions his mother by name in the *Confessions*. The ending of her name suggests a Greek strain in her family.

3 The Latin *fratres* included both masculine and feminine (not unlike the traditional use of the English "brethren"). I have rendered it here "my brother and my sister" to make Augustine's meaning clearer.

BOOK X
The examined life

1 The *Confessions* changes focus at this point and becomes more philosophical and theological. Here we begin to hear the self-examination of the bishop of Hippo and his interpretation of the nature of knowledge and of creation itself.

2 From Romans 4:5. Augustine understands *justifico* in the sense of making actually just (righteous). He recognizes the possibility of interpreting the word in the sense of being reckoned just, but uniformly adopts the former interpretation.

3 This book has been called one of the most honest soul inventories extant from the ancient world.

4 The praying Christian is pictured as a thurible, a vessel for burning incense in the Temple [or in the Church]. Cf. Psalm 141:2: "Let my prayer be counted as incense before thee."

5 From Cicero: "After Anaximander came Anaximenes, who taught that the air is God." *On the Nature of the Gods.*

6 Plotinus said that to admire, to take as an object of pursuit anything different from one's own nature, is to acknowledge one's inferiority to it.

7 The Latin word is *anima*—physical life. Augustine sees animals as possessing the *interior sensus,* which correlates the data of sense perception but lacks *ratio*—the reason, which forms judgments.

8 Augustine here is very near the Platonic teaching that learning is remembering. In his *Retractions* (I, 8:2) he gave up this opinion, saying rather that the mind has a natural affinity for the things of the intelligible world.

BOOK XII
Further inquiry into the mystery of creation

1 I have paraphrased this difficult passage for greater clarity.

2 A conflation of I Timothy 1:5 and 8. It reads in full: "Whereas the aim of our charge is love [charity] that issues from a pure heart and a good conscience and sincere faith. . . . Now we know that the law is good, if any one uses it lawfully. . . ."

BOOK XIII
From inquiry to praise

1 This peculiar expression, "waters without substance," is based on the Old Latin version of Psalm 124:5, which in turn came from a mistranslation of the Septuagint version of the Old Testament. Modern translators render this verse thus: "Then over us would have gone the raging waters" (RSV). Augustine regards sin as having no substance, and in these "waters without substance" the prodigal "wasted his substance," i.e., his very self. Cf. Augustine's sermon on Psalm 123:5 (KJV 124:5).

2 The reference here is to Mt. Hermon: "Therefore I remember you from the land of Jordan and Hermon . . ." Psalm 42:6

(KJV 43:8). The snow-capped height of Mt. Hermon made it a favorite symbol of God's majesty from ancient times.

3 Throughout his allegorical treatment of Genesis 1, Augustine uses the earth to refer to the godly, the faithful, and specifically, to the Church.

4 That is, the spiritual sluggishness of mankind makes preaching, especially evangelistic preaching, necessary. Included under the Latin word *sacramenta* are preaching, miracles and possibly the traditional sacraments. The *waters*, i.e., the unconverted, produce these signs in the sense that the world's need of them caused them to be given.

About Paraclete Press

Who We Are

Paraclete Press is a publisher of books, recordings, and DVDs on Christian spirituality. Our publishing represents a full expression of Christian belief and practice—from Catholic to Evangelical, from Protestant to Orthodox.

We are the publishing arm of the Community of Jesus, an ecumenical monastic community in the Benedictine tradition. As such, we are uniquely positioned in the marketplace without connection to a large corporation and with informal relationships to many branches and denominations of faith.

What We Are Doing

Books

Paraclete publishes books that show the richness and depth of what it means to be Christian. Although Benedictine spirituality is at the heart of all that we do, we publish books that reflect the Christian experience across many cultures, time periods, and houses of worship. We publish books that nourish the vibrant life of the church and its people—books about spiritual practice, formation, history, ideas, and customs.

We have several different series, including the best-selling Living Library, Paraclete Essentials, and Paraclete Giants series of classic texts in contemporary English; A Voice from the Monastery—men and women monastics writing about living a spiritual life today; award-winning literary faith fiction and poetry; and the Active Prayer Series that brings creativity and liveliness to any life of prayer.

Recordings

From Gregorian chant to contemporary American choral works, our music recordings celebrate sacred choral music through the centuries. Paraclete distributes the recordings of the internationally acclaimed choir Gloriæ Dei Cantores, praised for their "rapt and fathomless spiritual intensity" by *American Record Guide,* and the Gloriæ Dei Cantores Schola, which specializes in the study and performance of Gregorian chant. Paraclete is also the exclusive North American distributor of the recordings of the Monastic Choir of St. Peter's Abbey in Solesmes, France, long considered to be a leading authority on Gregorian chant.

DVDs

Our DVDs offer spiritual help, healing, and biblical guidance for life issues: grief and loss, marriage, forgiveness, anger management, facing death, and spiritual formation.

Learn more about us at our Web site:
www.paracletepress.com, or call us toll-free at 1-800-451-5006.